The Bible Guidebook

The Bible Guidebook
The Gospel Life Guidebook Series

Joshua Caleb Hutchens

GOSPEL LIFE PRESS

The Bible Guidebook
Copyright © Joshua Caleb Hutchens, 2022

Published by
Gospel Life Press
An Imprint of
Gospel Life
PO Box 19, Hardin, KY 42048 USA
contact@gospellife.org | gospellife.org

All Scripture quotations are taken from the Christian Standard Bible®, Copyright © 2017 by Holman Bible Publishers. Christian Standard Bible® and CSB® are federally registered trademarks of Holman Bible Publishers.

Printed in the United States of America

ISBN-13: 979-8-9873104-0-3 (Hardback)
ISBN-13: 979-8-9873104-1-0 (Ebook)

To
my parents
who taught me the Bible

Contents

About the Gospel Life Guidebook Series	1
Abbreviations	3
To Teachers	5

Meet the Bible

Meet the Bible	9
Experience the Bible	11
The Bible's Story	15

How to Study the Bible

How to Study the Bible	21
How to Read Old Testament Stories	27
How to Read Old Testament Law	33
How to Read Old Testament Wisdom and Poetry	39
How to Read the Prophets	43
How to Read the Gospels	49
How to Read Acts	53
How to Read New Testament Letters	57
How to Read Revelation	63
How Not To Read the Bible	69

Ancient World History

The Sumerians	77

The Egyptians	81
The Canaanites	85
The Assyrians	89
The Babylonians	93
The Persians	97
The Greeks	101
The Romans	105

The Old Testament

About the Old Testament	111
Genesis	117
Exodus	125
About the Tabernacle and Temple	131
Leviticus	143
Numbers	147
Deuteronomy	151
Joshua	155
Judges	159
Ruth	163
1–2 Samuel	167
1–2 Kings	171
1–2 Chronicles	177
Ezra-Nehemiah	181
Esther	185
Job	187

Psalms	191
Proverbs	195
Ecclesiastes	197
Song of Songs	199
About the Prophets	203
Isaiah	205
Jeremiah	209
Lamentations	213
Ezekiel	217
Daniel	221
The Twelve (The Minor Prophets)	225
Hosea	227
Joel	229
Amos	233
Obadiah	235
Jonah	237
Micah	241
Nahum	243
Habakkuk	245
Zephaniah	249
Haggai	251
Zechariah	253
Malachi	255
About the Apocrypha and Other Books	257

The New Testament

The Time between the Old and New Testaments	267
About the New Testament	275
Matthew	279
Mark	283
Luke	287
John	291
Acts	295
About Paul and His Letters	298
Romans	304
1 Corinthians	308
2 Corinthians	312
Galatians	316
Ephesians	320
Philippians	324
Colossians	328
1 Thessalonians	332
2 Thessalonians	336
1 Timothy	338
2 Timothy	342
Titus	344
Philemon	346
Hebrews	348
James	352

1 Peter	356
2 Peter	360
1 John	362
2 John	364
3 John	366
Jude	368
Revelation	370

Extras

Bible Reading Plan	376
Biblical Measurements	380
Maps	381
Picture Credits	399
Notes	401

About the Gospel Life Guidebook Series

The Gospel Life Guidebook Series is written for global pastors. Most pastors around the world have very limited access to biblical training. Many do not have a clear understanding of the gospel and are easy prey for the wolves of heretical movements like the prosperity gospel. Their biblical and theological knowledge is limited to what they may have heard at a conference or on the radio and television.

We intend this series to give global pastors the basic knowledge they need to faithfully serve the church of the Lord Jesus Christ. This series is not meant to be exhaustive. Many others have explained the concepts found here more fully elsewhere. The goal is to communicate basic truths simply and clearly, as well as to avoid discussions and illustrations that only make sense in a North American or European context.

The Gospel Life Guidebook Series comes from our specific theological identity at Gospel Life. We are orthodox Christian, Protestant, Evangelical, and Baptist.

About the Guidebook Series

- **Orthodox Christian.** We hold to the orthodox Christian faith concerning the Trinity and the person of Christ as summarized in the Apostles', Nicene, and Chalcedonian Creeds.
- **Protestant.** We hold to the Protestant distinctives of justification by faith alone, the sufficiency of Scripture, and radical corruption.
- **Evangelical.** We hold to the Evangelical distinctives of biblical inerrancy, the exclusivity of the gospel, and the necessity of gospel proclamation.
- **Baptist.** We hold to the Baptist distinctives of regenerate church membership, believer's baptism, autonomy of the local church, religious liberty, and perseverance of the saints.

Within this theological identity and with careful attention to the text of Scripture, we hope to produce a series of books that communicates the essentials to the pastors of the world. Of course, by doing this, we hope that this series will also be found useful by Christians everywhere, whether in a Sunday School class in the United States, a jungle village in Papua-New Guinea, or our training centers in Malawi.

Dr. Joshua Caleb Hutchens, Ph.D.
President, Gospel Life
Zomba, Malawi

Abbreviations

Old Testament Books

Gen	2 Chr	Dan
Exod	Ezra	Hos
Lev	Neh	Joel
Num	Esth	Amos
Deut	Job	Obad
Josh	Ps/Pss	Jonah
Judg	Prov	Mic
Ruth	Eccl	Nah
1 Sam	Song	Hab
2 Sam	Isa	Zeph
1 Kgs	Jer	Hag
2 Kgs	Lam	Zech
1 Chr	Ezek	Mal

New Testament Books

Matt	Eph	Jas
Mark	Phil	1 Pet
Luke	Col	2 Pet
John	1 Thess	1 John
Acts	2 Thess	2 John
Rom	1 Tim	3 John
1 Cor	2 Tim	Jude
2 Cor	Phlm	Rev
Gal	Heb	

To Teachers

To Teachers

The material in *The Bible Guidebook* can be divided and taught in various ways. Even in our own program at Gospel Life, we cover the material in this book differently in our separate programs. In our 5-year program for pastors who meet 3 weeks/year, we cover this material through five different courses:

1. Bible 1 (Genesis–Esther)
2. Bible 2 (Job–Malachi)
3. Bible 3 (Matthew–Acts)
4. Bible 4 (Romans–Revelation)
5. How to Study the Bible (Hermeneutics)
6. Ancient World History

In our 2-year (4 six-week semesters) program for young men who are called to the ministry, the material is covered through four courses:

1. Bible 1 (Old Testament)
2. Bible 2 (New Testament)
3. How to Study the Bible (Hermeneutics)
4. Ancient World History

To Teachers

I hope that you can see from the above examples that you can take the material here and shape it to fit the needs of your ministry, whether it is a pastor training course or a Sunday school class.

In this guidebook, after the introduction called "Meet the Bible," the material is divided into four units: How to Study the Bible, Ancient World History, Old Testament, and New Testament. There is so much more that can be said and has been said about the Bible, but I believe that the information contained in these pages are the basics that anyone needs to understand the Bible well. My goal in writing this material and in teaching it to my own students is to help them become more faithful preachers of God's word. I think the material here gives global pastors a starting place to understand the Bible and start teaching it to their churches.

Finally, if you are using this material to teach in another language, you have in advance our joyful permission to translate and use this material in your own setting with attribution. We only ask that you contact us by going to gospellife.org/books to inform us of your work. We are happy to share our resources (files, graphics, etc.) with you in your translation work.

I hope that the contents of this guidebook will help us all to testify like Paul: "Therefore I declare to you this day that I am innocent of the blood of all of you, because I did not avoid declaring to you the whole plan of God" (Acts 20:26–27).

Meet the Bible

Meet the Bible

Meet the Bible

The Bible is God's word.

This is the most important truth to understand before attempting to read and understand the Bible. It is a book like other books, but it is also unlike any other book in the world because it is God's word.

Paul explained this to Timothy, "All Scripture is inspired by God and is profitable for teaching, for rebuking, for correcting, for training in righteousness, so that the man of God may be complete, equipped for every good work" (2 Tim 3:16–17).

The Bible is also a book that contains books. The Bible contains 66 books written by over forty prophets and apostles in three languages (Hebrew, Aramaic, and Greek) over a period 1,500 years across three continents (Africa, Asia, and Europe). But it is the word of one, unchanging God who speaks to all people everywhere, calling them to faith in his only Son, Jesus Christ.

Today, most people are able to carry the Bible with them in a book of one- or two-thousand pages, but originally the books of the Bible were written on scrolls. Scrolls were long sheets of paper or animal skins that could be rolled up. Why were these 69 books collected and recognized as God's word? Why were other ancient books like the books of the Apocrypha in Catholic Bibles left out? The answer is that the people of God recognized these books as containing the authoritative and true word of God revealed through the prophets and apostles.

As God's word, the Bible is authoritative, true, clear, and sufficient. Since the Bible is God's speech, it is authoritative. It must be believed and obeyed because God must be believed and obeyed (Jas 1:22). It is true and without error because God cannot lie and his word is perfect (Num 23:19; Ps 19:7). God's word is clear. It is meant to be understood. God doesn't try to hide the meaning from us. Since he is all-powerful and all-wise, he is able to communicate clearly for us to understand (Ps 19:7). Finally, God's word is sufficient. The Bible tells us everything we need in order to know and love God (Deut 8:3; 2 Tim 3:14–17). We don't need prophets or apostles today to tell us new things that aren't in God's word. God has already told us everything we need in the Bible. We just need to open it up and begin to read.

Experience the Bible

When God inspired the prophets and apostles to write the Bible, he intended the Bible to be at the center of his people's lives. The blessed man in Psalm 1 has a fruitful and happy life because "he meditates on it day and night" (Ps 1:2). Moses told parents to talk about God's command with their children both at home and on the way, both in the morning and in the evening (Deut 6:7). The Bible should be a constant part of our lives, and so to experience the Bible fully we must engage with it in multiple ways. We must hear the Bible, read the Bible, pray the Bible, memorize the Bible, and study the Bible.

Hear the Bible.

Most of us first encountered the Bible through preaching. At church, we heard the Bible read and explained. Paul commanded his coworker Timothy, "Until I come, give your attention to the public reading, exhortation, and teaching" (1 Tim 4:13). God's plan is for the Bible to be read aloud weekly in churches for everyone to hear — especially for those who cannot read like children and the uneducated.

Paul also commanded Timothy, "Preach the word" (2 Tim 4:2)! True preaching is simply explaining the Bible clearly and helping people to understand what God expects of us. While hearing the Bible in worship is probably the first way you experienced the Bible, you will never outgrow your need to hear the Bible publicly read and preached.

Read the Bible.

For those who are able to read and have access to their own copy of the Bible, it is important to read the Bible daily. What a privilege it is to be able to read the Bible for ourselves! Men and women throughout history, and even around the world today, have given their lives so that others can read God's word for themselves.

The Bible is a big book, and it can be intimidating to just pick it up and start reading. That's why a reading plan like the one in the appendix of this book can help you get started. Our plan gives you readings in the Old Testament, New Testament, Psalms, and Proverbs each day so you can read different parts of the Bible at the same time.

Pray the Bible.

In the Bible, God gives us words that he wants us to speak back to him. Most obviously are the words of the Lord's prayer. Jesus said, "Whenever you pray, say …" (Luke 11:2; Matt 6:9–13). The book of Psalms contains 150 prayers that God wants us to make our own and pray back to him. Paul fills his letters with many prayers that can teach us how to pray (see Rom 15:5–6; 1 Cor 1:4–9; Eph 1:15–23).

When we begin to pray, we often don't know what to say or even how to start. We know that when we pray the prayers of the Bible as our own we are praying according to God's will since he inspired the very words we are praying.

Memorize the Bible.

The psalmist says, "I have treasured your word in my heart so that I may not sin against you" (Ps 119:11). We want God's word to become part of us so that it guides us in our daily lives. This requires memorizing God's word. When we memorize something, we think about it repeatedly and carefully. We are able to meditate on the meaning of each phrase or word in a way that we aren't able to when reading quickly. By memorizing, we treasure God's word.

Study the Bible.

Most of this book is dedicated to helping you study the Bible. When we are reading large portions of the Bible (like when we follow a reading plan), we aren't able to notice the specific details of each passage or book. Reading large portions is important because it helps us become better acquainted with the Bible as a whole, but studying smaller portions is also important so we can know God's word deeply.

Studying the Bible isn't something reserved for preachers. It is good for every believer, and studying the Bible shouldn't be too difficult. Bible study is simply reading a portion of the Bible slowly and repeatedly so that we think carefully about its meaning. Through Bible study, we can experience more of what God wants us to know about him from his word.

Meet the Bible

The Bible's Story

Have you ever flipped to the back of a book to find out how a story ends? For most books, skipping to the end would ruin the story, but with the Bible, it is actually helpful to know the end to understand the entire story. The Bible ends with God's eternal and perfect kingdom being established on earth. The Apostle John writes, "Then I heard a loud voice from the throne: Look, God's dwelling is with humanity, and he will live with them. They will be his peoples, and God himself will be with them and will be their God" (Rev 21:3).

This voice from the throne summarizes God's goal for his creation. He wants a people who will bear his image as his own unique people. He wants a people to live with and love, as they also love and worship him. God's goal is for God's people to dwell in God's presence under God's covenant.

The way God is accomplishing this goal is through the victory and rule of his chosen king, his own Son — Jesus, the seed of Abraham and the heir of David. So God is rescuing a people for himself through the establishment of his kingdom. Jesus has inaugurated God's kingdom by his victory over sin and death through his crucifixion and resurrection.

This establishment of God's kingdom through Jesus is the main story of the Bible. What is God's kingdom?

God's kingdom is God's people in God's presence under God's covenant.[1]

God wants to possess a people for his own, and to dwell with them as their God in his own holy place. He wants to enjoy an everlasting, unbreakable relationship with his people that is established through a covenant.

What is a covenant? A covenant is a formalized and binding agreement between two parties that establishes a relationship between them. This relationship is formed through the giving of promises and the acceptance of obligations. Throughout the Bible, God makes covenants with his people. He makes covenants with Noah, Abraham, Israel, David, and ultimately he makes a new covenant through Jesus Christ.

By making covenants between himself and his people, God is establishing a relationship with them that will ultimately bring about his kingdom. The vision of John in Revelation will come true. God will dwell forever with his people in his kingdom, because he has made them his people by giving them his unbreakable promises. God's people will dwell with God forever as his obedient and loving children through faith in what Jesus has done for them.

This kingdom story is split into four main parts:

1. **Creation.** God created his kingdom by putting his people (Adam and Eve) in his presence (in the garden of Eden) under his covenant.
2. **Fall.** Adam and Eve, however, broke God's covenant through disobedience and were removed from God's presence, being exiled from the garden. All of humanity has inherited their rebellion and separation from God.
3. **Salvation.** God began to reestablish his kingdom by making a covenant with Abraham. God reaffirmed his promises to Abraham by making a covenant with his descendants, the nation of Israel, at Sinai. He then began to fulfill his covenant promises by establishing his people in the promised land where he would dwell with them. Israel, however, broke God's covenant through disobedience, and like Adam and Eve, they were exiled from God's presence. Despite Israel's disobedience, God gave the prophets a promise of a new covenant that would finally

accomplish God's goal. Finally, he would dwell with his people. God sent his own Son, Jesus, to establish the new covenant and inaugurate his kingdom. Jesus cleansed God's people through his sacrifice on the cross. Now, by faith in Jesus, we become part of God's new covenant kingdom as it expands to include all the nations of the world.

4. **Restoration.** When Jesus returns, God will bring about his perfect kingdom forever. God's people (everyone who places their faith in Jesus) will live in God's presence in the new creation under God's new covenant.

While the Bible contains many different stories, all the stories make up this big story of creation, fall, salvation, and restoration. All the stories of the Bible find their fulfillment in what Jesus has done to save God's people, establish God's covenant, and inaugurate God's kingdom to bring God's people into God's presence forever.

Meet the Bible

The Bible's Story

God's Kingdom is	God's People	in God's Presence	under God's Covenant
Creation	Adam and Eve	Eden	God's commands God's provision God's presence
Fall	No One	Exile from Eden	Rebellion against God Struggle in a broken creation Removal from God's presence
Salvation *God chose Israel.*	Israel	Promised land	God's law God's king Sacrifices and God's presence
Salvation *Israel fell.*	Idolaters	Exile from the promised land	Rebellion against God Removal of the kings Removal from God's presence Destruction of the temple
Salvation *God foretold his kingdom.*	Redeemed, Born Again, International People	New creation	New covenant New king God's presence
Disappointment: *The return of the exiles did not bring God's perfect kingdom.*			
Salvation *God began his kingdom.*	Jesus	Jesus	Jesus
Salvation *God expands his kingdom.*	The church	The church	The church
Restoration	Redeemed, Resurrected, International People	New creation	No sin, no death God's king God's presence

How to Study the Bible

How to Study the Bible

Understanding any book that was written thousands of years ago can be a challenge, but when the task before us is not only to understand the book as testimony to history, but also to understand and obey it as the word of God to us today, then the task becomes doubly difficult. Studying the Bible is not an exact science. You can't simply follow steps 1–3 and produce the understanding that you need.

Studying the Bible is an active conversation with the Living God. Through the words of the Bible, God himself speaks to us today just as clearly and forcefully as he spoke to the prophets and apostles through whom he revealed his word. Even so, people often miss what God is saying because they do not pay careful attention to God's word. Often, in our pride, we make God's word say what we want it to say instead of humbly listening to how God is confronting our brokenness and sinful desires.

Paul exhorted Timothy to handle the Bible carefully: "Be diligent to present yourself to God as one approved, a worker who doesn't need to be ashamed, correctly teaching the word of truth" (2 Tim 2:15). He warned Timothy that people would seek teachers who told them what they wanted to hear rather than what the Bible actually says: "For the time will come when people will not tolerate sound doctrine, but according to their own desires, will multiply teachers for themselves because they have an itch to hear what they want to hear. They will turn away from hearing the truth and will turn aside to myths" (2 Tim 3:3–4).

The Basic Method of Studying the Bible

In one sense, studying the Bible is simple. Studying the Bible is simply reading portions of the Bible *slowly* and *repeatedly*. But to do this well, we need to follow a basic method that will guide us to clear understanding.

The basic method of studying the Bible is actually common sense. Imagine that you are walking down a road and a large truck weighed down by a heavy load is driving full speed toward you. What will you do in such a situation? First, you will see. You will look down the road and gather the facts of the situation: (1) There is a truck driving down the road. (2) It is a large truck with a heavy load. (3) It is coming quickly. (4) It is driving straight toward me. Then you will begin to process the information and understand the meaning of what you have seen: If I stay where I am, and if this truck continues to drive quickly toward me, it will hit me, and I will die. Finally, you will use this understanding to make a choice: RUN! Get out of the road!

When we study the Bible, we follow these same three steps from real life. First, we *read*, carefully seeing what the Bible actually says. Second, we seek to *understand* the meaning of the Bible, and third, we must *obey* the Bible.

Read. What does the Bible say?

The most important step of studying the Bible is learning to read it carefully. This step is the most important because if we mess up in this step then we cannot succeed in the other steps. So, we must begin with the question: "What does the Bible say?"

To answer this question, first we need God's help. God is not dead. He is speaking to us through his word, but because we are imperfect, we need the help of his Spirit to understand what he is saying to us. If you read and enjoyed a book, wouldn't you be excited to get to meet the author and ask him about everything you didn't understand completely? We don't only have the opportunity to meet the author of the Bible. We have the author dwelling within us as the Holy Spirit. We should pray like the songwriter of Psalm 119, "Help me to understand your instruction, and I will obey it and follow it with all my heart" (Ps 119:34).

But to know what the Bible says, we must also know some of the background about the particular book or section of the Bible we are studying. I hope this guidebook will help you in this area. In this book, you will find basic facts about each book of the Bible. For example, if you are trying to understand Philippians 4, you first need to know who was writing Philippians, who he was writing to, and what was the main idea that he was communicating.

Finally, the way to really answer the question "What does the Bible say?" Is to read *slowly* and to read *repeatedly*. During your daily Bible reading, it is okay to read through large portions of Scripture quickly, but when you are sitting down to understand the Bible deeply, you cannot expect to read the passage you are studying once and to understand it fully. Read the section you are studying slowly. But then read it over and over again. Read it until you almost have it memorized. You don't have to understand it yet. You just need to see it. You want to see every detail as clearly as you can so that you can start to understand.

Understand. What did the Bible mean?

Once you have read the section slowly and repeatedly, you can begin to seek to understand the meaning. As you seek to understand the meaning, there are three essential rules to remember:

1. *A passage will never mean what it never meant.* God never changes. Therefore, his word is trustworthy and unchanging. The words that God spoke to Moses still mean what they meant when God spoke them 3,400 years ago. New ideas and current events cannot alter the meaning of the Bible. Notice that the question we are asking in this step is "What *did* the

Bible mean?," not "What *does* the Bible mean?" To understand what the Bible means to us today, we must first understand what it meant to the original audience.

2. *Scripture interprets Scripture.* Some parts of the Bible are hard to understand, but thankfully God has given us the answer to every question that we need to know an answer to in the Bible itself. We will always have questions about things that God hasn't revealed to us, but if God hasn't told us the answer in the Bible, it is because in his wisdom he knew we didn't need to know the answer. Everything that we need to know to love and serve him is contained in the Bible. So when we come to a difficult verse or idea in the Bible, we do not have to speculate and formulate our own answers to the meaning. Instead, we need to ask the Bible itself for the answers. The clearer passages of the Bible help us to understand the difficult passages, if we will just take the time to ask and search the Scriptures.

3. *The entire Bible is about Jesus.* If we keep this simple rule in mind, it will save us from a lot of misunderstanding. The purpose of the Bible is to reveal Jesus and his kingdom to us. It isn't teaching us simply how to overcome our struggles or grow wealthy or have an easy life. It is teaching us who Jesus is and what he has done for us so that we will believe and be transformed into the likeness of Jesus. In the Old Testament, every passage is in some way pointing forward to Jesus' coming. In the New Testament, every passage is explaining the significance of who Jesus is and what he has done. No matter what section of Scripture we are studying, we must constantly be looking for Jesus there.

With those rules in mind, how do we find the meaning of the section of the Bible we are studying? Ask questions and seek answers! Read through the section again, and simply list every question that comes to mind. Imagine you were studying John 3:16, "For God loved the world in this way: He gave his one and only Son, so that everyone who believes in him will not perish but have eternal life." Here might be some of our questions: (1) What is the world? (2)

Who is the Son? (3) How do you believe in the Son? (4) What does it mean to "perish"? (5) What is eternal life?

To find the answers to these questions, you should first look within the chapter of the Bible that you are studying. In John 3, you would find that "to perish" is to be judged and condemned by God (John 3:17–18). If you can't find the answer you are seeking in the chapter, look for it in the rest of the book. For example, John more clearly explains who the Son is in John 1:14–18. If you can't find your answer in that book, then begin to search the rest of the Bible.

Finally, once you have answered all the questions that you can from the Bible itself, read the passage again with your new understanding. To help summarize your new understanding, write a sentence that explains the main idea of the passage in a simple and clear way.

Obey. What should I do?

James warned his readers, "But be doers of the word and not hearers only, deceiving yourselves" (Jas 1:22). God wants us to read and understand his word, but he wants us to read and understand *so that* we will obey his word. We are never finished until we have prayerfully sought to answer the question, "What should I do?"

Every passage of the Bible speaks to us and points us to reasons why we should worship God, truth about ourselves, commands God wants us to obey, ways we should treat other people, or prayers that we should pray. Jesus said that the entire Bible depends upon two commands: Love the Lord your God, and love your neighbor (Matt 22:37–40). We should always ask, "How does this passage teach me to love God more completely?" and "How does this passage teach me to love my neighbor more selflessly?"

Just get started.

The best way to learn how to study the Bible is to study the Bible. Don't be intimidated by these three steps. Today, I sometimes laugh at some of the ideas I came up with in my early attempts to study the Bible. Now I have greater understanding, and I wouldn't make the same mistakes that I made then. But I have that understanding because I did the hard work of studying and made those mistakes, learning from them through the years.

Always remember that you aren't studying the Bible alone. You are part of a church that loves God's word too. God gives us brothers and sisters, as well as pastor-teachers, to help us. We understand God's word better when we seek to understand it together as God's people than we could ever understand it alone.

Finally, remember that Jesus promises that the Spirit would guide us into all the truth (John 16:13). The Spirit honors humble hearts that work diligently to read, understand, and obey his word. He will shepherd us through his word and bring us gradually into greater and greater understanding of his truth.

Don't worry about being perfect. Put your faith in God, and get started!

How to Read Old Testament Stories

No matter where you go in the world, people love stories. However, how people tell stories differs from culture to culture. For example, a recent book reads differently than the ancient Greek poem by Homer *The Iliad*. As we approach the stories of the Old Testament, we find them as familiar as any story we've ever heard, but on the other hand, we can learn to understand these stories better if we know the way ancient Israelites told stories.

The following eight instructions help unlock the meaning of the stories of the Old Testament:[2]

1. Read the Old Testament as history.

The Old Testament authors knew they were writing history, not legend. Furthermore, with the exception of Genesis 1-11, these authors were writing relatively recent history. This is important because of what it says about God.

The God revealed to us in the Old Testament is a God who interacts with humans within history. Their experience with God wasn't primarily mystical — occurring in visions or dreams (although these did happen) — but historical. God, who transcends time and space because he created it, enters into time to perform mighty deeds for his people.

2. Admire the one Hero.

The God who reveals himself through his historical actions is the Hero of every story. He is the main character. What about Abraham, Moses, David, or Elijah? They are important, but God is always at the center. As you read the Old Testament stories, always ask first: what does this story teach me about God?

3. Understand that people are always the same.

There are many differences between how we live today and the lives of the people portrayed in the Old Testament. Despite these differences, we share many of the same experiences, like temptation, victory, pain, suffering, comfort, and joy to name a few.

While these stories occur in ancient history, they are not limited to telling us facts about history. They speak to universal human experiences, and they testify to a universal solution to the human problem. Everyone needs the merciful God of Abraham, Isaac, and Jacob to act on their behalf.

4. Identify the conflict.

Every story possesses a conflict of some kind. Otherwise, a story isn't really a story. It's just a list of related events. The conflict is a problem that needs a resolution. Here are a few examples of conflicts in the Old Testament:

- The serpent tempts the woman to eat the fruit (Gen 3).
- Goliath challenges Israel to a contest (1 Sam 17).
- Nebuchadnezzar demands that everyone worship his statue (Dan 3).

A correct understanding of the meaning of the story depends on a correct understanding of the conflict. Take time to identify the conflict in your mind.

5. Divide the story into scenes.

Hebrew stories typically present the action in a series of scenes. Let's take the story of the fall of humanity in Genesis 3 as an example:

- Scene 1: At the tree of knowledge of good and evil. The serpent tempts. The woman and man eat (Gen 3:1–6)
- Scene 2: Somewhere in the garden. The humans sew fig leaves as clothing (Gen 3:7).
- Scene 3: Somewhere in the garden. God is coming. The humans hide. God speaks (Gen 3:8–19).
- Scene 4: Somewhere in the garden. The man believes. God covers his nakedness (Gen 3:20–21).
- Scene 5: The heavenly council. God declares the need to remove humans from the garden (Gen 3:22).
- Scene 6: East of the garden. God drives the humans out and places guardians at the entrance (Gen 3:23–24).

To understand a story well, it helps to identify each scene and attempt to understand what each scene contributes to the story as a whole.

6. Study the characters.

Characters are important for any story, but in Old Testament stories, characters often help to interpret one another. Sometimes characters parallel one another. The most obvious example is Elijah and Elisha. Elisha imitates his predecessor Elijah. Similarly, Daniel parallels Joseph as an exiled wise interpreter of dreams within a gentile court. At other times, characters contrast with one another. Take Saul and David for example. Saul looks like a king. David doesn't. Saul is unfaithful. David is a man after God's own heart.

7. Listen to what is being said.

In many Old Testament stories, the action only serves to set the scene for the dialogue. The most significant aspects of the story and its meaning often occur in what the characters say.

The first spoken words of a story will often define the conflict. Let's take David's slaying of Goliath in 1 Samuel 17 as our example. In 1 Samuel 17:8-10, Goliath defines the conflict by challenging the armies and the God of Israel.

Many times, an author will emphasize an important point by repetition in the dialogue. In the David and Goliath story, Goliath's taunt is referred to twice more, even though it is not repeated word-for-word (1 Sam 17:8–10, 36, 45).

Through the dialogue, the conflict becomes clear: Goliath challenges the supremacy of Israel's God. Saul and Israel's army simultaneously do not trust their God, and choose to hide in their tents. Only David, the Spirit-anointed king, will have faith enough in God to take up Goliath's challenge.

Finally, at the crucial point in the story, the dialogue will often reveal the main point. When David speaks to Goliath in 1 Samuel 17:45-47, he reveals the point of the action. As the Yahweh's anointed, David will slay the giant, but why? David kills Goliath so "that all the earth will know" the God of Israel.

If you miss the dialogue, then you miss the story.

8. Remember that not everything done in the story is right.

Many Old Testament stories tell about sinful things that were done by characters in the Bible, but not every story tells whether or not that action was the right action. For example, when David sleeps with Bathsheba and murders her husband Uriah, the Bible says, "The LORD considered what David had done to be evil" (2 Sam 11:27). The story itself clearly tells us that David's actions were wrong.

But what about when Jephthah sacrificed his own daughter to God because he made a rash vow in Judges 11? The story itself does not actually tell us whether Jephthah's sacrifice was right or wrong. To discover whether or not we should imitate Jephthah's sacrifice of his daughter, we have to look at the rest of the Bible. When we do, we find that (1) human sacrifice is condemned by God (Jer 33:35), (2) God gave the Israelites a way to escape the consequences of rash vows (Lev 5:4–6), and (3) the story of Jephthah is placed in the book of Judges to show the increasing wickedness of the people of Israel (see the notes on Judges).

Not every story is given to us as a positive example to imitate, and we must be careful to read each story to uncover what the author means to teach us.

How to Study the Bible

How to Read Old Testament Law

It is hard to read the Old Testament law with its long, detailed descriptions about skin diseases and sacrifices. However, the law remains relevant for the Christian.

With a few helpful hints, the Old Testament law can become easier to read and more beneficial. The following seven hints will help you read the law better:

1. Read the law as part of the story.

The record of Israel's laws occurs within the context of the Exodus from Egypt and the wandering in the wilderness. Therefore, these are not abstract moral principles but the specific demands God makes upon his people as their Savior. Throughout the law, God constantly reminds Israel that he is the one who has brought them up out of Egypt. God demands obedience as Savior, not as dictator.

2. Receive the law as instruction.

The Hebrew word we most often translate "law" (*torah*) has a much broader meaning than simply legal restrictions or rules. "Instruction" may be the best translation. We often think of "law" as negative. The law binds, restricts, and limits. But the idea of "instruction" can help us see God's good intention in giving the law. Instruction helps, trains, and grants freedom.

3. Understand the law as an act of grace.

Understanding the place of the law in the story of Israel can help us see the law as an act of God's grace. The Old Testament law was not given so that Israel could earn a relationship with God. Obedience to the law was meant to flow from a people undeservedly rescued from slavery. The use of the law by the Pharisees and others in the New Testament should not be confused with the intention of God in giving the law. Salvation has always been by grace through faith, and this not of ourselves (Eph 2:8). The law instructs God's people how to live holy because their God is holy. The law condemns us because of our failure to keep the law, not because of the law's failure to communicate God's holiness and grace.

4. View the law as a boundary marker.

As God's rescued people, the law codified perpetual distinction between God's people and the surrounding nations. We may not always understand why God gave a specific instruction (like not boiling a baby goat in its mother's milk; Exod 23:19), but we know that God's command would distinguish Israel from the nations. Sometimes you hear that God gave certain regulations because they were healthier (like the regulations for the Kosher diet), but this cannot be clearly proven in most cases. What we can know, however, is that many of God's regulations would have made Israel different from other nations.

5. Look for two types of commands.

Not every command is the same, and when interpreting the commands of the law it can be helpful to categorize them into two different categories: (1) Direct Commands and (2) Case-by-Case Commands. Direct Commands give a straightforward command about what a person should or should not do. The ten commandments are the perfect example of these commands. They are absolute. "Do not _____" (Exod 20).

Case-by-case commands, by contrast, are conditional. Most of them come in the form of, "if this happens, then that." Deuteronomy 15:7-8 is a good example:

> "If there is a poor person among you, one of your brothers within any of your city gates in the land the LORD your God is giving you, do not be hardhearted or tightfisted toward your poor brother. Instead, you are to open your hand to him and freely loan him enough for whatever need he has."

This may seem like a minor distinction, but the point is that even in ancient Israel the various commands had differing levels of relevance. Some had absolute relevance to all people everywhere, while others were conditional upon certain situations.

6. See the covenant structure.

The law is more than just a code. It comes in the form of a covenant. In the ancient near east, a covenant was commonly an agreement between a conquering king and a conquered king, which created a relationship between the two through promises and obligations. These agreements had a common structure would have been recognized by the nation of Israel. Covenants include an identification of the parties, review of their history, list of obligations, identification of witnesses, consequences for unfaithfulness, and plans for reviewing the covenant. These various elements are evident throughout Exodus, Leviticus, Numbers, and Deuteronomy.

- **Identification of the parties.** This section lists those who are entering into covenant with each other. Take for example the first words of the ten commandments: "I am the LORD your God..." (Exod 20:2).
- **Review of their history.** The second section tells the history of the relationship between the parties: "...who brought you out of the land of Egypt..." (Exod 20:2).
- **List of obligations.** The obligations were the demands that the conqueror made upon the conquered. In political relationships, this often involved the

paying of tribute to the conqueror. In the Mosaic covenant, the commands themselves are the obligations.
- **Identification of witnesses.** Those who bore witness to the covenant would enforce the agreement. At times, these witnesses were more symbolic. For example, Jacob and Laban set up stones to bear witness to their covenant not to cross over to pursue one another (Gen 31:45-50). Various witnesses are given for the Mosaic covenant: creation (Deut 30:19), the words of the book itself (Deut 31:26), the people themselves (Josh 24:22), and the stone erected at Shechem (Josh 24:27).
- **Consequences for unfaithfulness.** In secular covenants, sanctions enumerated the benefits of keeping the covenant, and the punishments for violating it. Similarly, in the Mosaic covenant, there are blessings for obedience and curses for disobedience (Deut 28-33).
- **Plans for reviewing the covenant.** A covenant needed to be regularly reviewed and remembered. The Mosaic covenant was to be reviewed at various times in various ways. After entering the promised land, the people were to renew the covenant at Shechem (Josh 24). The law predicted that God would give Israel a king, and the king was to make a copy of the covenant (Deut 17:18-19). Also, the Levites were to read the covenant annually at the Feast of Booths (Deut 31:9-13).

The benefit of understanding the covenant structure of the law is that it helps one to understand how the law operated in the relationship of Israel to Israel's God.

7. Know that you are free from the law.

Should Christians stone people who blaspheme the name of God (Lev 24:16)? Are Christians required to rest on the Sabbath? Should Christians avoid pork or observe the Old Testament feasts?

The relationship of the Christian to the law of Moses has been a controversial topic since the earliest days of the church (Acts 15; Gal). The question is an important one. If we accept the Old Testament as Scripture, then shouldn't we obey all the commands of the law of Moses?

The Thirty-Nine Articles of the Anglican Church, the Westminster Confession (followed by Presbyterians), and the Second London Baptist Confession all give what has become the standard answer for Protestants: The law of Moses can be split into three categories: Ceremonial, Civil, and Moral. Ceremonial laws governed Israel's worship. Civil laws governed their community life, and moral laws told them right from wrong in a universal way. According to this explanation, Christians must still obey the moral laws, while the ceremonial and civil laws are no longer binding.

The problem with this explanation is that neither the Old Testament nor the New Testament neatly divide the law of Moses into these three categories. How can we know where every law fits? Is the command about observing the Sabbath, for example, ceremonial, civil, or moral? It can be argued that it is all three. The lines between the categories are not clear.

When we are talking about the Christian and the law of Moses, we are really talking about the view of the Apostle Paul toward the law, since he more than any other New Testament author speaks to the issue, and Paul never divides the law into these three categories.

Paul does three things with the law: He rejects it, replaces it, and uses it.[3]

Paul rejects the law as covenant.

The Christian is no longer under the dominion of the law. As far as the law operated for ancient Israel as the covenant agreement between them and God, it is no longer in effect, and the Christian is free from the law. As Paul says in Galatians 5:18, "But if you are led by the Spirit, you are not under the law." We are under the new covenant that Jesus established by fulfilling the demands of the law for us.

Paul replaces the law.

Our relationship with Jesus Christ has replaced the law. Our relationship to Christ becomes a new "law" for us. Paul describes this in various ways: the law of faith (Rom 3:27); the law of the Spirit of life (Rom 8:2); the law of Christ (1 Cor 9:21; Gal 6:2). Consider how Paul puts it in Gal 6:15, "For both circumcision and uncircumcision mean nothing; what matters instead is a new creation." Paul means that the demands of circumcision under the law are no longer binding upon believers in Christ. The important thing is that we have become a new creation through faith in Christ.

Paul uses the law as prophecy and wisdom.

The law is not completely irrelevant for the Christian. The law continues to be applicable as prophecy and wisdom. As prophecy, the law testified to the coming of Christ. Take, for example, Paul's statement in Romans 3:21, "But now, apart from the law, the righteousness of God has been revealed, attested by the law and the prophets." In these last days, God has clearly revealed his one, unchanging plan for salvation through faith in Jesus. We know that this is God's perfect plan because hundreds and even thousands of years before Jesus came, the Old Testament, including the law of Moses, pointed forward to Jesus' coming.

As wisdom, the law continues to give principles for Christian life. Interestingly, in Ephesians, Paul says that the law has been abolished (Eph 2:15), but at the end of the letter, he directs children to obey the law to honor their parents (Eph 6:1-3). So which is it? Is the law abolished, or does it still speak to us? While we are free from the law as a covenant because Christ fulfilled the law for us, the law continues to speak wisdom to us. It testifies to unchanging principles that God had put into creation. God intends for children to grow to maturity and wisdom by honoring and obeying their parents. This remains just as true today as it was when God spoke it from the cloud at Sinai.

How to Read Old Testament Wisdom and Poetry

The books of Old Testament wisdom, especially Psalms and Proverbs, have helped many Christians endure the difficulties of life by faith. Here are seven ways you can learn to read them for your own benefit:

1. Recognize that these books confront life in all its complexity.

Job and most of the Psalms demonstrate for us the life of faith in the midst of suffering. Yet Proverbs often reminds us that when we follow God's wisdom, things will generally go well for us. Ecclesiastes answers the question, "Is there meaning to life?" Song of Songs celebrates the joys of romantic love. For every high and low in our lives, there is something in the wisdom books that speaks to it.

2. Open your heart to these songs.

Most of the wisdom books are written as poetry or in song form. Songs are meant to engage our emotions. These books remind us that God made us to be more than just brains who think the right thoughts. He gave us hearts to feel deeply. As you read the Psalms, especially, don't just try to understand what is being said. Try also to feel the mood of the song.

Psalm 97 commands us, "Rejoice in the LORD, O you righteous, and give thanks to his holy name" (Ps 97:12). When we read that, we need to do it! But at other times, we read, "My God, my God, why have you forsaken me? Why are you so far from saving me, from the words of my groaning" (Ps 22:1)? When we read these words, we can remember times that we've felt abandoned too. Sometimes the emotions are complex, as when Psalm 2 commands us: "Serve the LORD with reverential awe and rejoice with trembling" (Ps 2:11).

3. See the pictures being created.

Songwriters have always used pictures or metaphors to communicate their ideas and emotions. When David writes, "Save me, O God! For the waters have come up to my neck," he does not mean that he is literally drowning as he writes. He's expressing that he feels like he is drowning because of the difficulties that he faces. Psalm 23 uses the picture of a shepherd to remind us of how God lovingly cares for us.

4. Notice the repetition.

In many languages, we recognize poetry because it rhymes. Hebrew poetry, however, does not rhyme. What makes it poetry then? Hebrew poetry is identified by it's repetition, which is called parallelism. For example, Psalm 141:3 consists of two lines that mean the same thing:

(1) LORD, set up a guard for my mouth;
(2) keep watch at the door of my lips.

David wants God to help him control his speech, but he makes his request in this poetic way by repeating himself.

Sometimes the repetition includes two lines that say opposite things to make a single point. We see this a lot in the book of Proverbs. For example,

(1) Whoever loves discipline loves knowledge,
(2) but one who hates correction is stupid (Prov 12:1).

This contrast between the ones who love and who hate correction makes the single point that a wise person accepts correction as good.

5. In the Psalms, look for Jesus and his kingdom.

The Psalms begin with the hope of a righteous king who will extend God's kingdom to the ends of the earth. Psalm 1 tells us of a blessed man who loves God's law. Psalm 2 speaks of God's chosen king who will defeat the nations. Both of these psalms together point forward to Jesus as the righteous king in the line of David. They are like the lenses of a pair of glasses through which we should read the Psalms. If we look through these lenses, we will begin to see Jesus and his kingdom throughout the book.

6. In Proverbs, look for guiding principles, not promises.

Most of the proverbs are short, two-line sayings that are meant for easy memorization. It is easy to remember that "there is a way that seems right to a person, but its end is the way to death" (Prov 14:12). By putting these memorable sayings in our hearts, they can become part of us and guide us in our reactions and decisions.

To create these memorable sayings, the authors of the proverbs paint in black and white. They show us a clear picture of life without too much complexity. There is good and evil, wisdom and folly. There are two ways to choose from.

This means that Proverbs is not meant to give us a guarantee or a promise but a guiding principle. Proverbs says, "Start a youth out on his way; even when he grows old he will not depart from it" (Prov 22:6). But we have all seen families where the parents did their best to teach their children, but the children grew stubborn and rebellious anyway. Do situations like this mean that Proverbs 22:6 is false? No. The proverb does not give a guarantee. It simply teaches that in general, when parents teach their children the right way, the children will follow the path set out before them.

7. In Job, Ecclesiastes, and Song of Songs, follow the story or the argument.

You cannot pull verses out of these books and understand them correctly. Ecclesiastes, for example, begins by saying, "Absolute futility. Everything is futile" (Eccl 1:2). Should we quote this verse to prove that this life is meaningless? Yes and no. Yes, the teacher of Ecclesiastes is teaching that life apart from God is meaningless, but when we read the entire book, we actually find that there is meaning in life when we live for God (Eccl 12:13–14).

Similarly, most of the book of Job is a conversation between Job and his friends. Job's friends are actually offering the wrong interpretation of Job's suffering. They think that Job deserves what has happened because he has sinned, but what they are saying is wrong. At the end of the book, God himself rebukes them (Job 42:7–9). When we pull verses out of these books without understanding how they fit in the book as a whole, then we risk believing that something wrong is right.

How to Read the Prophets

Most people have a difficult time reading the prophets because they think prophecy is simply foretelling the future. While the prophets often did foretell future events, they did much more than that. By understanding the role of prophets, as well as when and how they spoke, you will be able to better understand these important books of the Bible.

1. See the prophets as enforcing God's covenant.

Most of the time, the prophets aren't pointing to the future, but to the past. Their job was to remind Israel about the covenant they had made with God at Sinai. God's people were failing to keep God's covenant, and therefore they were in danger of falling under the curses of the covenant. Deuteronomy 28 had a strong influence over the prophets. In Deuteronomy 28, Israel is told that if they obey God, then God will bless them in the promised land, but if they disobey God, then God will curse them and ultimately remove them from the land.

The prophets identified the sins of God's people — idolatry, immorality, and injustice — and warned that soon Israel would face the consequences for their disobedience. At some point, God would remove the people from the land. Therefore, the prophets repeatedly called Israel to repentance and faith in God's word.

Isaiah 1, the first chapter of the prophetic section of the Bible, gives us the perfect example. First, Isaiah identifies Israel's sinfulness: "O sinful nation, people weighed down with iniquity, brood of evildoers, depraved children! They have abandoned the LORD; they have despised the Holy One of Israel; they have turned their backs on him" (Isa 1:4). He then calls the people to repentance: "Wash yourselves. Cleanse yourselves. Remove your evil deeds from my sight. Stop doing evil" (Isa 1:16).

Isaiah begs God's people to remember and obey God and his covenant, but Isaiah is also told by God that his work will be ineffective to change Israel. When God calls Isaiah as a prophet in chapter 6, he says, "Go! Say to these people: keep listening, but do not understand; keep looking, but do not perceive. Make the minds of these people dull; deafen their ears and blind their eyes; otherwise they might see with their eyes and hear with their ears, understand with their minds, turn back, and be healed" (Isa 6:10). Isaiah's preaching will ultimately serve to show the justice of God's judgment against Israel.

2. Know when the prophet spoke.

In general, we must understand the historical backgrounds of biblical books to read them well, but this is even more the case with the prophets. The prophetic books were written between 800–400 B.C. A lot happens and changes over four hundred years, and the situation that Amos spoke to is quite different from the situation that Malachi spoke to.

While the Bible speaks of many prophets who did not write their prophecies down (for example, Nathan, Elijah, Elisha, etc.), the first writing prophets arose around the 700s B.C. Amos, Hosea, Jonah, Micah, and Isaiah spoke during the divided kingdoms of Judah and Israel. God called these prophets to identify the increasing sinfulness of God's people and warn of the future exiles of both Judah and Israel. The northern kingdom of Israel would be defeated by Assyria and exiled in 723/22 B.C.

Jeremiah, Nahum, Zephaniah, Obadiah, Joel, and Habakkuk spoke as Babylon was growing powerful. They warned Judah that their own exile was imminent (586 B.C.). Ezekiel and Daniel prophesied during the Babylonian exile, calling God's people to commit themselves to God anew and look forward to a promised restoration. The final group of prophets — Haggai, Zechariah, and Malachi — spoke after Jews had begun to return to the promised land from exile, and called God's people to recommit themselves to God in the land.

3. Understand the different ways prophets spoke.

Not all prophets spoke in the same way. One of the most common ways that prophets spoke was to give a direct revelation from God. Jeremiah often says, "The word of the LORD came to me" (for example, Jer 1:4, 11; 2:1) or "This is the LORD's declaration" (for example, Jer 1:19; 2:3; 3:10). The words that Jeremiah then records are the direct speech of God himself. When the prophet gives a direct revelation from God, the prophet's words are God's words.

The prophetic books also contain large sections of historical stories. For example, Isaiah tells about events from Hezekiah's reign (Isa 36–39) or Daniel tells stories about himself and his friends seeking to live faithfully to God in Babylon (Dan 1–6). Much of what you've read in "How to Read Old Testament Stories" applies to these stories too. But it is also important to see that these stories help you understand the other revelations that God gives the prophets.

Some prophets received God's revelation through visions. Isaiah sees God enthroned and calling him to prophetic ministry (Isa 6). Ezekiel sees a valley of dry bones resurrected (Ezek 37). Daniel sees God appoint one like a son of man to be ruler of the earth (Dan 7). Visions help God's people to see and feel God's revelations. For example, Ezekiel could have simply said that God was going to transform and resurrect his people, but the vision of bones brought back to life is much more powerful.

At other times, the prophets themselves became the visual aid to their revelations. For example, God tells Hosea to "marry a woman of promiscuity and have children of promiscuity, for the land is committing blatant acts of promiscuity and abandoning the LORD" (Hos 1:2). Hosea's family then becomes a visual aid to help Israel understand what they were doing by disobeying God and worshiping idols.

Finally, much of the prophetic books are written in the form of poetry. They did this because poetry is easy to memorize. Much of what you've read in "How to Read Old Testament Wisdom and Poetry" will help you understand the prophets as well.

4. Pay attention when prophets do foretell the future.

While the prophets are not always foretelling future events, sometimes they do. In fact, Moses taught that this was an important test of whether or not a prophet was truly sent by God: "You may say to yourself, 'How can we recognize a message the LORD has not spoken?' When a prophet speaks in the LORD's name, and the message does not come true or is not fulfilled, that is a message the LORD has not spoken" (Deut 18:21–22). By this standard, many self-appointed prophets today whose predictions never come to pass are revealed as false prophets and liars. What the biblical prophets spoke always came to pass.

At times, however, the fulfillment of a prophesy can be quite complicated. Many prophecies were fulfilled twice. One "fulfillment" would be immediate and partial, but the perfect fulfillment would still await in the future. The initial fulfillment serves to emphasize God's commitment and ability to bring about the perfect fulfillment in the future.

For example, in Isaiah 7, God instructs King Ahaz of Judah to ask him for a sign that God will deliver him from the military threat of the northern kingdom of Israel and Aram. Ahaz refuses to ask God for a sign, but God gives him a sign anyway: "Therefore, the LORD himself will give you a sign: See, the virgin will conceive, have a son, and name him Immanuel" (Isa 7:14). God then says that before this child is grown the military threat will be no more (Isa 7:15). In chapter

8, Isaiah tells how his wife gives birth to a child. Isaiah's child is the first fulfillment of this prophecy, the sign given to Ahaz that God will defeat Judah's enemies. But in chapter 9, Isaiah foresees the birth of another child: "For a child will be born for us, a son will be given to us, and the government will be on his shoulders. He will be named Wonderful Counselor, Mighty God, Eternal Father, Prince of Peace" (Isa 9:6). The perfect fulfillment of Isaiah 7:14 came at the birth of this child who can also be called Mighty God, the child who is Immanuel ("God with us") and born of a virgin, Jesus (see Matt 1:23).

How to Study the Bible

How to Read the Gospels

Matthew, Mark, Luke, and John each wrote down the things Jesus said and did. We call their books gospels because of their focus on the good news about Jesus. Because the gospels include many stories about Jesus that follow the tradition of Hebrew storytelling in the Old Testament, many of the instructions for reading Old Testament stories will be helpful for reading the gospels and Acts as well.

But the gospels are also unique because there are four of them, and because they tell us about our Lord and Savior Jesus Christ. The following six suggestions will help you to read them so you can see Jesus clearly.

1. See how the 4 perspectives reveal the same good news.

The full titles of these books are the Gospel according to Matthew, the Gospel according to Mark, the Gospel according to Luke, and the Gospel according to John. When you see these longer titles side-by-side, it becomes clear that we are reading about 1 gospel, which is being told to us from 4 perspectives. This is no accident. The life and teachings of Jesus are so important that it takes four accounts to even begin to communicate it well.

Each gospel has its own personality and emphases. Matthew, Mark, and Luke share a lot of the same stories and teaching, often word-for-word. But each one is different. Mark is short and to-the-point. Luke gives us the historical details, and Matthew is focused on how Jesus fulfills the Old Testament and became the Savior of all nations. John was written last because the apostle John wanted to include stories and teaching that weren't found in the other three. John also spends more time explaining the significance of who Jesus is and what he did. God knew we needed all four accounts to get a clear picture of who Jesus is.

2. Look for the meaning on two levels.

Each of the gospels speaks to us from two different levels. First, there is the level of Jesus in the historical events and teaching recorded by the writers. We can ask, "What did Jesus mean when he said that? Why did Jesus do that? What was Jesus trying to teach us?"

But Jesus did much more than is written in the Bible. John says at the end of his gospel, "And there are also many other things that Jesus did, which, if every one of them were written down, I suppose not even the world itself could contain the books that would be written" (John 21:25). This reminds us that each of the gospel writers had to pick and choose which stories and teachings of Jesus to include and which to leave out.

This is the second level of the gospels, the level of the gospel writers. By choosing what to include and arranging them the way they did, the gospel writers are trying to teach us, too. We should ask, "Why did Matthew put these stories together? Or what did Luke want to teach us by including this detail?"

For example, in Mark 4:35–5:43, Mark arranges four stories about Jesus side-by-side. He tells us how Jesus calmed a storm (Mark 4:35–41), cast out an army of demons from a man (Mark 5:1–20), healed a woman (Mark 5:25–34), and raised a girl from the dead (Mark 5:21–24, 35–43). Mark puts these stories together to give us a full picture of Jesus' power. He has power over creation, demons, disease, and even death!

3. Understand that the gospels often show rather than tell.

Sometimes the gospels tell us clearly what we need to learn about Jesus like when John begins his gospel by telling us that Jesus is God (John 1:1), but at other times, the gospels invite us to be like the people who first observed Jesus in Galilee. We get to see him at work, marvel at him, and slowly grow in our understanding of who he is.

After Jesus calms the storm in Mark 4:35–41, the disciples ask, "Who then is this? Even the wind and the sea obey him" (Mark 4:41)! Mark doesn't give us the answer to this question. He wants us to experience the surprise that the disciples experienced, and, like the disciples themselves, we can slowly come to the realization that Jesus must be the creator God if creation obeys him.

4. Ask, "What does this show me about Jesus?"

Everything in the gospels is meant to show us who Jesus is, and everything about Jesus leads to the crucifixion and resurrection. While the four gospels tell us many different things about Jesus, they all come to the same end of the story: Jesus was crucified, and on the third day he rose again. Whatever we are reading in the gospels, we should be looking for what it teaches about Jesus.

5. Know that Jesus' kingdom is already but not yet.

Most of the disciples' problems came from their misunderstanding of Jesus' kingdom. They expected Jesus to go to Jerusalem and establish his kingdom in glory and power. Peter rebuked Jesus when he said he would be crucified (Matt 16:22). They argued about who was the greatest (Matt 18:1). James and John had their mother ask for them to sit at his right hand (Matt 20:20).

Jesus clearly preaches that "the kingdom of God has come near" (Mark 1:15). Jesus' ministry of healing and casting out demons gave evidence of the coming of the kingdom of God. But while Jesus' kingdom has already come in part, it has not yet come in full. Jesus tells Pilate, "My kingdom is not from here" (John

18:36). Jesus came the first time to inaugurate his kingdom. Now we are announcing the gospel of Jesus' kingdom. At Jesus' second coming, he will establish his kingdom forever with his people dwelling in a new creation.

6. Look for the main point of the parables.

Jesus told many stories to illustrate spiritual truths, which we call parables. Parables can be difficult to understand correctly. In some parables, every part of the story represents something. For example, in the parable of the four soils, Jesus says that the seed is the word of God, and then he goes on to explain that the four types of soil are four types of people who hear the word of God (Luke 8:4–15).

But in other parables, not every aspect of the story represents something. In most parables, Jesus is trying to teach us one simple point. The parable of the mustard seed, for example, simply shows how something small and insignificant can grow (Matt 13:31–32). In the same way, the kingdom of God may not look powerful at first, but in God's perfect timing, Jesus' kingdom will grow and fill the entire earth.

Often the main point of the parable comes when there is a surprising twist in the story. Jesus' listeners would have been surprised to hear of a Samaritan man caring for his enemy, a Jewish man (Luke 10:25–37). Similarly, no respectable father would shame himself to run through the village to embrace a rebellious son. But when Jesus shows this in his story of the prodigal son, he shows a beautiful picture of God's love for us (Luke 15:11–32).

How to Read Acts

Acts is an exciting book to study, as we see how the apostles obeyed Jesus' command to be witnesses to the ends of the earth in the power of the Spirit (Acts 1:8), but Acts can also be a difficult book to understand. On the one hand, the book of Acts tells of a period that is very much like our own. Jesus has ascended to heaven. Apostles and missionaries are preaching the gospel. People are being baptized and churches planted. Today, we are engaged in the same mission as the apostles were 2,000 years ago.

At the same time, many of the events recorded in the book of Acts are unique. Acts records a transitional time when all the blessings of the new covenant are just beginning to be realized. The Holy Spirit is poured out. Churches are established. Samaritans and gentiles are included in God's people.

These similarities and differences between the book of Acts and our own day create a difficulty for us. We must constantly ask the question: Of the things we read about in the book of Acts, what was unique to that transitional period, and what is normal for all churches in all places at all times? For example, should we only baptize believers as we see in Acts? Should we supernaturally speak in other languages? Should missionaries today adopt the strategy and practices of Paul?

To answer such questions, we must read Acts carefully by keeping three truths in mind.

1. Luke is writing history.

Luke's main purpose is to record the advance of the gospel from Jerusalem to Rome. While the history of the church has much to teach us about what God intends our churches to be, Luke is not writing a manual for how to do church. Because Luke is recording the way things were in the earliest churches, he isn't always intending to tell us how churches should be. We should, therefore, be cautious when applying Luke's history to our own situations.

2. Look for what is normal in the book of Acts itself.

When asking what should be normal in churches today, the first place to start is simply to ask, "What is normal in the churches described in the book of Acts?" If the churches in the book of Acts itself differ from one another in certain ways, then we should expect that our churches might differ in those areas as well.

In the first weeks following the outpouring of the Spirit on the day of Pentecost, the Jerusalem church shared all their property in common, with the wealthier members selling property to provide for members in need (Acts 2:42–47; 4:32–37). But we don't read about any of the other churches in Acts doing the same thing. This kind of radical devotion to God and one another was part of the unique outpouring of the Spirit transitioning the world into the new covenant era. While the Jerusalem church's generosity remains a good example to us, it is not something that we should mandate or enforce.

On the other hand, throughout Acts baptism follows repentance and faith. There is no instance in which the apostles baptized someone before they believed, whether they be adults or children incapable of professing faith. (The baptism of households refers to the extended family along with servants and slaves, and should be understood through the lens of the other examples of baptism of believers. See Acts 11:14; 16:15, 31; 18:8.) Since the practice of believers baptism is normal within the book of Acts itself, it remains the normal, biblical practice for churches today.

3. Think through 3 levels of application.

Christians will, of course, disagree on what applies today and what does not from the book of Acts. Pentecostals insist that Christians today should speak in tongues. Baptists believe that believers baptism is the only proper baptism today. While we cannot solve every issue, it is helpful for us to divide our applications into three levels.

Not Required At All. Some practices that we read about in Acts are not requirements for the church today. This is because Acts records a unique period in God's plan for establishing the new covenant and taking the gospel to the gentiles. Some of the things we read about were never meant to be repeated. For example, supernaturally speaking in other languages (or tongues) occurs three times in Acts, but at other times when people believe and receive the Holy Spirit, they do not speak in other languages (Acts 2:4; 10:46; 19:6). So even if someone believes that Christians can speak in tongues today, they should not understand speaking in tongues as a requirement for everyone who receives the Holy Spirit.

Not Required But Good. Other practices in Acts don't rise to the level of commands, but they are good examples to us. While the Bible may nowhere tell us that what we read is the one and only right way, there may be good reasons for the practice in the book of Acts. One example of this is the practice of baptizing people quickly after they believe. On the day of Pentecost, 3,000 believers were baptized that very day (Acts 2:41). Philip baptized the Ethiopian immediately after belief (Acts 8:36–39), and Paul baptized Lydia and the jailer immediately in Philippi (Acts 16:15, 33).

Today many churches delay the baptism of new believers in order to reduce the number of false professions of faith, and to ensure that new believers understand the significance of baptism. On the other hand, in the New

Testament, baptism clearly marked the decisive change in a person's life. As Paul shows us in Romans 6:1–11, New Testament Christians didn't look back to a day when they said a prayer for salvation as the turning point in their life. They looked back at their baptism, and surely there is wisdom in this New Testament approach, even if it isn't a mandate.

Required. There are some practices we read about in Acts, which should be practiced by all churches everywhere at all times. This is especially the case when there are commands or other instructions about the practice in other parts of the New Testament. Acts simply gives us the picture of how it was done. For example, the New Testament says much about baptism, and Jesus commands his disciples to baptize new disciples (Matt 28:19). The Greek word translated baptism means to put something completely under water. So baptism of believers by immersion, which we see happening in Acts, is not simply a good idea. It is what God expects the church to practice. It should be the normal practice in churches today.

How to Read New Testament Letters

The letters of the New Testament are some of the most important and cherished books of the Bible. Paul's letter to the churches in Rome clearly explains the gospel, which is the power of God for our salvation. The letter of Hebrews gives us a beautiful picture of Jesus as our priest who has compassion for us and intercedes on our behalf.

In some ways, studying the letters of the New Testament is easier than studying books like the Prophets or Revelation. The letters are easier for us because we live in the same period of salvation history as when they were written. Like the first readers, we also have the full message of Jesus Christ. We meet in churches. We work to proclaim the gospel throughout the world. We await Jesus' return. Therefore, a lot of what is written in the letters applies directly to Christians today.

At the same time, reading the letters can be difficult. To help with these difficulties, pay attention to these three suggestions:

1. Know the background of the letter, if possible.

Have you ever heard someone talking on the phone and tried to guess what was being said on the other end? Sometimes you can guess accurately what the conversation is about, but sometimes you will get it completely wrong. In the same way, when we are reading the letters, we are reading one side of a conversation. When possible, it is good to put together the evidence to understand why the author is writing the letter, but at other times, it simply isn't possible to know the circumstances that caused the letter to be written.

In his letter to Titus, Paul makes it very clear who he is writing to and why. Titus is one of Paul's sons in the faith, one of his young disciples and co-workers (Tit 1:4). Paul left Titus on the island of Crete to finish the work of planting churches there by appointing pastors (Tit 1:5). Paul makes clear that it is important for Titus to appoint godly pastors because ungodly, false teachers are already spreading their false teaching in Crete (Tit 1:10–14).

While the circumstances of Titus are fairly clear, the circumstances surrounding the letter of James are much less clear. James writes his letter "to the twelve tribes dispersed abroad" (Jas 1:1). If we take this literally, it sounds like he is writing to Jewish Christians scattered outside of Judea, but it is also possible that he is using the idea of "the twelve tribes" symbolically to refer to Christians as God's new covenant people. Since James was a prominent leader in the Jerusalem Church (see Acts 15:13–21), it's possible that he is writing a letter to the Christians from Jerusalem who were scattered during Saul's persecution (Acts 8:3–4). While imagining the letter as being written to Christians scattered by persecution helps us to make sense of a lot of what James writes in his letter, at the end of the day, it is only a theory. James doesn't give enough information to accurately reconstruct the background to the letter.

If there is enough evidence to reconstruct the background to the letter, it is very helpful in understanding the meaning of what the author wrote, but if there is not sufficient evidence, then we must simply do our best to understand the letter without knowing the background.

2. Understand the structure of ancient letters.

When I was in school, our teacher taught us to write a letter by writing the date, addressing who we were writing to, writing the content of our letter, and then closing with our name. One of my early letters may have looked like this:

> January 4, 1995
>
> Dear Mom,
>
> Thank you so much for taking care of me. Can I have a new toy car for my birthday?
>
> Love,
> Josh

The letters we read in the Bible have many of these same features, but they wrote their letters differently than we do today. Let's take James' letter as an example. He begins:

> James, a servant of God and of the Lord Jesus Christ:
> To the twelve tribes dispersed abroad.
> Greetings (Jas 1:1).

Here we see three important aspects of most of the letters of the Bible. The letter begins with the author's name and self-description. This is followed by a declaration that identifies the recipients of the letter, and then the author gives his greetings. Sometimes an author will take many verses to describe himself. In Romans, Paul's self-description runs from 1:1–6. Often, the authors of New Testament letters will give a more theological greeting, like when Paul writes in many of his letters, "Grace to you and peace from God our Father and the Lord Jesus Christ" (for example, Rom 1:7; 1 Cor 1:3; 2 Cor 1:2). At other times, the author will skip these introductory aspects altogether like in Hebrews or 1 John.

In some of the letters, the introduction is followed by a prayer of thanksgiving for the readers or by a prayer of blessing toward God. In

Ephesians, Paul writes, "Blessed is the God and Father of our Lord Jesus Christ…" (Eph 1:3), and he continues this prayer of praise until verse 14. In 1 Thessalonians, Paul begins by giving thanks to God for the Thessalonica Church (1 Thess 1:2–10).

Typically, the main content, or body, of the letter follows this prayer of thanksgiving or praise. At the end of the letter, some authors add greetings. For example, Hebrews ends with news about Timothy being released from prison and the following greetings: "Greet all your leaders and all the saints. Those who are from Italy send you greetings" (Heb 13:24).

Knowing the structure of New Testament letters will help you identify where you are when reading the letter. At other times, noticing that the author skips a common aspect of letter writing will help you to better understand the letter, like when Paul skips a thanksgiving in Galatians and proceeds directly to scolding his readers (Gal 1:6–9). This guidebook should help you to identify the structure of each letter so you can better understand them.

3. Look for the logical flow of the letter.

The letters of the New Testament weren't written simply to conduct business, or for trivial matters. The authors of these letters wrote in order to teach their readers. Often, they wrote because of problems in the churches that needed correction. At other times, they wrote primarily for the encouragement of the readers. But in every circumstance, they wanted to teach their readers important truths.

This means that each letter makes a logical argument. To understand the letter well, you need to follow the flow of the author's logic. While some letters are more clearly organized than others, they all have a flow of logic. For example, James is a lot like the book of Proverbs. James addresses various topics such as wisdom, favoritism, and speech. While James isn't making the same type of sustained argument that can be found in other letters, everything he writes is nevertheless unified around the theme of living joyfully when we experience trials (Jas 1:2).

On the other hand, many of Paul's letters are carefully planned and organized. Romans is one of the best examples. The book is easily split into two halves: Chapters 1–11 explain the gospel that Paul preaches and the results of faith in the gospel. Chapters 12–16 teach how Christians should live since they have believed the gospel. If you don't understand the connection between these two sections, you won't be able to fully appreciate what Paul is teaching. For example, Paul writes, "Let love be without hypocrisy. Detest evil; cling to what is good" (Rom 12:9). We might be tempted to teach this command in a way that encourages people to try to prove themselves to God by their good works, but in Romans 1–5, Paul makes clear that no one can be saved by works. God saves us through our faith in what Jesus has done for us. We don't obey a command like Romans 12:9 to earn God's favor. We obey it because God has transformed us through the gospel, and we now see our lives as a sacrificial offering given joyfully to the God who has justified us (Rom 12:1–2).

How to Read Revelation

The book of Revelation is easily one of the most difficult books in the Bible to understand. In Revelation, the Apostle John receives a vision that takes him from earth to the heavenly throne room, then back to earth and on into the new creation. Throughout this journey, John sees strange heavenly creatures, a dragon, a beast rising from the sea, and even God's glory in the new creation.

One reason Revelation is so difficult for us to understand is because we don't encounter this type of writing today. Books like Revelation that contain strange, symbolic visions are part of a category of writings called apocalyptic, a name which comes from the Greek word for "unveiling." Revelation isn't the only book in the Bible that uses this style of writing. Both Daniel and Ezekiel see similar heavenly visions.

One major misunderstanding of apocalyptic writings is that they aren't meant to be understood. Some people say that we just weren't intended to understand books like Revelation. However, the very name apocalyptic reminds us that these books are "unveilings" of heavenly realities. Yes, they take a lot of work to understand, but God has given them to us to study and understand.

To help you understand what God has revealed, start by following these three pieces of advice.

1. Understand what apocalyptic writing is and how it works.

Revelation isn't telling us a story in the same way that a historical book like Genesis is. When spies communicate, they often write to one another in a secret code that only they can understand. This is a little bit like how the book of Revelation works. Revelation speaks to us through a code of visions, symbols, and Old Testament references. Thankfully, the code isn't secret, but it does require us to do the work of breaking the code to understand the meaning of the book.

Here are four of the features of Revelation that contribute to the code in which John is writing:

Visions. As has already been mentioned, apocalyptic writing consists of a human prophet receiving visions from God. Usually, the prophet is guided on this vision by an angelic or heavenly being. For John, he was worshiping while imprisoned on the island of Patmos when Jesus himself appeared to him (Rev 1:9–20). Later he is taken to the heavenly throne room (Rev 4:1–3). From there, he begins to witness a series of visions revealing "what must soon take place" (Rev 1:1).

Symbols. John's visions consist of symbols that communicate important truths. Some of the symbols are animals, like the four living creatures around God's throne that represent the whole of creation worshiping God (Rev 4:6–9), the dragon that represents Satan (Rev 12), or the beast that represents the person whom Paul calls the man of lawlessness and John calls in his letters the antichrist (Rev 13). But the most important animal symbol in the book is the symbol of Jesus as both the Lion of Judah and the Lamb who was slain (Rev 5).

Numbers are also important symbols in the book. There are several series of 7 throughout the book, which help us to follow the structure of the book: 7 churches, 7 seals, 7 trumpets. In chapter 7, we hear of a census of 144,000 Israelites. The number comes from there being 12,000 from each of the 12 tribes.

144,000, therefore, represents the perfection of the nation of Israel, not a literal number of people. John hears about perfect Israel as God had always intended it to be, but then he sees "a vast multitude from every nation, tribe, people, and language, which no one could number." God's perfect Israel is this innumerable multitude of people from every nation who have believed in Jesus.

The symbols in the book are not always easy to understand, but it is important to consider each one carefully rather than jumping to strange theories. For example, people often ask, "What is the mark of the beast in Revelation 13:16–18?" Throughout the centuries, people have come up with numerous theories, being fearful that they might accidentally receive the mark and be condemned forever. However, when we look at the mark of the beast, first and foremost as a symbol, we see it contrasted with the seal that is placed upon God's people in Revelation 7:3. Then when we think about the symbolism of the forehead and the hand, we are reminded of God's instruction in Deuteronomy 6 that the people of Israel should bind God's word "as a sign on your hand" and as "a symbol on your forehead" (Deut 6:8). God's people were to think (head) and act (hand) on the basis of God's word. The mark of the beast is that people are committed to thinking and acting according to the antichrist's ways, and those who will not conform to the thinking and acting of the antichrist will be rejected.

Use of the Old Testament. Revelation is filled with references to the Old Testament, but it doesn't quote Old Testament verses directly. Instead, we should think of John as a painter, and the paint he uses is the Old Testament. Let's take John's vision of Jesus in Revelation 1:9–20. To describe what he is seeing, John uses Old Testament images from multiple passages: God speaking to Israel from Sinai in Exodus 19, Joshua's encounter with the commander of the Lord's army in Joshua 5, Daniel's vision of the heavenly man in Daniel 10, and Zechariah's vision of the lampstand in Zechariah 4, to name a few. In Revelation 1, John isn't quoting these passages. He is painting with them. He is taking elements from them and reworking them to give us a picture of Jesus.

Revelation 1 isn't unique. John paints with the Old Testament again and again throughout the book. The best way to prepare to understand Revelation, therefore, is simply to read the Old Testament over and over in order to become so familiar with the Old Testament that you are able to see the colors John is painting with.

2. Look at the big picture of each vision.

While understanding the symbols of each vision is important, we can easily get distracted by the details. In seeking to understand the trees, we may miss the forest. It is less important that we understand every aspect of a vision than that we understand the big picture of the vision.

For example, there are many aspects of John's vision of the woman, the child, and the dragon in Revelation 12 that can be difficult to understand. Who is the woman? What is the heavenly battle referring to? What's the significance of the eagle wings in verse 14? While seeking to answer these questions is important, it is more important that we see the big picture. Revelation 12 teaches us that no matter how fierce and threatening Satan may appear, God himself will protect his people.

3. Remember the basic rule that clearer passages help us to understand more difficult passages.

Sometimes when people study Revelation, they forget their basic rules of Bible study and begin coming up with strange and wild interpretations, but the same rules that we learned in the basics of Bible study apply to Revelation as well. Perhaps most important is the rule that "Scripture interprets Scripture." This rule teaches that clearer passages in the Bible often shed light on more difficult passages.

There's no doubt that Revelation is a difficult book. Thankfully, there are many other passages that shed light on Revelation. Most importantly, perhaps, is Matthew 24–25, which contains Jesus' sermon on the Mount of Olives. In

Matthew 24–25, Jesus teaches the disciples in a clear and simple way about his return. A clearer passage like Matthew 24–25 can guide us to better understanding of Revelation.

How Not To Read the Bible

While we are attempting to learn how to read the Bible well and understand what the original authors wanted us to understand, many people make mistakes in the ways they understand and use the Bible.[4] It's important that we examine some of the most common mistakes we might encounter, so we can learn how *not* to read the Bible. Here are six mistakes people make when using the Bible:

1. Don't use the Bible to say what you want to say.

Preachers often make the mistake of having something to say and then looking for a verse that will support what they already wanted to say. When we do this, the Bible isn't allowed to speak with its own authority. Instead, we are simply using the Bible to say what we want to say.

One of the most abused verses of the Bible is Philippians 4:13, which says, "I am able to do all things through him who strengthens me." People use this verse to assure themselves that God will help them to accomplish their dreams. But when we use this verse to say what we want it to say, we miss the powerful message the Bible is trying to speak into our lives. Paul is actually teaching in Philippians that whatever situation we find ourselves in — rich or poor, easy-going or suffering — we can be content and faithful to God's call in our lives.

2. Don't ignore the context.

Most mistakes in interpreting the Bible arise from people ignoring the context of the verses they are quoting. The Bible isn't a list of random, unconnected sayings. We cannot be certain that we understand a particular verse if we don't understand how it fits into its paragraph, chapter, or book.

The false teachers known as Mormons, or the Church of Jesus Christ of Latter Day Saints, use most people's ignorance of context to promote their false teachings. One false teaching of Mormonism is that our souls existed before we were born. To prove their false teaching, Mormons will point to three verses:

> Jeremiah 1:5, I chose you before I formed you in the womb; I set you apart before you were born. I appointed you a prophet to the nations.
>
> Acts 17:28, For in him we live and move and have our being, as even some of your own poets have said, "For we are also his offspring."
>
> Hebrews 12:9, Furthermore, we had human fathers discipline us, and we respected them. Shouldn't we submit even more to the Father of spirits and live?

After citing these verses apart from their context, Mormons will say, "See. God is the Father of our souls, and our souls existed before we were born." But if we take the time to look at each verse in context, we will see very quickly that these verses do not support Mormon false teaching.

Jeremiah 1:5 is speaking about God choosing Jeremiah as a prophet before he was even born. In Acts 17, Paul is teaching the Athenians that God provides for human beings, and therefore, he doesn't have any needs humans can meet. Hebrews 12:9 compares God's discipline of believers with the discipline we experience from earthly parents. None of these passages are discussing whether or not our souls existed before birth.

3. Don't talk about the Bible without citing the Bible.

Have you ever heard someone claim that the Bible teaches something without actually opening the Bible and showing you? We can all be tempted to take this shortcut. Someone might say, "The Bible teaches that everyone who has the Holy Spirit speaks in tongues." This sounds very impressive, and since we probably know the Bible talks about the Holy Spirit and about speaking in tongues, we might be convinced by this statement. But it is important to ask the simple question, "Where? Where does the Bible teach this?"

We can make whatever claim we want to about the Bible, but if we can't show where our claim is taught in the Bible, then our claim is worthless. Someone might say, "The Bible teaches that we were created by green men from outer space." But if we open our Bibles, we won't find this claim supported anywhere. We should always ask people who teach to show us the truth from the Bible.

4. Don't create important teachings based on difficult passages.

Another mistake people make is to create important teachings around unclear and difficult passages. For example, the Mormons practice baptism on behalf of dead relatives. They base this on 1 Corinthians 15:29 where Paul mentions in passing baptism for the dead. Unfortunately, Paul doesn't explain what he means by baptism for the dead and the concept isn't explained elsewhere in the New Testament. We can't be sure what Paul is referring to. Therefore, we shouldn't take this difficult verse and create an important teaching based on it.

5. Don't make things symbolic that aren't symbolic.

Some books of the Bible, like Daniel and Revelation, use symbols to communicate important truths. But most of the Bible is meant to be read literally.

That means we aren't supposed to look for hidden or symbolic meanings behind the obvious meaning of the text.

Some false teachers claim that the forbidden fruit in Genesis 2–3 isn't actually fruit but is sex, and the sin of Eve wasn't biting a piece of fruit. It was actually having sex with the serpent. The problem with this strange interpretation is that it just isn't what Genesis 2–3 says. Unlike Revelation, Genesis is a book written as history. It is telling what happened in plain language. So when it says that the woman took a bite of the fruit, it means that the woman took a bite of the fruit. Nothing more.

6. Don't add to the Bible.

Some people claim to have great respect for the Bible, but allow other things to have a greater level of authority than the Bible in what they believe and how they live. By adding another authority to the Bible, they are actually rejecting the authority of the Bible. Sometimes this takes the form of false teachers who add extra books or prophecies to the Bible, like the way Muslims follow the Quran, the Mormons the Book of Mormon, the Seventh-Day Adventists the prophecies of Ellen G. White, or some pentecostals the prophecies given in their church services.

Some churches elevate the traditions of their church to having greater authority than the Bible itself. Even though it is clear from both the Bible and church history that the early church baptized believers by immersion, the Roman Catholic Church affirms the sprinkling of infants on the basis of church tradition. Since Christians began at some point to sprinkle infants and the church accepted the practice into its tradition, it is now a proper baptism, even though it wasn't what the apostles did.

While we are thankful for the teachers God gives us to understand the Bible, and the traditions passed down to us by other Christians, the Bible alone is our authority. Those things are only meant to help us understand the Bible, and if anything ever contradicts the Bible, we must reject that teaching and keep the Bible itself. The Bible speaks to us the authoritative words of God.

How to Study the Bible

Ancient World History

Ancient World History

The Sumerians

Basic Facts
Time Period: about 3100 B.C.–1700 B.C.
Location: southern Mesopotamia (modern Iraq)
Principal Cities: Ur, Babylon, Erech, Akkad
Alternative Names: Sinara (Gen 10:10; 11:2); Kaldeya (Gen 11:31)
Biblical Connections: Abraham was originally from a Sumerian city, Ur of the Chaldeans (Gen 10:31).

Dates with B.C. and A.D.

During the Old Testament period, years are marked by the letters B.C., such as 1446 B.C.

B.C. stands for "Before Christ." So 1446 B.C. is one-thousand four-hundred forty-six years before the time of Jesus Christ. Because these dates are counting down to the time of Christ, they decrease in value as time passes. For example, the year after 1446 B.C. is 1445 B.C., and the year after 1445 B.C. is 1444 B.C.

The years after the coming of Jesus are sometimes marked with the letters A.D., such as A.D. 33. A.D. stands for the Latin phrase *"anno domini,"* which means "Year of our Lord." Because these dates are counting up from the time of

Christ, they increase in value as time passes. For example, the year after A.D. 33 is A.D. 34 or 2020 is followed by 2021.

History

For much of its history, Sumeria consisted of **independent city-states**. Each city was ruled by its own governor or king, and some cities even elected their officials. Competition for wealth and natural resources, however, eventually led to stronger cities conquering weaker cities.

Sargon of Akkad (about 2100 B.C.) was the king of the powerful city of Akkad, and he began establishing his own empire by conquering the surrounding cities. He is believed to be the first ruler to conquer the entire territory of Sumeria.

Like Sargon before him, **Hammurabi of Babylon** (about 1720 B.C.) began as the king of Babylon, but then started conquering surrounding cities until he was the king of most of the region of Sumeria. Hummurabi famously wrote down his laws on pillars, which were erected in each city for the people to read. In some ways, his laws are similar to the law given to Moses in the Bible, but his laws often contain much more severe punishments than can be found in the Bible.

Hammurabi of Babylon

Religion

The Sumerians worshiped **many gods**. Each city had one god that was the primary god worshiped in that city. For example, Nanna, the god of the moon, was the primary God of the city Ur, Abraham's hometown.

Sumerian temples are called **Ziggurats**. They were a type of pyramid. By going up toward the sky, the Sumerians believed they could offer their worship closer to the gods. The Tower of Babel may have been a type of Ziggurat.

Technology

The Sumerians were the first (or one of the first) civilizations to invent a system of writing. The system is called **cuneiform** and used pen-sized sticks to make impressions in wet clay. Then the clay would dry.

After inventing writing, the Sumerians were able to produce the first **literature** of human history by writing down the myths about their gods. The most famous of these is called the Epic of Gilgamesh, which records legends about a mythical king named Gilgamesh..

Cuneiform Tablet

Ancient World History

The Egyptians

Basic Facts
Time Period: about 3100 B.C.–600 B.C.
Location: the Nile River (modern Egypt)
Principal Cities: Zoan, Memphis, Thebes, Tahpanhes
Biblical Connections: Egypt shows up throughout the Bible. Abraham went to Egypt to escape famine (Gen 12:10–20), and Joseph was sold into slavery and then ruled Egypt (Gen 37–50). Moses delivered the Israelites from slavery in Egypt (Exod). Later, Solomon married an Egyptian princess (1 Kings 3:1). In the New Testament, Joseph and Mary escaped to Egypt to keep the baby Jesus safe (Matt 2:14–15).

Geography
The **Nile River** is the reason why Egypt existed as an empire at all. Egypt is surrounded by the Sahara Desert. The Nile River, however, flooded each year, making the soil along its banks rich. The ancient Egyptians, therefore, settled in a place perfect for farming.

Originally, Egypt was divided into two separate kingdoms: **Upper Egypt** in the south and **Lower Egypt** in the north at the Nile Delta. Early in Egyptian history, the two regions became united under a single ruler. For most of Egyptian history, Upper Egypt was dominant, but Lower Egypt also had times of dominance.

History

The Egyptian kings are called **Pharaohs**, and the long history of ancient Egypt can be divided into five basic periods: The Early Kings, the Old Kingdom, the Middle Kingdom, the New Kingdom, and Egypt as a Conquered Kingdom.

Among **the Early Kings** period (2900–2575 B.C.), the greatest king was **Pharaoh Menes** (about 2900 B.C.). Menes was the first Pharaoh to unite Lower and Upper Egypt. He put his capital at Memphis on the border of the two regions. The first pyramid was built at the end of this period.

The Old Kingdom (2575–2150 B.C.) is sometimes called the Age of the Pyramids because the greatest of the pyramids were built during this period. **Pharaoh Khufu** (reigned 2589–2566 B.C.) built the Great Pyramid of Giza near modern Cairo for his tomb. The Old Kingdom seems to have collapsed into a time of famine and chaos. For about 100 years (2150–2040 B.C.), Egypt split back into two regions, Lower and Upper Egypt.

The Middle Kingdom (2040–1640 B.C.) began when **Pharaoh Mentuhotep II** (reigned 2060–2010 B.C.) reunited Lower and Upper Egypt. This is the kingdom that was visited by Abraham, and in which Joseph would rise to prominence, but the Middle Kingdom collapsed when Egypt was invaded by a people called the Hyskos. We know very little about the Hyskos, but their invasion may be the reason why the Pharaoh in Exodus did not know about Joseph (Exod 1:8). Between Genesis and Exodus, there is a transition from the Middle Kingdom to the New Kingdom with the major interruption of the Hyskos invasion.

The New Kingdom (1550–1075 B.C.) began with **Pharaoh Amhose I** (reigned about 1550–1525 B.C.) who reunited Egypt under Egyptian rather than Hyskos rule. This is the time period of the Exodus, but it is difficult to know with absolute certainty which Pharaoh ruled during the time of the Exodus. Nevertheless, by comparing the Bible with Egyptian history, we can attempt to make a good guess. **Pharaoh Thutmose I** (reigned 1520–1492 B.C.) was likely the Pharaoh who decreed the death of the Israelite sons. His daughter **Hatshepsut** may have been the one who adopted Moses. She later ruled Egypt after the death of her husband and half-brother, Thutmose II. **Pharaoh Amenhotep II** (reigned 1450–1425 B.C.) was possibly the Pharaoh who refused to let the people of Israel go with Moses. Interestingly, after he died the kingdom passed to one of his younger sons, Thutmose IV. If

Pharaoh Amenhotep II

Amenhotep II was the pharaoh of the Exodus, then his oldest son died in the final plague. **Amenhotep III** (reigned 1386–1349 B.C.) is another important pharaoh from the period. He conquered much of northeast Africa and brought Egypt to the height of its power and prosperity.

Beginning in the 600s B.C., Egypt began to lose it's power and began to be **conquered** and ruled by other kingdoms. Egypt was first conquered by the Assyrians in 671 B.C., but they only held Egypt temporarily. In 605 B.C., King Nebuchadnezzar of Babylon conquered the country. The Babylonians ruled Egypt until they were conquered by the Persians in 525 B.C. In 332 B.C., Alexander the Great conquered Egypt for the Greeks. For the next 300 years, Egypt was ruled by Greeks who established the great city of Alexandria. In 47 B.C., Julius Caesar conquered Egypt for the Romans, making it a part of the Roman Empire.

Religion

Egyptians worshiped **many gods**. Some of the most important were Ra (the sun god and ruler of the gods), Isis (the mother goddess), Osiris (god of the dead), Horus (god of the sky), and Thoth (god of knowledge). The Nile River was also considered a god named Hapi. Hapi gave the Egyptians life through allowing the growth of their crops by flooding every year.

The Egyptians invented **mummification**, a way to preserve dead bodies by removing the dead person's organs and wrapping them in cloths. They believed that the preservation of the body enabled the soul to continue to exist in the afterlife.

Hieroglyphics

Technology

Egyptians developed a system of writing that used pictures instead of an alphabet called **hieroglyphics**. For centuries, scholars were unable to read Egyptian hieroglyphics, but in 1799, French scholars discovered the Rosetta Stone, a portion of a stone pillar that contained the same decree written in three versions: Greek, ancient Egyptian in an alphabet called Demotic, and ancient Egyptian in hieroglyphics. The Rosetta Stone became the key to understanding hieroglyphics.

The Canaanites

Basic Facts
Time Period: about 3000 B.C.–100 B.C.
Location: the land of Canaan (modern Israel, Jordan, Syria, and Lebanon)
Principal Cities: Jerusalem, Jericho, Ugarit, Gaza, Tyre
Biblical Connections: Canaan was the land promised to Abraham and conquered by Joshua. Almost all of the events in the Bible take place in the land of Canaan.

Geography
The land of Canaan is a diverse land consisting of seas, mountains, and an important river. To the west was the **Mediterranean Sea** or sometimes called the Great Sea (see Num 34:6). While the Israelites were a land-loving nation, some Canaanites, especially the Phoenicians, became great explorers of the sea.

The terrain between the Mediterranean Sea and the Jordan River rises to the **mountains of Judah**. To the east of these mountains, the **Jordan River** flows out of the Sea of Galilee in the north and down to the Dead Sea. The Dead Sea is a salt sea and has no living animals in it. It is the lowest point on the face of the earth.

East of the Jordan River, in what is today the country of Jordan, the terrain rises again and is mountainous. These mountains stretch out and meet the Arabian dessert, which is uninhabited.

Different Nations

The term **"Canaanites"** does not refer to one, unified nation. Instead, it refers to a number of nations that inhabited the land of Canaan. For much of its history, Canaan consisted of independent city-states, each ruled by its own king. The peoples who lived in Canaan shared a lot of common traditions and practices, but each nation was also unique. Like with Israel itself, these nations became less important once larger empires like Assyria and Babylon began to invade Canaan.

The **Hittites** are not really Canaanites. They came from Anatolia (modern Turkey). They expanded their territory into an empire from about 1600-1100 B.C. But even after the Hittite empire fell, many Hittite people remained in the cities of Canaan.

Various Canaanite people groups lived in the mountains of Judah. Most prominent among these were the Amorites and the Jebusites. The **Amorites** were originally from Mesopotamia, but settled in Canaan around 2100 B.C. It is uncertain whether the **Jebusites** were simply a clan of the Amorites or were a separate people. The Jebusites were the original inhabitants of Jerusalem.

One of the most significant people groups mentioned in the Bible are the **Philistines**. The Philistines lived on the southern coast of Canaan along the Mediterranean Sea. They may have originally come from the island of Cyprus in the Mediterranean Sea, but this is uncertain. The Philistines lived in five independent city-states that cooperated with one another: Ashdod, Gaza, Ashkelon, Gath, and Ekron. The Philistines were known for having a highly trained military with chariots, foot soldiers, and archers. They grew to their strongest during the time of the judges (about 1200 B.C.), as is evident in the stories of Samson and Samuel. David is credited with subduing them (about 1000 B.C.). 1 Samuel 5 talks about the Philistine god Dagon. Very little is known about

Dagon, and Dagon may be the Philistine name for the Canaanite god Baal. Whatever the Philistines believed about Dagon, the God of Israel demonstrated his greater power over their idol by beheading Dagon's statue (1 Sam 5).

The **Phoenicians** lived north of the promised land in the cities of Tyre and Sidon. They became a great sea-faring people and settled colonies across the Mediterranean Sea. Their most famous colony was Carthage in North Africa, modern Tunisia.

East of the Jordan River dwelled three important nations: the Edomites, Moabites, and Ammonites. The **Edomites** were the descendants of Esau. They lived in the southern part of the mountains east of the Jordan River. This region is called both Edom (Isa 63:1) and the land of Seir (Gen 32:3) in the Bible. The **Moabites** were descendants of Lot (Gen 19:30–38). They lived just north of the Edomites in the land of Moab. Ruth was a Moabite, and later Solomon built a place of worship for their god Chemosh after his heart turned away from the God of Israel (1 Kings 11:7). The **Ammonites** also descended from Lot (Gen 19:30–38). They lived in the northern part of the mountains east of the Jordan River. Solomon built a place of worship for their god Milcom (1 Kings 11:1–8).

Religion

The Canaanites worshiped many gods, and when we read the Old Testament we encounter some of their gods, which were a constant temptation to the Israelites. In Canaanite religion, **El** was the highest of the gods and the creator. El is simply the word for "god" in Hebrew and related languages. Even the Arabic name Allah, which the Muslims use for God, comes from the same root. El was seen as distant and unapproachable, so he wasn't the focus of the worship of the people.

Most often the Israelites were tempted to worship Baal and Asherah. **Baal** simply means "Master." He was the god

Baal

of fertility. He was worshiped so that rain would fall on the crops, and so that both people and animals would give birth. His connection to family and farming explains why he was the primary god of Israelite idolatry. **Asherah** was the wife of El and the mother of Baal. She was the goddess of fertility. Because of this, Asherah worship was often paired with the worship of Baal.

The Assyrians

Basic Facts
Time Period: about 2000 B.C.–605 B.C.
Location: northern Mesopotamia (modern Syria and Iraq)
Principal Cities: Ashur, Nineveh, Calah (see map on p. 389)
Biblical Connections: The Assyrians became a threat to the divided kingdoms of Judah and Israel. The Assyrians eventually conquered the northern kingdom of Israel and sent many of its citizens into exile. Jonah prophesied to the Assyrian city of Nineveh.

History
Assyrian history can be divided into three periods: the Early Assyrians, the First Great Assyrian Empire, and the Neo-Assyrian Empire. The **Early Assyrian** period began around 2000 B.C., but during this period the Assyrians did not become a large empire. This changed around 1300 B.C.

The First Great Assyrian Empire (about 1300 B.C.–1000 B.C.) lasted for about 300 years. The greatest king of the period was **Tiglath-pileser I** (reigned 1115 B.C.–1077 B.C.). He conquered territory from the the Tigris and Euphrates rivers all the way to the Mediterranean Sea. But eventually this empire weakened, and for about 100 years the Assyrians did not exercise great influence.

Adad-nirari II (reigned 911 B.C.–891 B.C.) reunited the Assyrian empire, leading to its most powerful and prosperous period, known as the **Neo Assyrian Empire** (about 900 B.C–605 B.C.). In the Bible, we encounter **Tiglath-pileser III** (reigned 744 B.C.–727 B.C.), who became a great conqueror. He is also called Pul (2 Kings 15:19). He instituted the policy of deportations, or moving conquered people from their home territory to another territory. He thought that moving people to foreign lands would cause them to lack the unity and knowledge to revolt against him. Eventually, this policy led to the deportation of the northern kingdom of Israel. His conquests caused the northern kingdom of Israel to ally with the kingdom of Syria (or Aram) based in Damascus. Syria and Israel attempted to conquer Ahaz king of Judah, but Ahaz appealed to Tiglath-pileser III for help (2 Kings 15–16; 2 Chron 28; Isa 7–8), which resulted in Assyria conquering Israel and Syria.

After the northern kingdom of Israel rebelled against Assyrian rule, **Shalmaneser V** (reigned 726 B.C.–722 B.C.) conquered the capital city of Israel, Samaria, in 723 B.C. (2 Kings 17–18) and exiled the people of the northern kingdom. One Assyrian document states that this consisted of about 27,000 people.

The next Assyrian king mentioned in the Bible is **Sennacherib** (reigned 704 B.C.–681 B.C.). When Sennacherib came to power, much of the empire was in revolt. King Hezekiah of Judah also asserted his independence from Assyria at this time. This led Sennacherib to invade Judah in 701 B.C. (2 Kings 18–20; 2 Chron 32; Isa 22). Sennacherib conquered the Jewish city of Lachish and then besieged Jerusalem. Eventually, however, the Assyrians withdrew

Ashurbanipal on a Lion Hunt

after the angel of the Lord defeated them (2 Kings 19:35–36). Sennacherib was murdered by his own sons in 681 B.C. (2 Kings 19:37).

The greatest king of the Neo-Assyrian period was **Ashurbanipal** (reigned 668 B.C.–627 B.C.). Ashurbanipal brought about the time of greatest prosperity for the Assyrian empire. After his death, however, Babylon and other territories began to rebel. In 612 B.C., the Babylonians and the Medes conquered the capital, Nineveh. In 605 B.C., the Assyrians and Egyptians met the Babylonians and the Medes in the Battle of Carchemish. The defeat of Assyria and Egypt at this battle marks the end of the Assyrian empire and the rise of Babylon.

Religion

The Assyrians shared the same gods as many of the other nations in Mesopotamia, such as the Babylonians. However, each city and nation emphasized certain gods more than others. **Asshur** was the primary god of the Assyrians, and the one after whom their first city and their civilization were named. Asshur was the god of war. **Ishtar** was the wife of Asshur and the goddess of love and war.

Technology

Shalmaneser created a **library at Nineveh**, which may have been one of the largest libraries ever built in ancient times. Modern archaeologists have uncovered over 30,000 tablets from the former site of the library.

Tiglasth-pileser III built **roads** throughout his empire. While these roads helped with trade, his primary purpose in building roads was so that his armies could travel quickly to any area in the empire.

The Assyrian army was able to dominate

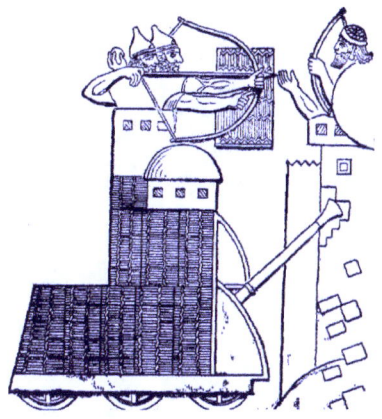

Assyrian Siege Machine

their enemies in part because of the invention of **siege machinery,** including covered ramps that allowed soldiers to scale city walls, and towers that could ram walls. Assyrians were known in the ancient world for their brutality. After conquering a city, they would often dismember people or impale captives on stakes.

The Babylonians

Basic Facts
Time Period: about 626 B.C.–539 B.C.
Location: central Mesopotamia (modern Iraq)
Principal City: Babylon (see map on p. 390)
Biblical Connections: After conquering Assyria, Babylon became the primary threat to the southern kingdom of Judah and eventually conquered Jerusalem. Daniel and his friends served in ancient Babylon after being carried into exile.

History
The city of Babylon enjoyed an early period of domination as part of the Sumerian civilization. To distinguish between the earlier Babylonian empire and the one that rose after the fall of Assyria, historians often call the second rise of Babylon the Neo-Babylonian period.

King **Nabopolassar** (reigned 626 B.C.–605 B.C.) rebelled against Assyrian rule, eventually bringing about the fall of the Assyrian empire and the emergence of the Babylonian empire. After Nabopolassar died, his son **Nebuchadnezzar II**

Nebuchadnezzar II

(reigned 605 B.C.–562 B.C.) continued to expand the empire and consolidate his power. His reign marks the height of the Babylonian empire. Nebuchadnezzar conquered Jerusalem three times:

> **605 B.C.** Nebuchadnezzar defeated King Jehoiakim and took prisoners back to Babylon, including Daniel and his friends (Dan 1).
>
> **597 B.C.** Nebuchadnezzar besieged the city, and King Jehoiachin surrendered himself. Nebuchadnezzar took many of the temple treasures to Babylon. He also took many of wealthy and skilled persons into exile (2 Kings 24:8–17).
>
> **587 B.C.** Nebuchadnezzar burned the city, destroyed the temple, and captured King Zedekiah (2 Kings 24:10–17).

Despite the difficulties he caused in Judah, Nebuchadnezzar brought much peace and prosperity to the Babylonian empire, but as Nebuchadnezzar himself learned in Daniel 4, this was part of God's plan.

Nabonidus (reigned 556 B.C.–539 B.C.) was a man devoted to study, and for much of his reign, he abandoned his role as king. He retreated to the city of Tema in the Arabian desert, leaving his son **Belshazzar** (reigned 553 B.C.–539 B.C.) as ruler of the empire in his place. Belshazzar was never, therefore, officially king of Babylon because his father was alive, but he ruled as king due to his father's absence. Belshazzar's foolishness is shown in Daniel 5, and it was during his reign that Cyrus the Great of Persia invaded Babylon.

In 549 B.C., Cyrus conquered the neighboring kingdom of Media, establishing the Medo-Persian empire in what is today the country of Iran. After Cyrus defeated Belshazzar in battle, Belshazzar retreated to Babylon, which he considered an impenetrable fortress. According to some accounts, Cyrus' army redirected the Euphrates River, which flowed under the walls of the city. Cyrus' army then marched into the city on the dry river bed in 539 B.C.

Religion

The Babylonians worshiped the same gods as the Sumerians and Assyrians before them. The only difference were the gods they revered most. **Marduk** was the primary god of Babylon and was regarded as the supreme god over all other gods. Babylonians believed that Marduk created the world. He is sometimes called Bel or "Master" (Isa 46:1; Jer 50:2). This name shows that he was the Babylonian equivalent to the Canaanite god Baal. The name Bel is the root for both Belshazzar and Daniel's Babylonian name Belteshazzar.

Ishtar Gate of Babylon

Technology

The Hanging Gardens of Babylon is considered one of the seven wonders of the ancient world. Nebuchadnezzar married Princess Amytis from the Zagros Mountains in modern Iran. Babylon was on a flat, river plain, and the princess missed the green mountains of her homeland. So, at least according to legend, Nebuchadnezzar built a towering garden in Babylon to remind her of the Zagros Mountains.

The Persians

Basic Facts
Time Period: about 560 B.C.–330 B.C.
Location: Persia (modern Iran)
Principal Cities: Susa, Persepolis, Babylon (see map on p. 391)
Biblical Connections: Cyrus the Great conquered Babylon and allowed the Jewish exiles to return home. Daniel remained a counselor of Cyrus after the fall of Babylon. Eventually, Nehemiah and Ezra would return to Judah to reestablish the Jewish nation and rebuild Jerusalem. Esther became Queen of Persia and saved her people from slaughter.

History

The rise of **Cyrus the Great** (reigned 560 B.C.–530 B.C.) was prophesied by Isaiah who lived 200 years earlier (Isa 44:28–45:6). Cyrus united the nations of Persia and Media under a common king, which gave them the strength to challenge and eventually conquer the Babylonian empire. Sometimes his empire is called the Medo-Persian Empire.

He conquered Babylon in 539 B.C. He then expanded his empire to much of the Middle East, spanning from modern Pakistan and Afghanistan in the east to Turkey in the west. After conquering Babylon in 539 B.C., Cyrus decreed that the Jews could return to Jerusalem and the land of Canaan (2 Chron 36:22–23; Ezra

Darius I

1:1–4). He is the same king identified by the alternative name Darius the Mede in Daniel 6.

Darius I (reigned 521 B.C.–486 B.C.) attempted to invade Greece but was defeated by the Greeks at the Battle of Marathon (490 B.C.). The desire of the Persian kings to invade Greece would ultimately lead to the downfall of their empire. Darius I also funded the reconstruction of the temple in Jerusalem (Ezra 4–6).

Xerxes I (reigned 485 B.C.-465 B.C.) like his father Darius I attempted to invade Greece. He famously won the Battle of Thermopylae, but then was turned back a few days later after defeat in the naval Battle of Salamis (480 B.C.) near Athens. Xerxes is called Ahasuerus in the Bible. After dismissing his wife Vashti for insubordination, he married a Jewish young woman named Hadassah, better known as Queen Esther.

Xerxes was followed by **Artaxerxes I** (reigned 465 B.C.–424 B.C.). Nehemiah served as the cupbearer to Artaxerxes, and Artaxerxes commissioned Nehemiah to return and rebuild the walls of Jerusalem (Neh 2). He also supported the return of Ezra to teach the Jewish people the law of God (Ezra 7).

Later, **Darius III** (reigned 336 B.C.-330 B.C.) became king at a time of great unrest in the Persian empire. The Greeks had long desired to take revenge on the Persians for their earlier invasions. After the Greeks were united under the rule of Alexander the Great, they began a conquest of the Persian Empire. The armies of Darius were repeatedly defeated by Alexander. At the Battle of Issus (333 B.C.), Alexander even captured the family of Darius. Eventually, Darius was captured by Alexander's soldiers and died in 330 B.C. The Persian empire died with him.

Religion

Sometime before 1000 B.C. the **Prophet Zoroaster** led the Persians away from worshiping many gods to worshiping the supreme god Ahura Mazda. The religion of Persia is called Zoroasterianism.

Ahura Mazda

Ahura Mazda, or the Wise Lord, was regarded by the Persians as the supreme god and the creator of the world. According to Zoroaster, Ahura Mazda created two opposing spirits: Spenta Mainyu, the good spirit, and Angra Mainyu, the evil spirit. These two spirits are at conflict in the universe and within each human being, and this will remain so until Ahura Mazda will bring the world to an end.

Because of the influence of these spirits, people are equally good and bad. The task of each human being is simply to say no to evil and have good thoughts, good words, and good deeds.

The religion of Zoroasterianism, especially the belief in one god, has much in common with the faith of the Jews in the God of Abraham, Isaac, and Jacob. These similarities may explain why the Persian kings dealt so kindly with the Jewish people, even funding the rebuilding of the temple and the city walls of Jerusalem.

Ancient World History

The Greeks

Basic Facts
Time Period: about 336 B.C.–167 B.C.
Location: Greece, but spreading all the way to India in the east and Egypt in the west.
Principal Cities: Athens, Thessalonica, Sparta, Corinth; later, Antioch in Syria and Alexandria in Egypt (see map on p. 392)
Biblical Connections: The Greek Empire emerged during the time between the Old and New Testaments, but it was foretold by Daniel in Daniel 7–12. By the time the New Testament begins, the Greek kingdoms had fallen to the Romans. However, much of their empire continued to influence the world of the Bible. Most important among these influences was the Greek language, which the apostles used to write the New Testament.

History
Greek civilization emerged as early as 800 B.C. However, Greeks were not a united people during this period. Each city was an independent city-state. Some like Sparta were ruled by kings. Others like Athens were democracies ruled by city councils. These city-states often fought among each other. But when the Persians attempted to invade Greece, it forced these city-states to join together. This period of **independent Greek city-states** (about 800 B.C.–336 B.C.) is

Alexander the Great

considered the height of Greek culture. During this period, the Greeks produced great literature, philosophy, and artwork.

Phillip was king of the northern part of Greece called Macedonia, but he began to conquer the cities to the south, uniting the Greeks under one king. After Phillip was assassinated in 336 B.C., his son Alexander became king of all of Greece at only 20 years old. Because of his great accomplishments, he became known as **Alexander the Great** (reigned 336 B.C.–323 B.C.). Alexander himself may have plotted the murder of his father.

Alexander immediately began fighting against the Persians in modern Turkey, down the Mediterranean coast, and into Egypt. With the death of Darius III of Persia in 330 B.C., Alexander became the ruler of the entire Persian Empire. He continued fighting to the east into modern Afghanistan, Pakistan, and India. But when he neared the Ganges River in India in 326 B.C., his army revolted and refused to go any further. He and his army returned to Persia and then to Babylon. In 323 B.C., Alexander died in Babylon at only 32 years old.

When he died, he had no clear heir, and, as Daniel had prophesied, his empire was divided among four of his generals—Cassander (Greece), Lysimachus (Anatolia; modern Turkey), Ptolemy (Egypt), and Seleucus (Syria and Persia) (Dan 7; 11:3–4).

During the time between the Old and New Testaments, two of these Greek kingdoms exercised influence over the Jews in the land of Canaan: **The Ptolemies in Egypt and the Seleucids in Syria**. These two kingdoms continually fought to dominate the Jewish people. Eventually, however, the Jews enjoyed a period of independence after revolting under the leadership of Judas Maccabeus (167 B.C.). The independent Jewish kingdom later fell to Rome in 63 B.C.

Religion

The Greeks worshiped numerous gods, and each city had a god that they worshiped the most. **Zeus** was the king of the gods and was worshiped across Greece. **Athena** was the primary goddess of Athens and was the goddess of wisdom. Other important Greek gods were **Hera** (the queen of the gods), **Poseidon** (god of the sea), **Hermes** (the messenger of the gods), **Ares** (the god of war), and **Hades** (the god of the underworld).

The Parthenon, Temple of Athena

In the city of Athens, some Greeks began to focus less on the gods and more on the important questions of life like "Why are we here?", "What is good and evil?", or "What is the best way for society to work?" These men were called **philosophers**, which means "lovers of wisdom." Important Greek philosophers include Socrates, Plato, and Aristotle. In Acts 17, when Paul visits Athens, he speaks to the heirs of the Greek philosophical tradition, arguing with them that Jesus is the Savior of the world.

Ancient World History

The Romans

Basic Facts
Time Period: 63 B.C.–A.D. 395
Location: Italy, but conquering the entire Mediterranean region.
Principal Cities: Rome, Alexandria, Antioch, Corinth, Ephesus (see map on p. 396)
Biblical Connections: The entire New Testament was written under the reign of the Roman Emperors.

History
In its earliest days, Rome was ruled by kings, but these kings became so corrupt that eventually the people rebelled and established **the Roman Republic** (about 500 B.C.–27 B.C.). For almost 500 years, Rome was led by rich leaders who were elected by the citizens of Rome to the Roman Senate. Under the Roman Republic, the city began to expand its power. After conquering all of Italy, Rome came into conflict with the north African city of Carthage. Once Rome defeated Carthage, it became the undisputed power in the Mediterranean and continued to expand. However, during times of unrest, Rome would often turn over power to great generals. This weakness led to the fall of the republic and the establishment of the empire.

Augustus Caesar

Under the Roman Republic, **Julius Caesar** became a powerful general. He conquered parts of modern France, England, and Germany for Rome. He later conquered Egypt. After defeating rival generals, he returned to Rome as the ruler of the Senate. Roman senators believed that he was about to declare himself king, and they assassinated him to stop him in 44 B.C.

After his death, a civil war broke out between those loyal to Julius Caesar and his assassins. Eventually, Julius Caesar's adopted son Octavian emerged as the victor and ruler of Rome. Octavian took the name **Augustus Caesar** (reigned 27 B.C.–A.D. 14) and became the first Roman emperor. He was the emperor when Jesus was born (Luke 2:1). He united the Roman Empire from England in the west to Judea in the east. The Mediterranean Sea became known as the Roman lake because of the domination of Rome. His rule brought about a period of peace and prosperity to the empire known as the **Pax Romana** or Roman Peace.

In many regions, Augustus allowed local rulers to rule independently as long as they submitted to requests from Rome and sent tax money to Rome. King **Herod the Great**, who was king of Judea at the birth of Jesus, and his sons after him were such rulers.

Tiberius (reigned A.D. 14–A.D. 37) largely followed the path set out by Augustus. He was the emperor during Jesus' earthly ministry and crucifixion (Luke 3:1). Caligula (reigned A.D. 37–A.D. 41) followed Tiberius. He became known for his extravagant parties and also for being mentally insane. He is not referred to in the New Testament.

Claudius (reigned A.D. 41–A.D. 54) was emperor during much of the ministry of the apostles. He was an able emperor who brought peace back to the empire after Caligula's chaotic reign. During Claudius' reign, Jews in the city of Rome began to persecute Christians. Claudius didn't fully understand the reasons for the unrest among the Jewish community and expelled the Jews from Rome in A.D. 49 (Acts 18:2).

Claudius was replaced by **Nero** (reigned A.D. 54–A.D. 68), who began his reign as a good emperor but later became enthralled with a lavish lifestyle and paranoid that his enemies wanted to destroy him. In A.D. 64, a section of Rome burned. Rumors, likely true, began to circulate that Nero himself had started the fire, clearing the land for an extravagant palace. To deflect criticism, Nero blamed the fire on a small group of people called Christians who followed a different king named Jesus. During this persecution, both Paul and Peter were killed by Nero, probably around A.D. 67 or 68.

After the death of Nero, several men competed to become emperor. Ultimately, **Vespasian** (reigned A.D. 69–A.D. 79) won and became emperor. The Jews revolted against Roman rule, and Vespasian saw the suppression of this revolt. In A.D. 70, Vespasian's son Titus led an army that reconquered Jerusalem and destroyed the temple. The Jews were largely scattered from their homeland for centuries after this. Although the destruction of the temple occurred after most of the New Testament was already written, it was prophesied by Jesus (Luke 21:20).

After the New Testament period, the Roman Empire continued for about 300 more years. Eventually, the Germanic peoples from the north invaded and brought about the end of the Roman Empire.

Religion

The Romans worshiped the Greek gods but gave them Latin names. Zeus became **Jupiter**, Hera became **Juno**, Ares became **Mars**, Hermes became **Mercury**, etc.

As a large empire, however, Rome adapted itself to the religions of the many cultures it conquered. It did not require conquered peoples to worship the Roman gods but practiced a form of **religious toleration**. Most people in the empire continued to worship their own local gods. Rome also allowed the Jews to worship their God freely. They only required the Jews to make a regular sacrifice on behalf of the emperor. Christians were only persecuted because the Romans saw them as political rebels who declared a different king and a different kingdom (Acts 17:7).

Beginning with Augustus, the emperor was seen as god-like, and after the death of each emperor, it was believed that the emperor became a god. Statues of the emperors were worshiped throughout the empire. While Jews were allowed to not partake in **emperor worship** since they only worshiped one God, non-Jewish gentile Christians were required to partake in emperor worship or face persecution.

Roman Road

Technology

The Romans connected their empire with wide **roads** that allowed them to march armies quickly across their broad empire. These roads also allowed missionaries like the Apostle Paul to travel easily and quickly from city to city to proclaim the gospel.

The Old Testament

The Old Testament

About the Old Testament

Basic Facts
Number of Books: 39
Language: Hebrew. Portions of Ezra and Daniel are in Aramaic.
Places Written: The Sinai wilderness, Canaan, Babylon and Persia
Dates Written: about 1450–400 B.C.

The Big Idea of the Old Testament

While there are many important ideas in the Old Testament, one idea is the most important:

THROUGH HIS COVENANTS, GOD PROMISES HIS KINGDOM.

At creation, the garden of Eden looks like it will be the perfect kingdom of God that will last forever, but human sin causes God to exile Adam and Eve from the garden. God promises Abraham that he will give his descendants his perfect kingdom and establishes a covenant with Abraham that is passed down to his descendants through Isaac and Jacob.

God's kingdom begins to take shape as he rescues Israel from Egypt, making them his own people, and guides them to the promised land where he will dwell in their midst in the tabernacle. God even anoints a king who loves him, named

David, and he makes a covenant with David promising that one of his sons will reign forever.

The prosperity of Solomon's kingdom looks like God's perfect kingdom, but Israel's sin causes God to exile Israel from the promised land. The Assyrians and the Babylonians come and take the people away from God's place. Nevertheless, God continues to promise Israel his perfect kingdom through the prophets.

The Old Testament, however, ends, and God's promise remains unfulfilled. Only the coming of Jesus Christ recorded in the New Testament could bring about God's perfect kingdom. The Old Testament gives us God's promises while the New Testament shows us the fulfillment of those promises.

Old Testament: PROMISE → New Testament: FULFILLMENT

The Order of the Books

Today books are made by sewing or gluing pages together. A modern book can contain thousands of pages. In ancient times, books were written on scrolls, which were long sheets of paper or animal skins that could be rolled up. Originally, books of the Bible would have been written on separate scrolls. Therefore, the exact ordering of the books of the Old Testament was less important than it is today in our modern Bibles.

Nevertheless, by the time of Jesus, the Old Testament was organized into three major sections: the Law, the Prophets, and the Writings. Jesus often referred to the Old Testament as "the law and the prophets" (see Matt 5:17; 22:40). In Bibles today, we organize the Old Testament into four sections: Law, History, Wisdom, and Prophets. See the charts to the right to see which books were part of each division.

An Ancient Scroll

About the Old Testament

Jewish Divisions of the Old Testament

Law	Prophets	Writings
Genesis	*Early Prophets*	Psalms
Exodus	Joshua	Proverbs
Leviticus	Judges	Job
Numbers	1 Samuel	Song of Solomon
Deuteronomy	2 Samuel	Ruth
	1 Kings	Lamentations
	2 Kings	Ecclesiastes
		Esther
	Later Prophets	Daniel
	Isaiah	Ezra-Nehemiah
	Jeremiah	1 Chronicles
	Ezekiel	2 Chronicles
	The Twelve (Hos–Mal)	

Modern Divisions of the Old Testament

Law	History	Wisdom	Prophets
Genesis	Joshua	Job	*Major Prophets*
Exodus	Judges	Psalms	Isaiah
Leviticus	Ruth	Proverbs	Jeremiah
Numbers	1 Samuel	Ecclesiastes	Lamentations
Deuteronomy	2 Samuel	Song of Solomon	Ezekiel
	1 Kings		Daniel
	2 Kings		
	1 Chronicles		*Minor Prophets*
	2 Chronicles		Hosea
	Ezra-Nehemiah		Joel
	Esther		Amos
			Obadiah
			Jonah
			Micah
			Nahum
			Habakkuk
			Zephaniah
			Haggai
			Zechariah
			Malachi

Dates with B.C. and A.D.

During the Old Testament period, years are marked by the letters B.C., such as 1446 B.C.

B.C. stands for "Before Christ." So 1446 B.C. is one-thousand four-hundred forty-six years before the time of Jesus Christ. Because these dates are counting down to the time of Christ, they decrease in value as time passes. For example, the year after 1446 B.C. is 1445 B.C., and the year after 1445 B.C. is 1444 B.C.

The years after the coming of Jesus are sometimes marked with the letters A.D., such as A.D. 33. A.D. stands for the Latin phrase *"anno domini,"* which means "Year of our Lord." Because these dates are counting up from the time of Christ, they increase in value as time passes. For example, the year after A.D. 33 is A.D. 34 or 2020 is followed by 2021.

Seeing Jesus in the Old Testament

The Old Testament points forward to the coming of Jesus Christ, but it points to Jesus in multiple ways. It doesn't merely predict his coming, but it also shows us what he will be like and why he must come. By understanding these four ways we can see Jesus in the Old Testament, you will be able to read all the books of the Old Testament as preparing us for the coming of Christ.

1. The Old Testament foretells the coming of Jesus.

Throughout the Old Testament, God gives his people direct promises and prophecies of Jesus' coming. He tells Adam and Eve that an offspring of the woman will crush the head of the serpent (Gen 3:15). He tells David that one of his sons will reign over the entire world forever (2 Sam 7:12–16). God even reveals specific details about Jesus' life like the fact that he would be born in Bethlehem (Mic 5:2). While all of these direct promises and prophecies are important, they aren't the only way that the Old Testament points forward to Jesus.

2. The Old Testament tells a big story in which Jesus is the main character.

Another way that the Bible points forward to Jesus is through its big story. God creates humanity, but humanity sins. God chooses Abraham's family, delivers them from Egypt, gives them the promised land, and anoints kings to rule over them. But Israel sins. Jesus is the offspring of Abraham who will fulfill all of God's promises to Israel. Jesus will expand God's kingdom to all nations and all of creation. The Old Testament is a story without an ending. It awaits the coming of Jesus to bring the ending to the story so we can say, "And they all lived happily ever after."

3. The Old Testament creates pictures that point to Jesus.

In addition to promises and the story of the Old Testament, the Old Testament also creates pictures that point forward to Jesus. These pictures are often called "types," and interpreting them is called "typology." In the Old Testament, God establishes people, events, and institutions that are fulfilled in a greater way in Jesus than they were in the Old Testament.

One example is the priesthood and the Day of Atonement in Israel (see Lev 16). Jesus is both our high priest and the atoning sacrifice for our sins (see Rom 3:25; Heb 7–10). Actually, the Old Testament sacrifices could never truly take away sin. Their entire purpose was to point forward to the superior ministry of Jesus (Heb 10:4).

People in the Old Testament also picture Jesus. Jesus is the greater Moses who teaches God's people (Matt 5:1–2). Jesus is the greater David who rules God's people (Rom 1:3–4). Even events point forward to the coming of Christ. Our salvation through Christ is pictured in Noah's salvation from the flood, or Israel's salvation from Egypt (see 1 Cor 10:1–5; 1 Pet 3:20–21).

4. The Old Testament reveals our need for Jesus.

The Old Testament also points forward to Jesus by exposing our need for a Savior. God gives Israel his perfect law, but the history of Israel reveals that it is

The Old Testament

impossible to fulfill God's law apart from inward transformation. Even Moses knew that Israel would fail to obey the law (Deut 31:27). Jesus, however, fulfills all the demands of the law on our behalf and transforms us into people who obey God (Gal 3:1–4:7; 5:16–26).

Genesis

Basic Facts
Author: Moses
Original Audience: the nation of Israel
Place Written: The Sinai wilderness
Date Written: about 1450-1410 B.C.

The Main Idea
God's kingdom was destroyed by sin, but God promised to establish his kingdom through a covenant with Abraham.

Structure
- 1-11. God creates, but sin destroys the world.
    - 1-2. God creates the world and humans.
    - 3-11. All nations fall under God's judgment.
- 12-50. God chooses Abraham to bless the world.
    - 12-25:18. God promises to bless all nations through Abraham.
    - 25:19-36:43. Isaac and then Jacob inherit the promise of Abraham.
    - 37-50. God preserves the family of promise by grace.

The Old Testament

Big Events & Ideas

God created everything.

Genesis 1:1 says, "In the beginning God created the heavens and the earth." Genesis teaches that God is the creator of everything, and that he is the only God. Since God is the creator of everything, he is also the king over everything.

God created everything for his own glory. Romans 11:36 says, "For from him and through him and to him are all things. To him be the glory forever. Amen" (Rom 11:36). The world is the place God made to show his greatness and goodness so that creatures would glorify and enjoy him.

God created humans and made them rulers of the world.

Humans are the creatures God made to glorify and enjoy him forever (see 1 Cor 10:31). God created humans "in his image" (Gen 1:27). In God's image, humans were made to be rulers of the world under God the king.

> God blessed them, and God said to them, "Be fruitful, multiply, fill the earth, and subdue it. Rule the fish of the sea, the birds of the sky, and every creature that crawls on the earth" (Gen 1:28).

God created humans "male and female" (Gen 1:27). God created man and woman equally in his image, so man and woman have equal value before God. But God gave man and woman different roles for glorifying him as rulers of the world. In Genesis 2:18–25, God leads the man to feel his need for someone who is like him, but is also different. The man needed "a helper corresponding to him" (Gen 2:18). God made the man to lead, provide, and protect the family, and he made the woman to help her husband, bear children, and nurture the family.

God placed the man and the woman in the garden of Eden. God's kingdom was established: God's people were in God's place, and they lived under God's covenant. God gave them a command to obey. If they obeyed it, then they would enjoy life forever in God's presence within the garden, but if they disobeyed, then they would die and be exiled (Gen 2:16–17).

Humans sinned against God and were exiled from the garden of Eden.

In Genesis 3:1, we meet God's enemy, the serpent. Revelation 12:9 and 20:2 reveals that this serpent was actually a fallen angel called Satan, or the devil. Satan is the leader of the fallen angels, and he continues to rebel against God by tempting and accusing God's people (Isa 14:12–15; see Job 1–2; Zech 3:1–2; 1 Pet 5:8).

Satan suggests to the woman that God's word is untrustworthy by asking, "Did God really say, 'You can't eat from any tree in the garden'" (Gen 3:1)? Then he assaults God's goodness:

> "No! You will not die," the serpent said to the woman. "In fact, God knows that when you eat it your eyes will be opened and you will be like God, knowing good and evil" (Gen 3:4–5).

According to Satan, God has lied to the man and woman. God is not a loving king. He is an evil dictator. The man and the woman join Satan's rebellion by eating the forbidden fruit.

This is the first human sin. Sin is rebellion against God and his good rule in what we do, say, or think. Death is God's righteous judgment against sin. Through death, God separates sinners from the blessings of life. Death occurs in 3 stages: spiritual, physical, and eternal. At the moment the man and woman sinned, they died spiritually. They became separated from God and hid from him (Gen 3:8; see Eph 2:1–2). Eventually, the man and woman would die physically (Gen 3:19). Later the Bible tells that the final stage of death is separation from God's blessings forever in hell (see Rev 20:14).

Because the man and the woman had died spiritually, God removed them from his presence in the garden of Eden. "He drove the man out and stationed the cherubim and the flaming, whirling sword east of the garden of Eden to guard the way to the tree of life" (Gen 3:24).

Despite the sorrow of that day, God gave humanity a promise that one day he would destroy the power of sin.

> I will put hostility between you and the woman, and between your offspring and her offspring. He will strike your head, and you will strike his heel (Gen 3:15).

Adam believed this promise of an offspring of the woman who would be humanity's future Savior, and he showed his faith by naming the woman "Eve," or "Life," on the same day that death entered the world (Gen 3:20).

God used Noah to save humanity and made a covenant with him.

In Genesis 4–6, sin grows and grows to the point that God decides to destroy humanity with a flood. Why does God judge humanity's sin? God judges sin because he is holy, righteous, and good. If God allowed sin to continue without judgment, then he would not be holy, righteous, and good.

In his mercy, God chose to save a portion of humanity through Noah, a man who obeyed God. God revealed to Noah the way of salvation: an ark.

After saving Noah from the flood, God established a covenant with him. A covenant is a formalized and binding agreement between two parties that establishes a relationship between them. God promised Noah never to destroy humanity with a flood again (Gen 9:11). The covenant of Noah preserves the earth for the duration of God's plan of salvation.

Even though Noah obeyed God when building the ark, Noah had the same problem as Adam. He was a sinner, and like Adam, he died (Gen 9:20–29). After the flood, humanity continued to rebel against God, even building a tower to make themselves a great name (Gen 11:1–9). Humanity needs God to change their hearts.

God chose Abraham and made a covenant with him.

God chose a man named Abram (which he later changed to Abraham) and made him a promise.

> The LORD said to Abram, "Go out from your land, your relatives, and your father's house to the land that I will show you. I will make you into a great nation, I will bless you, I will make your name great, and you will be a blessing. I will bless those who bless you, I will curse anyone who treats you with contempt, and all the peoples on earth will be blessed through you" (Gen 12:1–3).

God's promise was to recreate his kingdom through Abraham's family. Even though Abraham had no children, he would become a great nation, and God's people would live in God's place, the land of Canaan that God showed to Abraham. Through this kingdom, God would bring his blessing to all of humanity.

God guaranteed this covenant with the shedding of blood (Gen 15), and began to fulfill his promise by giving Abraham and Sarah a son, Isaac. From Isaac, God passed the promise on to Jacob, and from Jacob, the promise was given to his twelve sons.

God used Joseph to save Israel.

Abraham's family only survived and grew because of God's care and protection. God would not abandon Abraham's family because God would never abandon his covenant promise. The story of Joseph in Genesis 37 and 39–50 shows God's power at work to care for Abraham's family.

Because of the sins of favoritism and jealousy in Jacob's family, Joseph was sold into slavery in Egypt. But God had a greater purpose, to save God's people from famine. Joseph explains this to his brothers, "You planned evil against me; God planned it for good to bring about the present result—the survival of many people" (Gen 50:20).

Genesis begins by teaching that God is the creator and king of everything. Even though sin entered the world and damaged God's creation, God remains king over everything, and he is in complete control of everything (see Pss 115:3;

135:6; Dan 4:35). In his wisdom, God always chooses what is best to glorify himself and bring good to his people (see Ps 104:24; Rom 11:33).

Seeing Jesus

Genesis is a genealogy. Of course, it contains several detailed genealogies. But it is important to understand that Moses designed the book in sections that each begin with genealogical statements:

- Genesis 1:1, "In the beginning, God..." – This marks off the introduction of the book.
- Genesis 2:4, "These are the records of the heavens and the earth, concerning their creation. At the time that the LORD God made the earth and the heavens"
- Genesis 6:9, "The family records of Noah"
- Genesis 10:1, "These are the family records of Noah's sons, Shem, Ham, and Japheth"
- Genesis 11:10, "These are the family records of Shem"
- Genesis 11:27, "These are the family records of Terah"
- Genesis 25:12, "These are the family records of Ishmael"
- Genesis 25:19, "These are the family records of Isaac son of Abraham."
- Genesis 36:1, 9, "These are the family records of Esau (that is, Edom)."
- Genesis 37:2, "These are the family records of Jacob."

This repetition throughout the book shows that Moses thinks of Genesis as one long genealogy. The narrative sections simply fill out the significance of the genealogy.

Why the focus on the genealogy? The answer comes early in the book:

> I will put hostility between you and the woman, and between your offspring and her offspring. He will strike your head, and you will strike his heel (Gen 3:15).

The genealogy points forward in faith to the fulfillment of God's promise. The serpent, sin, and death would all be overcome by the offspring or seed of the woman. This emphasis continues in the lives of Abraham, Isaac, and Jacob. They receive a promise that is both a promise *of* offspring and *to* offspring (for example, Gen 12:7; 13:15; 15:5). The flow of the story shows us that the offspring promised to Abraham, Isaac, and Jacob is the same offspring promised to the woman in Genesis 3:15. Through this family, God will save the creation.

The New Testament clearly and adamantly claims that the offspring of the woman and of Abraham is Jesus Christ (see Gal 3:16). The genealogy of Genesis points us toward the fulfillment of all of God's promises in Jesus! Jesus has crushed the head of the serpent. In Jesus, all the families of the earth have been blessed. Through Jesus, God has multiplied Abraham's offspring.

The Old Testament

Exodus

Basic Facts
Author: Moses
Original Audience: the nation of Israel
Place Written: The Sinai wilderness
Date Written: about 1450-1410 B.C.

The Main Idea
God delivered Israel from Egypt and made them his people.

Structure
- 1–18. **God delivers Israel from Egypt.**
    - 1–4. God delivers Moses in order to make him the deliverer.
    - 5–15:21. God defeats Egypt and frees Israel.
    - 15:22–18:27. Israel journeys to Mount Sinai.
- 19–40. **God makes a covenant with Israel at Sinai.**
    - 19–24. God establishes his covenant with Israel.
    - 25–31. God gives instructions for the tabernacle.
    - 32–34. Israel forsakes God, but Moses intercedes for them.
    - 35–40. Israel builds the tabernacle.

Big Events & Ideas

God uses Moses to save Israel from Egypt.

The book of Exodus begins with God saving the future savior. Pharaoh attempts to kill all the boys born to the Israelites, but Moses escapes destruction when his parents placed him in an ark in the Nile River and Pharaoh's daughter drew him out of the water (Exod 1:1–2:10; see Heb 11:23). Moses grows up in Pharaoh's household, but after killing an Egyptian, he escapes to Midian and lives as a shepherd for forty years.

God speaks to Moses from a burning bush and commands him to return to Egypt to deliver Israel. Through Moses, God judges Egypt with plagues and shows his superiority over Egypt's idols (Exod 7:4–5).

God is I AM.

At the burning bush, Moses asks God to reveal his name. "God replied to Moses, 'I AM WHO I AM. This is what you are to say to the Israelites: I AM has sent me to you'" (Exod 3:14). From "I AM" comes God's personal name in Hebrew, Yahweh (older scholars mispronounced God's name as Jehovah and many Christians still use this version today). The name Yahweh is sacred, and most Bible translations identify the name with the title LORD in capital letters.

By identifying himself as I AM, God wants Moses and Israel to know that he is independent. God does not need us or anything. He simply is (see Job 41:11; Ps 50:10–12; Acts 17:24–25). He is also unchangeable. He is always loyal and perfect. He always is what he is, and he will never change (see Ps 102:25–27; Mal 3:6; Jas 1:17). Finally, God is eternal or timeless. He is outside of time (see Job 36:26; Ps 90:2; Isa 46:9–10; Rev 1:8; 4:8). There is no god like the one, true God whose name is I AM.

God saves Israel and judges Egypt on Passover and at the Red Sea.

In Exodus 11–12, God sends the final plague that kills the firstborn sons of Egypt. God saves Israel from this judgment through the death of a lamb. Each family is instructed to kill a lamb and paint its blood over their doorposts. When God sees the blood, he passes over that house (Exod 12:13).

After the death of the firstborn in Exodus 14, Pharaoh releases the Israelites. God leads them to the banks of the Red Sea. Pharaoh then changes his mind and traps Israel at the sea. God, however, creates a way through the sea to save Israel, and then drowns Pharaoh's army. "That day the LORD saved Israel from the power of the Egyptians, and Israel saw the Egyptians dead on the seashore" (Exod 14:30). By saving Israel, God claims the people as his own.

God chooses Israel and gives Israel his law.

Through God's rescue of Israel, Israel becomes God's own people.

> You have seen what I did to the Egyptians and how I carried you on eagles' wings and brought you to myself. Now if you will carefully listen to me and keep my covenant, you will be my own possession out of all the peoples, although the whole earth is mine, and you will be my kingdom of priests and my holy nation.' These are the words that you are to say to the Israelites (Exod 19:4–6).

God's people should reflect God's own holy character. So God gives his people his law. The law of God is the instruction God gives to teach his people to live for his glory. It is summarized by these two commands: First, love God with all your heart, soul, mind, and strength. Second, love your neighbor as yourself (see Matt 22:37–40).

Israel worships a golden calf.

God had delivered Israel, chosen them as his own people, and given them his law. But when Moses is on Mount Sinai, the people ask Moses' brother Aaron to fashion a god for them. Aaron makes a golden calf and then says, "Israel, these are your gods, who brought you up from the land of Egypt" (Exod 32:4)! Then Israel worships the idol.

The worship of the golden calf foreshadows the entire history of Israel. Despite all that God had done, the nation is idolatrous. They would reject the one, true God, and the sin of idolatry would eventually lead to the exile of the nation from the promised land.

God shows Moses his glory.

In Exodus 33:18, Moses asks God to show him his glory. When God passes by Moses, he proclaims the glory of his character:

> The LORD — the LORD is a compassionate and gracious God, slow to anger and abounding in faithful love and truth, maintaining faithful love to a thousand generations, forgiving iniquity, rebellion, and sin. But he will not leave the guilty unpunished, bringing the fathers' iniquity on the children and grandchildren to the third and fourth generation (Exod 34:6–7).

God's glory is the great beauty of God, which he displays by revealing himself as creator, judge, and savior. God reveals himself to Moses as righteous and just. He always does what is right (see Deut 32:4; Isa 45:19; Rom 3:25–26), and he always punishes sin (see Gen 18:25; Ps 7:11; Job 8:3; Nah 1:6). But God is also full of love and mercy. God lovingly gives himself away to others (see Zeph 3:17–18; 1 John 4:8–10), and he forgives sinners (see Exod 33:19; Ps 103:8–10; 2 Cor 1:3; 1 Pet 5:10).

God dwells with Israel in the tabernacle.

In Exodus 25–31 and 35–40, God reveals his plans for the tabernacle, and Israel builds the tabernacle. The tabernacle was a tent where God would dwell among his people and be worshiped by them. When the tabernacle is completed and dedicated, "the glory of the LORD filled the tabernacle" (Exod 40:34). God's presence lives among his people, and God's presence is the source of blessing to God's people.

Exodus

Seeing Jesus

The Exodus is the salvation act of the Old Testament. When ancient Israelites thought about salvation, they thought about the Exodus. However, even within the pages of the Old Testament, the prophets made clear that the Exodus was insufficient. What God's people needed was a second Exodus, a comprehensive salvation event. The New Testament answered this longing. The Exodus was a shadow. Christ is the substance!

In Exodus, Abraham's family was enslaved to the most powerful nation in the world, Egypt. The Israelite situation was impossible. Only the God of Abraham, Isaac, and Jacob could deliver them, and that is exactly what happened. God, using his servant Moses, fought for his people and defeated Pharaoh.

But even within the pages of Exodus itself, it became apparent that God's people were enslaved in another way. They were enslaved to sin. The long history of Israel from the Exodus to the exile simply repeated this fact: Israel is not free. It is enslaved to sin.

So God's judgment must ultimately come through the exile, but by the prophets, God gave hope that he would one day deliver his people from their slavery. He would liberate the Jews from the exile to Babylon just as he did from Egypt (see Jer 23:7-8). But this new Exodus would bring about more than physical liberation. God would liberate his people from their sins and give them his Spirit (see Isa 44; Jer 31; Ezek 36).

Jesus has liberated us from sin, Satan, and death by paying the penalty of death and giving us his Spirit (see Heb 2:10-15). Every time a new Christian passes through the waters of baptism, he or she testifies to a reality more miraculous than when Israel passed through the Red Sea. Every time a church eats the Lord's supper, they bear witness to a deliverance greater than the one commemorated by the Passover. The Lamb has been slain, and his people are free!

The Old Testament

About the Tabernacle and Temple

God instructed Moses to build the tabernacle, or tent of meeting, so God could dwell in the midst of his people. The ultimate goal of God's covenant was that he would be with his people as their God. Because the tabernacle was central to God's covenant with Israel, it became the center of Israel's worship to God through the priests that served, the sacrifices offered, and the feasts celebrated there.

David desired to convert the tabernacle into a permanent structure in Jerusalem, and his son Solomon would complete the project by building the first temple in 960 B.C. The temple, while consisting of stone and precious metals, continued to follow carefully the pattern of the tabernacle revealed to Moses. The Babylonians destroyed Solomon's temple in 586 B.C.

When the Jews returned from Babylon, they began to rebuild the temple in Jerusalem under the leadership of Zerubbabel in 520 B.C. In 20 B.C., Herod the Great remodeled Zerubbabel's humble temple, which resulted in the magnificent building and courtyards described in the Gospels and Acts. This second temple, however, would be destroyed by the Romans in A.D. 70. Today, the Muslim

The Old Testament

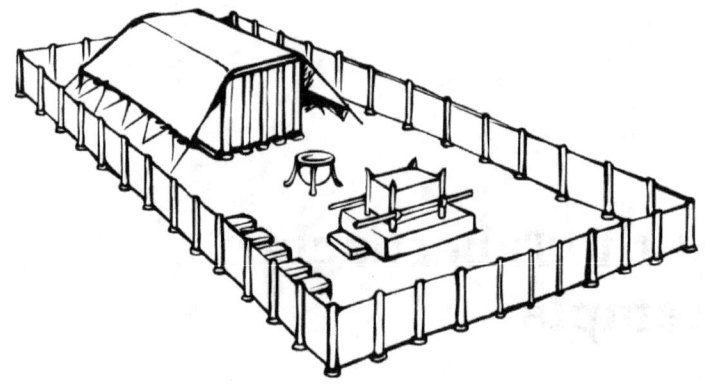

The Tabernacle

Dome of the Rock and al-Aqsa Mosque stand where the the temple once stood in Jerusalem.

Even though a temple no longer stands in Jerusalem, God still dwells among his people. The New Testament teaches that the new covenant people of God, the church, are God's temple since he dwells in us through the Holy Spirit (1 Cor 3:16; 1 Pet 2:1–8).

The Tabernacle and Temple Among the People

The placement of the tabernacle in the Israelite camp during their wanderings in the wilderness, as well as the placement of the temple in the promised land, held great significance. God instructed that the tabernacle was to be erected at the center of the Israelite camp with three tribes camping on each of the four sides of the tabernacle. Naphtali, Asher, and Dan camped to the north, Issachar, Judah, and Zebulun to the east, Gad, Simeon, and Reuben to the south, and Ephraim, Manasseh, and Benjamin to the west. The Levites were to dwell by their clans between the other tribes and the tabernacle, showing their role as priests who were to intercede on behalf of the nation (Num 2).

About the Tabernacle and Temple

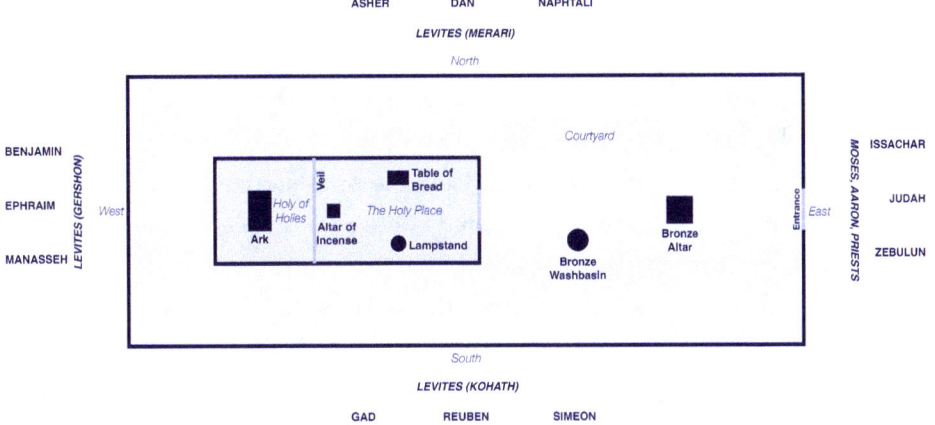

The Divisions of the Tabernacle and Israel's Camp

In the promised land, Israel set up the tabernacle at Shiloh, the geographic center of the promised land (Josh 18:1). Later, David moved it to Jerusalem, which was about 20 miles (32 kilometers) from Shiloh (2 Sam 6:17). When Solomon built the temple on Mount Zion in Jerusalem, the temple remained at the center of the promised land.

Through the tabernacle and temple's placement, God communicated his desire to dwell among his people. When John describes the coming of Jesus, he writes, "The Word became flesh and dwelt among us" (John 1:14). The word translated "dwelt" means to pitch a tent and live in it. John pictures Jesus himself as the new tabernacle in the midst of God's people.

The Divisions of the Tabernacle and the Temple

Both the tabernacle and temple were divided into three divisions: the courtyard, the holy place, and the holy of holies. To access **the courtyard**, one had to enter into the gates of the tabernacle, since the tabernacle was surrounded by a fence made of animal skins. While only the priests could enter the holy place, all Israelites were able to enter into the courtyard as long as they were ritually clean. This was the place where sacrifices were offered. In Jesus' day, the second temple's courtyard was divided into three sections: the court of the gentiles, the court of the women, and the inner courtyard. Only Jewish men could enter the inner courtyard.

Upon entering the tent or building itself, the priests came into a room called **the holy place.** Here the priests ministered at the altar of incense, the table of the bread of the presence, and the lampstand.

The holy place was separated from **the holy of holies** by a veil made of purple material. Two cherubim were embroidered on the veil, reflecting the cherubim God placed at the gate of Eden in Genesis 3:24. These two guardians of God's presence communicated that no sinful human was allowed to go through the veil into the holy of holies. Within the holy of holies was the ark of the covenant, which represented God's own presence among his people. Only the high priest was allowed to enter the holy of holies on the Day of Atonement to sprinkle blood upon the mercy seat or top part of the ark.

When Solomon built the temple, the building and decorations were covered with designs of trees and flowers (1 Kgs 6–7). The garden theme of the building was meant to remind worshipers of the garden of Eden, where God dwelled with man. The tabernacle and the temple were like a new garden of Eden where God reigned on earth, but sin remained a problem separating God and humanity, as the cherubim reminded the priests. Only through atoning sacrifices could the way be open for God to dwell with humanity. When Jesus died as the perfect sacrifice, the veil of the temple was ripped from top to bottom, demonstrating that God could now truly live among his people (Matt 27:51).

The Furnishings of the Tabernacle and the Temple

The various furnishings of the tabernacle and temple communicated important spiritual truths to the nation of Israel.

The courtyard contained two furnishings: the bronze altar and the bronze washbasin or sea. **The bronze altar** was the place where sacrifices were offered. The altar had four horns at each corner, which may have symbolized God's

About the Tabernacle and Temple

power over life and death (Exod 27:1–8; 38:1–7). Also in the courtyard was **the bronze washbasin or sea**. The priests were to wash their hands and feet in this washbasin before entering the holy place, symbolizing the necessity of holiness and purity to approach God (Exod 30:17–21; 38:8).

In the holy place, the priests ministered using three furnishings: the table of the bread of the presence, the lampstand, and the altar of incense.

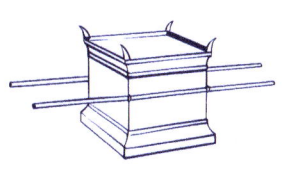

The Bronze Altar

The Table of the Bread of the Presence

Upon entering the holy place, **the table of the bread of the presence**, which was made of wood overlaid with gold, was placed to the right. Every Sabbath the priests were to place two stacks of six loaves of bread, symbolizing each of the twelve tribes, as well as pitchers to be utilized in drink offerings. The priests were to eat the bread during the week in the presence of God. This was a reminder of the meal that the elders of Israel ate in God's presence on Mount Sinai when God made his covenant with Israel (Exod 24:9–11). The bread symbolized God's constant provision for his people (Exod 37:10–16; Lev 24:5–9).

To the left side, opposite of the table, stood **the lampstand** made of gold. The lampstand consisted of six branches coming out from a central branch. At the top of each branch was a container where oil could be poured and burned. The priests were to keep these seven lamps burning constantly, both to give light to the room and remind God's people of God's guidance (Exod 25:31–40; 37:17–24).

The altar of incense stood directly before the veil

The Lampstand

135

and was made of wood overlaid with gold. Here the priests would burn incense each morning and evening. The incense used had to follow the exact recipe instructed by God. The sweet smell would fill the room. On the Day of Atonement, the high priest would take incense from this altar into the holy of holies. The sweet smelling incense represented the prayers of God's people (Exod 30:1–10, 34–38; 37:25–29; Rev 5:8).

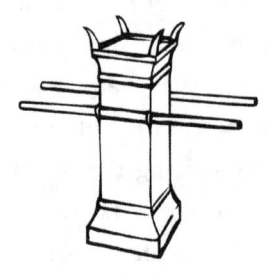

Altar of Incense

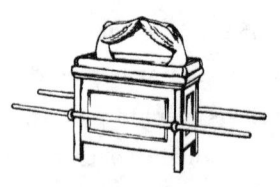

Ark of the Covenant

After going through the veil into the holy of holies, the high priest would see **the ark of the covenant**. The ark of the covenant was a wooden box overlaid with gold. The box could be opened by removing the lid from the top, and God instructed Moses to place four objects within the ark: the two stone tablets of the ten commandments, a jar of manna, and Aaron's staff that budded (Exod 16:32–34; Num 17:10; Deut 10:5). On the lid of the ark were two cherubim with their wings outstretched toward the center. Like the cherubim on the veil, these guardians reminded the high priest that God's presence was inaccessible to sinners, just as he had placed the cherubim at the entrance to Eden (Gen 3:34). The area between the cherubim was called the mercy seat. This was the place where the high priest was to sprinkle the blood of the sacrifice on the Day of Atonement. It represented God's throne on earth, the place where he dwelled in the midst of his people. The ark of the covenant was the greatest reminder of God's unique covenant with the people of Israel. The only true and holy God had chosen to dwell in the midst of a sinful

The Ark carried by Priests

About the Tabernacle and Temple

nation that he had saved from slavery, provided sacrifices for the covering of their sin, and given his law to as instruction to be a holy people (Exod 25:10–22; 37:1–9).

The Priests

God chose the tribe of Levi to minister before him in the tabernacle and the temple. The tribe of Levi was then divided into

The three divisions of Levi (left to right): Levite, high priest, priest

three main divisions: the Levites, the priests, and the high priest. The Levites refers to those members of the tribe who assisted the priests in their duties. They were divided into three divisions based on their descent from the three sons of Levi: Gershon, Merari, and Kohath (Num 3). Levites assisted the priests by carrying and constructing the tabernacle during the years in the wilderness, performing music, acting as temple guards, and cleansing the temple vessels.

The priests came specifically from the family of Aaron, the first high priest and brother of Moses who descended from Kohath. Only priests could offer sacrifices or serve in the holy place. Later David would divide the priests into 24 divisions to organize the worship of the temple (2 Chron 24). From among the priests would be appointed the high priest who would not only supervise the priests and the Levites, but also served as the mediator between God and Israel on the Day of Atonement.

The priests were to each wear undergarments, a tunic, a turban, and a sash. The undergarments, tunic, and turban were to be made of fine white linen, while the sash was to contain beautiful embroidery and was worn around the waist like a belt. Theses garments were meant to reflect God's own glory and beauty in the same way that Adam reflected God's glory as a perfect image bearer in Eden (Exod 28:39–43).

The high priest was to wear a robe, ephod, breastpiece, and turban. The robe was worn over the high priests white linen tunic and was dark blue with pomegranates embroidered at the bottom hem. Golden bells were then attached to this hem. The bells served the purpose of alerting those outside the tabernacle that the high priest had not been killed upon entering into God's presence (Exod 28:31–35). The ephod was worn on top of the robe and consisted of gold, blue, purple, and red yarn embroidered in linen. Two onyx (black) stones were placed into golden pouches on the shoulders of the ephod. The names of the tribes of Israel were engraved on these gem stones to symbolize that the high priest represented the entire nation before God (Exod 28:6–14). On top of the ephod, the high priest wore the breastpiece, which was a square made of gold, blue, purple, and red yarn embroidering linen. Twelve gems were mounted on this breastplate in four rows: *row 1* carnelian, topaz, emerald, turquoise; *row 2* lapis lazuli, diamond; *row 3* jacinth, agate, amethyst; *row 4* beryl, onyx, and jasper. Each stone was engraved with one of the names of the twelve tribes. The breastpiece was worn by the high priest, using gold chains attaching it to the ephod. The Urim and Thummim, which the priest could use to cast lots to discern God's will, was placed within the breastpiece. We do not know what the Urim and Thummim were made of or how they were used to discern God's will (Exod 28:15–30). Finally, the high priest wore a turban upon his head, which consisted of a golden band or crown. Upon this golden band was engraved "Holy to the LORD" as a reminder of God's declaration that his people were holy or set apart to him from among the nations (Exod 28:36–38).

The Offerings

The book of Leviticus describes five main offerings that the people of Israel were to offer to God for specific purposes. These were the burnt offering, the grain offering, the peace offering, the sin offering, and the guilt offering. **The burnt offering** involved the voluntary sacrifice of either a bull, sheep, goat, or bird. While the priests could keep the skin of the animal, the rest of the animal was completely consumed by the fire, with the blood being splattered on the sides of the altar. Worshipers would offer a burnt offering as an act of thanksgiving or accompanying vows or prayers to God (Lev 1).

In **the grain offering**, the worshiper gave a combination of flour or crushed grain kernels, oil, frankincense, and salt. This could be given either as raw ingredients or as a cooked loaf of bread. The priest would burn a handful on the altar, but the rest would be kept for the priests to eat. Grain offerings were often given along with burnt offerings or peace offerings for the same purposes, or they might be given alone as an act of thanksgiving for the harvest (Lev 2).

The peace or fellowship offering consisted of the sacrifice of a cow, sheep, or goat. In this offering, the worshiper, rather than the priest, killed the animal. The blood would be splattered on the altar, and portions of the animal would be burned completely upon the altar. The rest of the animal would be eaten by the worshiper and the priests, symbolizing the covenant relationship between God and the worshiper (Lev 3).

The sin offering was given to atone for sins committed by the worshiper, whether intentionally or unintentionally. The requirements for the sin offering differed based on who had committed the sin. When offered for a priest or the entire nation, the sin offering required the sacrifice of a bull while when offered for a leader or a common person, the requirement was a goat or a lamb. The blood of the animal would be smeared on the altar and sprinkled inside the holy place, while portions of the animal would be eaten by the priests with other portions burned. The Day of Atonement was the greatest of the sin offerings (Lev 4:1–5:13).

The guilt offering was given to atone for more serious sins. It served as a way of paying restitution to God for the wrong that the worshiper had done. The worshiper was to offer a ram whose blood would be poured on the sides of the altar while the meat was burned on the altar with the priests keeping some portions. This act of worship would accompany restitution paid to the victim of the worshipers sin. He was to pay back any damages done along with an extra 20% (Lev 5:14–6:7).

The Feasts

In addition to the weekly observance of **the Sabbath**, where the people rested from their work, and the monthly **new moon festival**, when trumpets were blown and sacrifices given (Num 28:11–15), the priests were to lead the nation in observing five annual feasts: Passover, Firstfruits, Weeks, Trumpets, the Day of Atonement, and Booths.

Passover occurred in the Spring (March/April according to the modern calendar). Passover reminded Israel that God had saved them from Egyptian slavery. Celebrations centered around the Passover meal eaten by families, especially the eating of unleavened bread (Lev 23:4–8).

Firstfruits followed one week after Passover (March/April). Through Firstfruits, worshipers placed their hope in God, praying that he would bring about the full harvest in the days to come. Firstfruits consisted of the waving of sheaves of grain before Yahweh, as well as a series of burnt, grain, and drink offerings (Lev 23:9–14).

Weeks (also known as the Feast of the Harvest or the Day of the Firstfruits; Exod 23:16; Num 28:26) was commemorated every year on the first day of Sivan, the third month (May/June). It is called Weeks because it occurs seven weeks, or fifty days, after Firstfruits. In the New Testament, it is called Pentecost, the Greek word for "fiftieth." By offering grain, peace, and sin offerings, the people gave thanks to God for their harvest (Lev 23:15–21).

Trumpets occurs on the first day of the seventh month, called Tishri (September/October). While it marks the beginning of a new agricultural year, its primary function is to prepare the people for the Day of Atonement. The day began with a blast of the trumpet that called the nation to assemble before God and offer sacrifices to him (Lev 23:23–25).

The Day of Atonement came on the tenth day of Tishri (September/October). On this day, the high priest would atone for the sins of the entire nation. He began by offering a bull for his own sins and the sins of his household. Then he was to cast lots over two goats. One goat was to be sent off into the wilderness, symbolizing that God had removed the people's sin from them. The other goat was killed as a sin offering. He would then enter into the holy of holies to sprinkle the blood of both the bull and the goat on the mercy seat of the ark. To remember the day, the people were to fast and do no work (Lev 16; 23:26–32).

Booths was the final feast of the Israelite year, celebrated a few days after the Day of Atonement on the 15th–22nd days of Tishri (September/October). Booths commemorated God's faithfulness to Israel during the Exodus. It was celebrated by building temporary shelters from tree branches and giving offerings. Israelites would live in these shelters for a week, remembering how their ancestors had lived as sojourners in the desert (Lev 23:33–36).

Later in Jewish history, two other festivals were added — Purim and Hanukkah.

Purim (the Hebrew word for "lots;" see Est 9:24) remembers the deliverance of the Jews from the plot of Haman by Queen Esther. It was celebrated annually on the fourteenth and fifteenth days of Adar (March) by the giving of gifts and reading the book of Esther.

Hanukkah remembers the rededication of the temple after its desecration by the Greek king Antiochus IV and its recapture by Jewish hero Judas Maccabeus in 167 B.C. It is also called the festival of lights because it involves the lighting of candles or lamps or the festival of dedication. Since it was created after the Old

The Old Testament

Testament was completed, it is only mentioned in the New Testament. Jesus celebrated it (John 10:22).

Leviticus

Basic Facts
Author: Moses
Original Audience: the nation of Israel
Place Written: The Sinai wilderness
Date Written: about 1450-1410 B.C.

The Main Idea
A holy God demands holiness from his people but also provides sacrifices to atone for their sin.

Structure
- 1–10. Rules for Offerings and Priests
- 11–15. Rules about Cleanness and Uncleanness
- 16–17. The Day of Atonement
- 18–25. Holy People and Holy Days
- 26. Blessings and Curses
- 27. Rules for Vows

The Old Testament

Big Events & Ideas

God is holy and demands holiness from his people.

Leviticus is about holiness. The word "holy" in its various forms occurs over fifty times in the book. After having saved Israel out of Egypt, God's will for his people is clear:

> Be holy because I, the LORD your God, am holy. (Lev 19:2; see Lev 11:44-45; 20:7, 26; 21:8).

God is holy, or separate from sin (see Isa 6:3). God's character should be reflected by the character of his rescued people. This is the great privilege given to Israel. Through their salvation, they have become God's people and his possession. A holy God has chosen to dwell in their midst in the tabernacle, spreading his blessing to his chosen possession.

God uses sacrifices to save his people from his judgment.

The greatest privilege of Israel is also their greatest danger. God's holiness demands that sin be judged. If God does not execute justice against sin, then he is no longer holy. Yet, the people of Israel, like all people born with Adam's nature, are sinful. God's presence — the source of their blessing — will become their curse because of their sin.

Therefore, in his mercy, God provides for the needs of his people. He gives them a priesthood, or men whose lives are devoted completely to holiness and are consecrated to approach God's presence in the tabernacle. Then he gives them sacrifices, the most important of which occur on the Day of Atonement (Lev 16). Atonement is when God punishes a substitute for human sin so that he can forgive and make humans holy.

Through these acts of worship, an innocent animal dies on behalf of a guilty people in order to satisfy God's holy wrath and righteous justice. Through these institutions, a holy God can dwell in the midst of an imperfect people, giving them grace and peace.

Seeing Jesus

Hebrews says that the priesthood and sacrifices described in Leviticus were only shadows. Christ is the substance (Heb 8:5; 10:1). Jesus Christ is the eternal high priest from a priestly order superior to the Levitical priests (Heb 4:14-7:28), and as a superior high priest, he offered a superior sacrifice (Heb 8:3-10:18). His sacrifice does not need to be repeated regularly as the sacrifices described in Leviticus because his sacrifice accomplished what the blood of bulls and goats could not (Heb 10:1-4). His sacrifice has taken away our sins and cleansed our consciences. His sacrifice has opened up the way to God fully and finally for all who would approach God through him (Heb 10:19-20). And what sacrifice was this? It was the sacrifice of himself on the cross, the spilling of his own blood.

Through the blood of Jesus, we have been declared "holy ones," or "saints." So we endeavor to live as who we are, just as Peter encourages us: "As obedient children, do not be conformed to the desires of your former ignorance. But as the one who called you is holy, you also are to be holy in all your conduct; for it is written, 'Be holy, because I am holy'" (1 Pet 1:14–16).

And one day, because of Jesus' death on our behalf, we will be who we are—holy, perfectly and forever. Then we will dwell in the presence of a holy God forever, praising him for his grace and enjoying his peace (Rev 21-22).

The Old Testament

Numbers

Basic Facts
Author: Moses
Original Audience: the nation of Israel
Place Written: east of the Jordan River
Date Written: about 1450-1410 B.C.

The Main Idea
God will never abandon his promises of blessing his people, even though they reject him.

Structure
- **1–10. Israel prepares to enter the land.**
  - 1–4. Moses conducts a census of the people.
  - 5–10. Rules for the Camp and the Tabernacle.
- **11–19. Israel rejects Moses, the land, and God**
  - 11. Israel complains against Moses and God.
  - 12. Miriam and Aaron oppose Moses.
  - 13–14. Israel refuses to enter the land.
  - 15. An Israelite violates God's law.
  - 16–17. Korah rebels against Moses.

- 18. God provides for the cleansing of his sinful people.
- **20–36. Israel travels from Kadesh to the Jordan River.**
  - 20–21. From Kadesh to Moab.
  - 22–24. Balaam is unable to curse Israel.
  - 25. Israel commits idolatry with the Baal of Peor.
  - 26–36. Moses conducts a new census and prepares the people for the land.

Big Events & Ideas

God will bless his people.

Numbers begins with one of the most beautiful descriptions of God's good intentions for his people. God gives the Aaronic priesthood the following blessing to speak over the people:

> May the LORD bless you and protect you;
> may the LORD make his face shine on you and be gracious to you;
> may the LORD look with favor on you and give you peace (Num 6:24–26).

However, Numbers isn't about the realization of this blessing. Numbers is about the execution of God's curse upon those delivered from Egyptian slavery.

Israel sins against God in the wilderness.

Four times in the central section of the book people reject the God-appointed leadership of Moses, and thus they rebel against God himself. First, the people cry out against Moses because they craved meat (Num 11). Second, his own brother and sister question Moses' leadership (Num 12). Third, and perhaps most importantly, the people refuse to enter the promised land after the bad report given by ten men who had spied out the land (Num 13-14), and, finally, a group of Levites led by Korah attempt a coup against the leadership of Moses and Aaron (Num 16-17).

Moses repeatedly responds to rebellion with humility, falling on his face in prayer (Num 12:3; 14:5; 20:6). God executes justice against those who rebel, but not fully. When the people refuse to enter the promised land, he would destroy them all, but Moses intercedes, praying that God might not destroy the people for the sake of his great Name (Num 14:13-19). Because of Moses' selfless intercession, God does not utterly destroy Israel. Instead, he swears in his wrath that the generation liberated from Egypt would die in the wilderness over a forty year period rather than enjoy God's peace in the promised land (Num 14:20-38).

God will never abandon his promises, even when Israel rejects him.

In his mercy, God refuses to revoke his promise to bless Israel. Even the pagan spiritualist, Balaam, cannot curse Israel, despite the fact that he desired the cash promised by Balak, king of the Amorites (Num 22-24).

Like their fathers, the second generation, those who would enter the promised land, rebel against God by engaging in the idolatrous orgies that passed for worship of the god Baal of Peor (Num 25). But Yahweh, in his mercy, continues to prepare this generation to enter the promised land by giving them battle plans, setting the boundaries of the land, and assigning cities for the Levites and for refuge (Num 33-35).

The book hints strongly at the defect in God's people. In Numbers 11:29, Moses laments, "If only all the LORD's people were prophets and the LORD would place his Spirit on them!" The people need the internal deliverance that only the Holy Spirit can provide.

Seeing Jesus

The rebellion of Israel reflected their fallen humanity. All of us can see ourselves in the thoughts and actions of this stubborn people. God's wrath burns against us, and yet an intercessor greater than Moses has stepped up — Jesus. He has turned away the wrath of God and saved us for the glory of God's Name. We are heirs of the promises of God just as we have become God's people by the indwelling and transformation of the Holy Spirit.

"Christ redeemed us from the curse of the law by becoming a curse for us, because it is written, 'Cursed is everyone who is hung on a tree.' The purpose was that the blessing of Abraham would come to the gentiles by Christ Jesus, so that we could receive the promised Spirit through faith" (Gal 3:13–14). Jesus saves us from the curse we deserve for our sin. This results not just in our forgiveness, but also our transformation! God forgives us of our sins, *and* he makes us into his own unique people by putting his own Spirit within us.

We who have believed in Christ have truly experienced the blessing of God: "May the LORD bless you and protect you; may the LORD make his face shine on you and be gracious to you; may the LORD look with favor on you and give you peace" (Num 6:24–26). As Paul often reminds us in his letters, we are the recipients of God's grace and peace through Jesus (for example Rom 1:7; 1 Cor 1:3; 2 Cor 1:2).

Deuteronomy

Basic Facts
Author: Moses wrote chapters 1–30. Joshua probably added chapters 31–34.
Original Audience: the nation of Israel
Place Written: east of the Jordan River
Date Written: about 1406 B.C.

The Main Idea
God made a covenant with Israel, but they needed circumcised hearts to keep it.

Structure
- 1–4:43. Moses' First Speech: The History of Israel
- 4:44–26:19. Moses' Second Speech: The Commands
- 27–30. Moses' Third Speech: Blessing and Cursing
- 31–34. Joshua replaces Moses as Israel's Leader.

Big Events & Ideas

God renews his covenant with a new generation.

Israel is poised to invade the promised land. The generation that God had delivered from Egypt refused to trust God and take the land, fearing that their "children" would become "plunder" (Num 14:3). But now their corpses are dead and buried in the wilderness. Their little ones have become the very ones who will enter the promised land by God's grace.

Israel will live in the promised land with God dwelling among them on the basis of their covenant with God. The book of Deuteronomy serves as a remedial education in the covenant God made at Sinai. The book is a long sermon in which Moses prepares the people for life in the land in hopes that they might escape the same fate as their fathers.

Obedience results in blessing, and disobedience results in curse.

The covenant stipulates what obedience to God looks like. To keep the covenant, they must trust and obey God. Simply put, this means they must "love the LORD" with all their heart, soul, and might (Deut 6:5). If they obey, then they will be blessed. They will be blessed in their cities and in their fields, in their families and in their flocks (Deut 28:1-14). On the other hand, Moses warns them,

> But if you do not obey the LORD your God by carefully following all his commands and statutes I am giving you today, all these curses will come and overtake you (Deut 28:15).

Their cities will be destroyed. Their fields will fail. Their families will disintegrate, and their flocks will miscarry. In the end, God would exile them from the promised land, just as he had exiled Adam and Eve from the garden of Eden (Deut 28:15-68).

Israel needs circumcised hearts.

In order to obey, Israel must circumcise their hearts. They are commanded to do so (Deut 10:16). However, Moses prophesies that they will fail to execute the command. The curses of the covenant will fall upon them. They will be exiled from the land (Deut 30:1-10). But in the last days, God will do for them what they could not and would not do for themselves. "The LORD your God will circumcise your heart and the hearts of your descendants, and you will love him with all your heart and all your soul so that you will live" (Deut 30:6).

Seeing Jesus

The prophets of the exile, Jeremiah and Ezekiel, looked forward to the day when God would circumcise the hearts of his people. Ezekiel said, "I will give you a new heart and put a new spirit within you; I will remove your heart of stone and give you a heart of flesh" (Ezek 36:26). Jeremiah clarified that this action characterizes a new covenant that God would make with Israel.

The covenant recorded in Deuteronomy testifies to human inability to keep a covenant with God. Israel was never able to keep the old covenant because Israel was enslaved to their own sinful nature. Hebrews says, "For if that first covenant had been faultless, there would have been no occasion for a second one" (Heb 8:7). Then Hebrews clarifies that the fault was not with the covenant ,but with the people (Heb 8:8).

But the old covenant stipulations, along with its curses and blessings, no longer apply to the Christian. Christ has freed us from the demands of that covenant by undertaking its curse on our behalf.

> Christ redeemed us from the curse of the law by becoming a curse for us, because it is written, "Cursed is everyone who is hung on a tree" (Gal 3:13; citing Deut 21:23).

Christ's blood has instituted the new covenant (Luke 22:20). If you are united to Christ by repentance and faith, then your heart has been circumcised. You have been born again. Your desires have been changed so that you now want to obey God. The law has been written on your heart, and God's Spirit dwells in you and directs you. You, who once hated God and loved sin, now love God and hate sin because of what Jesus has done for you and in you.

Joshua

Basic Facts
Author: Joshua wrote parts of the book (Josh 24:26), but an unknown person compiled the book into its final form.
Original Audience: the nation of Israel
Place Written: Canaan
Date Written: about 1300–1400 B.C.

The Main Idea
God gave Israel the promised land and calls them to serve him in the land.

Structure
- 1–5 Israel crosses the Jordan River into the land.
- 6–12. God gives the land to Israel.
- 13–21. God divides the land among Israel.
- 22–24. Israel is called to serve God in the land.

Big Events & Ideas

God gives Israel the promised land.

The book of Joshua is not about the superior military strategy of Joshua. It's about God's grace toward Israel. God gives them the promised land. God says to Israel, "I gave you a land you did not labor for, and cities you did not build, though you live in them; you are eating from vineyards and olive groves you did not plant" (Josh 24:13).

Even the Canaanite prostitute Rahab recognizes this at the beginning of the book: "I know that the LORD has given you this land" (Josh 2:9). The Gibeonites (Canaanites from the city of Gibeon) also know this truth when they seek to align themselves with Israel: "It was clearly communicated to your servants that the LORD your God had commanded his servant Moses to give you all the land and to destroy all the inhabitants of the land before you" (Josh 9:24).

God planned the first battle in the promised land to teach Israel this principle. The people of Israel are instructed to march around the mighty city of Jericho, and then the walls fall down. God delivered the mighty city into their hands just as he would do with the rest of the promised land. "The LORD fought for Israel" (Josh 10:14, 42).

Israel is called to serve God in the land.

Because God gave Israel the land, the people of Israel are obligated to serve God and worship him alone. God says to Israel, "I gave you the land ... Therefore, fear the LORD and worship him in sincerity and truth. Get rid of the gods your fathers worshiped beyond the Euphrates River and in Egypt, and worship the LORD" (Josh 24:13–14).

At the end of his life, Joshua demands that Israel make a choice. Either they will worship idols, or they will worship the one, true God. But they must choose (Josh 24:15). The people promise to worship God alone (Josh 24:16–18). Joshua, however, tells them, "You will not be able to worship the LORD, because he is a holy God. He is a jealous God" (Josh 24:19). Joshua, therefore, predicts the events that are recorded in the book of Judges.

Israel kills the Canaanites.

Why does God command Israel to destroy the Canaanites? How can we explain that such commands come from a God who is merciful and loving?

First, God is the creator and king of all places and all peoples. The Canaanites owed God worship. Instead, they worship numerous idols and lived wickedly (see Lev 18). Just as God destroyed the entire earth except for Noah's family with the flood, and just as he destroyed the wicked cities of Sodom and Gomorrah with fire from heaven, God had the right to destroy the wicked Canaanites.

Second, God often used other nations to execute his judgment. The nation of Israel is God's tool of judgment against the Canaanites. In the same way, God would later use the Assyrians and Babylonians to execute his judgment against Israel.

Third, God shows mercy to those Canaanites who put their faith in him like Rahab (Josh 2:9) and the Gibeonites (Josh 9:1–27).

Will God command nations today to utterly destroy another nation? No. First, God no longer gives prophetic revelation like he did in biblical times. There is no prophet that could give us the command to destroy a nation. Second, and more importantly, we live in a different part of salvation history. God's kingdom has come in Jesus, and God's desire is to include all nations in his kingdom through the preaching of the gospel. God will judge all peoples one day, but he will do that when Jesus returns, not through human warfare.

Seeing Jesus

At the end of Joshua, God's people are in God's place under God's covenant. It looks like God has fullfilled the promise to Abraham. God promised to make Abraham a great nation, and he promised to give Abraham a land (Gen 12:1–2). Now that this great nation dwelt in the promised land it looked like God's kingdom would come, and all the peoples on the earth would be blessed through Israel (Gen 12:3). But as Joshua predicted, Israel was not able to worship God faithfully (Josh 24:19; see Judges). The problem of sin, which had destroyed the kingdom that God created in the garden of Eden, would also destroy the kingdom in the promised land.

Israel needed a greater Joshua (the name Jesus is the Greek version of the Hebrew name Joshua). Hebrews says, "For if Joshua had given them rest, God would not have spoken later about another day. Therefore, a Sabbath rest remains for God's people" (Heb 4:8–9). This greater Joshua would bring God's people rest by destroying the power of sin. This greater Joshua would bring God's people not just into a promised land but into a new creation.

Judges

Basic Facts
Author: unknown, possibly Samuel.
Original Audience: the nation of Israel
Place Written: Canaan
Date Written: about 1050–1000 B.C.

The Main Idea
Israel needs a king who will lead them to keep God's covenant.

Structure
- 1–3:6. Israel begins to rebel against God.
- 3:7–16:31. Israel's rebellion gets worse and worse.
  - 3:7–11. Othniel
  - 3:12–30. Ehud
  - 3:31. Shamgar
  - 4–5. Deborah
  - 6–8. Gideon
  - 9. Abimelech
  - 10:1–2. Tola
  - 10:3–5. Jair

- 10:6–12:7. Jephthah
- 12:8–10. Ibzan
- 12:11–12. Elon
- 12:13–15. Abdon
- 13–16. Samson
- **17–21. Israel reaches the fullness of rebellion.**

Big Events & Ideas

Israel sins, God disciplines, and then God delivers.

Joshua's prediction was correct. Israel is not able to serve God alone (Josh 24:19). Instead, Israel imitates the Canaanite peoples, whom God had judged through Israel. They begin to worship the Canaanite gods:

> The Israelites did what was evil in the LORD's sight. They worshiped the Baals and abandoned the LORD, the God of their fathers, who had brought them out of Egypt. They followed other gods from the surrounding peoples and bowed down to them. They angered the LORD, for they abandoned him and worshiped Baal and the Ashtoreths (Judg 2:11–13).

Repeatedly, Yahweh disciplines his people by sending another nation to oppress them. Under the oppression, Israel cries out to Yahweh, and Yahweh raises up a judge to deliver Israel. But then Israel turns away from Yahweh again and the cycle starts all over: Sin → Discipline → Crying Out → Deliverance.

But each time Israel repeats this cycle, their sin becomes worse and worse. This cycle is actually a downward spiral. The early judges like Othniel, Ehud, and Deborah are portrayed mostly as righteous deliverers. The later judges like Gideon and Samson were increasingly sinful themselves.

In Judges 17–21, the author gives multiple stories that illustrate just how bad Israel's rebellion had become. These stories contain examples of idolatry, sexual immorality, murder, and civil war. Instead of living as a holy people, they've become as wicked as the people of Sodom, whose actions they imitate (compare Gen 19 with Judg 19). The people of Israel had drifted far away from their God and from the peace and prosperity of his kingdom.

Seeing Jesus

At the end of Judges, the author reminds us four times, "In those days there was no king in Israel; everyone did whatever seemed right to him" (Judg 17:6; see 18:1; 19:1; 21:25). The people of Israel could not escape the cycle of sin. They needed a king who would lead them to be faithful to God's covenant.

This was always part of God's plan. Jacob had prophesied, "The scepter will not depart from Judah" (Gen 49:10). God had even given Moses laws about Israel's kings long before there ever was a king (Deut 17:14–20). The primary duty of an Israelite king was to know and keep God's covenant. He was supposed to make a handwritten copy himself and read it daily (Deut 17:18–19).

Why then did God say that the people were rejecting him when they asked Samuel for a king in 1 Samuel 8? The people asked for "a king to judge us the same as all the other nations have" (1 Sam 8:5). The people had not asked for God's king who would lead them as God's unique and holy people. Instead, they asked to become like the other nations.

The people needed a righteous king after God's own heart. This king wouldn't just deliver the people from the nations that oppressed them. This king would deliver them from the cause of such oppression — sin. This king would change their hearts and lead them to keep God's covenant, securing them in God's place forever.

The Old Testament

Ruth

Basic Facts
Author: unknown
Original Audience: the nation of Israel
Place Written: Canaan
Date Written: about 1000–900 B.C.

The Main Idea
God cares for a family and brings about the birth of his chosen king.

Structure
- 1. Ruth returns to Bethlehem with Naomi.
- 2. Ruth gleans in Boaz's field.
- 3. Ruth asks Boaz to redeem her.
- 4. Boaz marries and has a son with Ruth.

Big Events & Ideas
God saves a gentile by faith.

Ruth was a gentile, a woman from Moab. The Moabites descended from Lot's incest with his daughter (Gen 19:37), and they were not allowed to join the people of Israel for worship (Deut 23:3). Ruth, however, professes faith in Yahweh when she says to Naomi, "Your people will be my people, and your God will be my God" (Ruth 1:16). As the story goes on to demonstrate, Yahweh accepts Ruth into his covenant people on the basis of her faith.

God controls all things for his glory and for the good of his chosen people.

The book of Ruth wants us to see that the right thing happens at the exact right time so that we will credit God with the blessing that came to Naomi and Ruth. Ruth just "happened to be in the portion of the field belonging to Boaz," the man who could change her circumstances (2:3).

All this happens "during the time of the judges" (1:1). This is a period of immense wickedness in Israel and great suffering. Despite the sinfulness of Israel, God never neglects his promise to Abraham. Even in the darkest days, God is working to bring about his kingdom in small and undetected ways.

God gives Ruth a redeemer.

Naomi identifies Boaz as a "close relative" and one of their "family redeemers" (2:20). A family redeemer was responsible to redeem the land of a dead relative in order to keep the land in the family (Lev 25:23–25). It might also involve marrying a brother's childless widow in order to raise an heir for the dead husband (Deut 25:5–6). Boaz shows kindness to his relative, Naomi, by redeeming her husband's property, marrying her son's widow Ruth, and raising a son who would inherit the property.

Through Boaz's redemption of Ruth, Naomi and Ruth experienced Yahweh's blessing. Naomi begins the story by renaming herself Mara or "Bitter" (1:20). She says, "I went away full, but the LORD has brought me back empty. Why do you call me Naomi, since the LORD has opposed me, and the Almighty has afflicted me" (1:21)? But after Ruth gives birth to Boaz's son, the women of the city say, "Blessed be the LORD, who has not left you without a family redeemer today. May his name become well known in Israel. He will renew your life and sustain you in your old age. Indeed, your daughter-in-law, who loves you and is better to you than seven sons, has given birth to him" (4:14–15).

Seeing Jesus

In Matthew 1:5, Matthew includes the family tree of Jesus: "Boaz fathered Obed by Ruth." Ruth, a woman from Moab who became an Israelite by faith, became the great-grandmother of King David, and from the family line of David came Jesus, Israel's Messiah and the Savior of the world.

Throughout the Bible, the family line of Jesus continues because of God's providential work and care. God gave Abraham and Sarah a son after they were old (Gen 15). Ruth had been married to Naomi's son for ten years without having children, indicating that she too was barren (Ruth 1:4). But after God brought her into his people and into the promised land by faith, she gave birth to a son. So too, when the Messiah would finally come from the line of Abraham and David, he would be born miraculously to a virgin (Matt 1:20–21).

God had a plan to fulfill the promise he made to Abraham to bring about his kingdom. God moved empires and armies to accomplish his plan, but he also moved seemingly insignificant people in small villages to prepare the way for his Son to enter the world.

The Old Testament

1–2 Samuel

Basic Facts
Author: unknown, possibly compiled by the prophets Samuel, Nathan, and Gad (1 Chron 29:29)
Original Audience: the nation of Israel
Place Written: Canaan
Date Written: about 900–700 B.C.
2 Books or 1? 1–2 Samuel are actually one book. It was split in two because it could not be easily contained on a single scroll.

The Main Idea
God gives his people a righteous king and promises to make his kingdom last forever.

Structure
- **1 Samuel. God gives Israel their king.**
  - 1–7. Samuel faithfully judges Israel.
  - 8. Israel asks for a king.
  - 9–15. God gives and then rejects Saul as king.
  - 16–31. God chooses and protects David.

The Old Testament

- **2 Samuel. God gives Israel his king.**
  - 1–4. David becomes the king of Israel.
  - 5–6. David claims Jerusalem as the city of God.
  - 7. God makes a covenant with David.
  - 8–10. David demonstrates both power and kindness.
  - 11–20. David sins and endures the consequences.
  - 21–23. David gives thanks to God in his final days.
  - 24. David sins by taking a census and receives forgiveness.

Big Events & Ideas

Israel sins against God by asking for an earthly king.

Because Samuel's sons had become corrupt like the sons of Eli before them (1 Sam 2:12–36; 8:1–3), the Israelites ask Samuel to "appoint a king to judge us the same as all the other nations have" (1 Sam 8:5). Samuel is offended at their request, but God tells him, "Listen to the people and everything they say to you" (1 Sam 8:6). God explains that this is not a rejection of Samuel, but another rejection of him as their God and king (1 Sam 8:7–8).

God, therefore, leads Samuel to appoint a king over Israel. But this king is exactly the type of king Israel had asked for — a king "the same as all the other nations" (1 Sam 8:5). Saul possesses the outward appearance of a king. "There was no one more impressive among the Israelites than he. He stood a head taller than anyone else" (1 Sam 9:2). Saul looks like an earthly king, and Saul acts like an earthly king. He does not obey God, and God rejects him as king (1 Sam 15).

God chooses David as his king.

After rejecting Saul as king, Samuel says that God has found a king "after his own heart" (1 Sam 13:14). This new king, unlike Saul, doesn't look like a king. God teaches Samuel, "Humans do not see what the LORD sees, for humans see what is visible, but the LORD sees the heart" (1 Sam 16:7).

God chooses a young shepherd from Bethlehem and put his Spirit on him (1 Sam 16:13). With the Spirit upon him, God empowers David to defeat Israel's enemies, the Philistines, and deliver Israel (1 Sam 17). Although David suffered for many years under Saul's persecution, eventually God exalted him to the throne and established his kingdom.

God makes a covenant with David.

Once David's kingdom is established, God makes a covenant with David. David wants to build a house for God (the temple; 2 Sam 7:5–7), but God promises instead to build a house for David (a line of kings from his family; 2 Sam 7:11).

The covenant with David isn't entirely separate from the covenant with Abraham. Instead, it gives greater clarity to the covenant with Abraham. God has promised to give Abraham a great name by giving him a land and making his descendants a great nation, through whom God would bless all the peoples on earth (Gen 12:1–3). God makes these same promises to David: God will give David a great name (2 Sam 7:9), and will plant the nation of Israel securely in the promised land (2 Sam 7:10).

To these promises made to Abraham, God adds, "Your house and kingdom will endure before me forever, and your throne will be established forever" (2 Sam 7:16). The kingdom promised to Abraham will now come through a son of David who will rule as king forever.

David sins but repents.

After God makes a covenant with David, David commits a horrific sin. He takes a married woman named Bathsheba and sleeps with her. When he finds out she is pregnant, he attempts to hide what he has done by having her husband Uriah killed in battle (2 Sam 11). But when the prophet Nathan confronts David about his sin, David repents and seeks God's forgiveness (2 Sam 12; Ps 51).

At the end of the book, David sins again. This time he takes a census of the fighting men of his kingdom. The sin in this action may not be as easy for us to discern as the adultery and murder that David commits in chapter 11. Why is David's census sin? Because he is seeking his security in his own power and kingdom rather than trusting God. When David is rebuked by the prophet Gad, he again repents and chooses to fall into the hands of God who is merciful (2 Sam 24).

David's sins demonstrate God's faithfulness to his covenant. God will certainly fulfill his promise to establish an eternal king in the line of David. David's sins, or the sins of David's descendants, cannot cause God to abandon his covenant promise.

Seeing Jesus

Jesus "was a descendant of David according to the flesh" (Rom 1:3; see Matt 1). The corruption of Eli's sons (1 Sam 2:12–36), Samuel's sons (1 Sam 8:1–3), and King Saul (1 Sam 15) showed Israel's need for a righteous king after God's own heart (1 Sam 13:14). David was that king. Because David trusted in God, God exalted David and saved him from his enemies. Even though David sinned, he humbled himself and repented (2 Sam 12).

God promised David, "Your house and kingdom will endure before me forever, and your throne will be established forever" (2 Sam 7:16). As Peter explained on the day of Pentecost, David "is both dead and buried, and his tomb is with us to this day" (Acts 2:29). One of David's descendants would be a righteous king like David, but he would be greater than David because his kingdom would be perfect and last forever—the Lord Jesus, the Messiah. His kingdom would encompass the whole world, fulfilling the promise to Abraham to bless "all the peoples on the earth" (Gen 12:3).

1–2 Kings

Basic Facts
Author: unknown, possibly Jeremiah or other prophets
Original Audience: the nation of Israel in exile
Place Written: possibly Babylon
Date Written: about 560–540 B.C.
2 Books or 1? 1–2 Kings are actually one book. It was split in two because it could not be easily contained on a single scroll.

The Main Idea
Israel rejects God, and God judges his people.

Structure
- **1 Kings. Israel rejects God and his kingdom.**
  - 1–4. Solomon becomes Israel's king.
  - 5–10. Solomon builds the temple.
  - 11. Solomon rejects God.
  - 12–14. The kingdom is divided.
  - 15–16. Israel falls into chaos without God.
  - 17–22. Elijah proclaims God's word in Israel but is rejected.

- **2 Kings. God judges Israel and Judah.**
  - 1–10. Elisha proclaims God's word in Israel but is rejected.
  - 11–12. King Joash of Judah repairs the temple.
  - 13–16. Both the kings of Israel and Judah reject God.
  - 17. God uses Assyria to judge Israel.
  - 18–20. King Hezekiah of Judah trusts in God.
  - 21. The kings of Judah reject God.
  - 22–23:30. King Josiah returns Judah to God.
  - 23:31–25:30. God uses Babylon to exile Judah from the land.

Big Events & Ideas

God dwells with Israel in the temple.

God had promised that David's son would build God's house (2 Sam 7:13). After God establishes Solomon's kingdom, Solomon builds the temple in Jersualem (1 Kgs 5–8). When the temple is completed, "the cloud filled the LORD's temple, and because of the cloud, the priests were not able to continue ministering, for the glory of the LORD filled the temple," just as when Moses dedicated the tabernacle (1 Kgs 8:10–11; Exod 40:34–38).

Solomon's prayer at the temple's dedication tells both the purpose of the temple and foreshadows the sorrows that come later in 1–2 Kings:

> May the LORD our God be with us as he was with our ancestors. May he not abandon us or leave us so that he causes us to be devoted to him, to walk in all his ways, and to keep his commands, statutes, and ordinances, which he commanded our ancestors. (1 Kgs 8:57–58).

Through the temple, God dwells with his people, Israel. But the day would come when Solomon's temple would be destroyed because God's people had rejected their God.

Solomon sins against God, and God divides his kingdom.

Solomon, the builder of the temple and wise king, leaves his wisdom behind in his old age:

> When Solomon was old, his wives turned his heart away to follow other gods. He was not wholeheartedly devoted to the LORD his God, as his father David had been. Solomon followed Ashtoreth, the goddess of the Sidonians, and Milcom, the abhorrent idol of the Ammonites. Solomon did what was evil in the LORD's sight, and unlike his father David, he did not remain loyal to the LORD.
>
> At that time, Solomon built a high place for Chemosh, the abhorrent idol of Moab, and for Milcom, the abhorrent idol of the Ammonites, on the hill across from Jerusalem. He did the same for all his foreign wives, who were burning incense and offering sacrifices to their gods (1 Kgs 11:4–8).

Because of Solomon's idolatry, God tells him that his kingdom will be divided (1 Kgs 11:11–13). When Solomon's son Rehoboam becomes king in Jerusalem, the northern ten tribes of Israel rebel and crown Jeroboam (2 Kgs 12).

God sends prophets.

The books of 1–2 Kings introduce us to many prophets. Some, like Jonah (2 Kgs 14:25) and Isaiah (2 Kgs 19–20), have their own books of the Bible that record their prophecies. Others, like Nathan (1 Kgs 1), Ahijah (1 Kgs 11–14), and Jehu (1 Kgs 16), are introduced to us as part of the story. Some are even unnamed altogether, like the prophet in 1 Kings 20.

Of all the prophets of 1–2 Kings, Elijah and Elisha are the most prominent. Elijah and Elisha are identified as true prophets of God by the fact that the predictions they make come to pass, and by the numerous miracles they perform. The number of miracles they do remind us of Moses, but also point forward to the coming of Jesus. They call fire down from heaven. They heal.

They provide food miraculously, and they even raise the dead. Elijah doesn't even die but goes to heaven in a chariot of fire.

Despite how clearly God's power works through Elijah and Elisha, they are rejected by God's people. Their suffering marks them out as true prophets of God. They are chased away. They have to survive in foreign lands or in the wilderness. They even begin to succumb to despair, like Elijah did on Mount Horeb (1 Kgs 19). Another prophet in the southern kingdom of Judah, Ahijah, was even killed for his prophecies against the sin of Israel (1 Kgs 14). True prophets are identified by the truth of their prophesies and the power of their miracles, but also by their rejection and suffering.

The northern kingdom of Israel sins, and God uses the Assyrians to exile them from the land.

Jeroboam doesn't want his people going to Jerusalem to worship at the temple, since doing so might turn their allegiance back to Rehoboam. So he erects idols of golden calves in the Northern Kingdom. The kings that follow Jeroboam only increase Israel's idolatry. Most notorious among Israel's kings is Ahab, who marries Jezebel, a princess from the Phonaecian city Sidon. Ahab and Jezebel promote the worship of Baal and Asherah.

God sends prophets like Elijah and Elisha to warn Israel that if they continue to worship idols, then he will judge them. But Israel rejects God's word through the prophets until it is too late.

> The Israelites persisted in all the sins that Jeroboam committed and did not turn away from them. Finally, the LORD removed Israel from his presence just as he had declared through all his servants the prophets. So Israel has been exiled to Assyria from their homeland to this very day (2 Kgs 17:22–23).

In 722 B.C., the Assyrians destroy the northern kingdom of Israel and take its people into exile.

The southern kingdom of Judah sins, and God uses the Babylonians to exile them from the land.

The southern kingdom of Judah has a more complicated history than the Northern Kingdom. Among David's descendants in Jerusalem, there are some good kings who turned to God, like Hezekiah and Josiah. But most of the kings of Judah worship idols just like the kings in the north. God sends the Babylonians in 597, 586, and 582 B.C. to destroy Jerusalem and take its people into exile.

Despite this, 1–2 Kings ends with hope. After thirty-six years in prison, Johoiachin, the king of Judah from David's family, is released from his imprisonment and treated kindly by the king of Babylon (2 Kgs 25:27–30). Jehoiachin's liberation gives Israel hope that God has not neglected his promise to David. A king from the family of David will rule one day over the entire world forever.

Seeing Jesus

At the beginning of his reign, it looked like Solomon would be the descendant of David who would reign over a perfect kingdom forever. He asked God for wisdom, and God gave him prosperity and peace as well (1 Kings 3). Solomon built the temple, and God's glory filled it (1 Kings 5–8). But Solomon sinned, and God divided his kingdom (1 Kings 11–12).

Despite Solomon's failure, God never abandoned his promises to Abraham and David. God would one day bless all the peoples on earth through Israel (Gen 12:3). One day God would establish the kingdom of David's descendant forever (2 Sam 7:16). But first, Israel would experience God's judgment against their sin. First, they would be removed from the promised land by the Assyrians and Babylonians. Despite Israel's faithlessness, God would remain faithful. One day the promised Messiah would come.

The Old Testament

1–2 Chronicles

Basic Facts
Author: probably Ezra or another priest.
Original Audience: the nation of Israel returning from exile
Place Written: Canaan
Date Written: about 450–400 B.C.
2 Books or 1? 1–2 Chronicles are actually one book. It was split in two because it could not be easily contained on a single scroll.

The Main Idea
God creates a kingdom that is destroyed by Israel's sin, but God's kingdom will still come in the future.

Structure
- **1 Chronicles. God creates a kingdom.**
    - 1–9. The Geneaology of Israel from Adam to the Twelve Tribes.
    - 10–29. King David reigns in Jerusalem and prepares for the temple.
- **2 Chronicles. Israel rejects the kingdom.**
    - 1–9. Solomon reigns in Jerusalem and builds the temple.
    - 10–36:21. God judges sinful Judah.

- 36:22–23. God moves King Cyrus of Persia to end the exile and rebuild the temple.

Big Events & Ideas

1–2 Chronicles is a summary of the entire Old Testament.

1–2 Chronicles repeats much of the information found in 1–2 Samuel and 1–2 Kings. Even so, we shouldn't just skip over it, since it has a unique message. In the Jewish ordering of the Old Testament (see "About the Old Testament"), 1–2 Chronicles was the last book of the Old Testament.

1–2 Chronicles begins with a geneaology that stretches all the way back to Adam (1 Chron 1:1), and it ends with the return of the Jews from exile (2 Chron 36:22–23). It, therefore, contains the history of the entire Old Testament. 1–2 Chronicles is meant to summarize the entire Old Testament and to remind the Jewish people that God's promises would still be fulfilled one day in the future.

God will send a king-priest like David.

In 1–2 Chronicles, David is presented as a king-priest who leads Israel to worship God. He brings the ark of the covenant back to Jerusalem and leads the nation in worshiping God before the ark (1 Chron 13, 15–16). David purchases the future site of the temple, prepares for its construction, and teaches Solomon what to do (1 Chron 21–22, 29). He organizes the Levites, priests, musicians, and gatekeepers for worship in the temple (1 Chron 23–26). Like Moses with the tabernacle, David receives the plans for the temple directly from God (1 Chron 28:19).

When God makes a covenant with David in 1 Chronicles 17, he promises David concerning his son, "I will appoint him over my house and my kingdom forever, and his throne will be established forever" (1 Chron 17:14). God promises that the future king who will bring God's forever kingdom will be like David — a king-priest over both God's temple and God's kingdom.

God will dwell with his people.

Solomon follows David's instructions and builds the temple (2 Chron 2–7). When Solomon dedicates the temple, "fire descended from heaven and consumed the burnt offering and the sacrifices, and the glory of the LORD filled the temple. The priests were not able to enter the LORD's temple because the glory of the LORD filled the temple of the LORD" (2 Chron 7:1–2).

1–2 Chronicles ignores the history of the Northern Kingdom and focuses only on the Southern Kingdom, where the kings in the family line of David reign and where the temple stands. The good kings of Judah like Joash and Hezekiah care for the temple (2 Chron 24:1–19; 29:3–36). The bad kings erect idols in the temple, allow it to be plundered, and disregard its holy places.

Because of his people's sin, God sends the Babylonians against Judah. Nebuchadnezzar destroys the temple in 586 B.C. But God is not finished with his people.

The book ends with hope. The temple will be rebuilt and God will be with his people (2 Chron 36:23).

Seeing Jesus

1–2 Chronicles was written at the end of the Old Testament period. Israel had received God's promises and seen a partial version of God's kingdom during the reigns of David and Solomon, but Israel also sinned against God and saw that kingdom destroyed. Israel's sin, however, did not cancel God's promises.

The hope that 1–2 Chronicles sets forth is that a king-priest in the family line of David would come and reign forever. As a priest, this individual would bring people into God's presence. As a king, this individual would lead God's people in loving obedience to God. When the king-priest comes, then God would finally dwell with his people.

Jesus is the king in the family line of David, but he is also our Great High Priest who has brought us near to God (Heb 4–10). Because Jesus is a perfect king-priest, his kingdom will have no end, and he will fulfill all the promises that

The Old Testament

God made to David. One day God will dwell with his people and sin will be no more (Rev 21:3–4).

Ezra-Nehemiah

Basic Facts
Author: Ezra, portions from Nehemiah's own records
Original Audience: the nation of Israel returning from exile
Place Written: Canaan
Date Written: about 450–400 B.C.
2 Books or 1? Ezra-Nehemiah appear as two separate books in Bibles today because of the different focus of each book, Ezra and Nehemiah respectively. But originally Ezra-Nehemiah was one book with one main idea.

The Main Idea
God returns exiled Jews to the promised land, but the kingdom of God does not come.

Structure
- **Ezra. God returns exiled Jews to the promised land.**
  - 1–6. God uses Cyrus and Zerubbabel to return the Jews to the land.
  - 7–10. God uses Ezra to return the Jews to the land and to God.
- **Nehemiah. God rebuilds Jerusalem, the city of the king.**
  - 1–7. God uses Nehemiah to rebuild the wall of Jerusalem.
  - 8–13. God uses Ezra and Nehemiah to return the people to him.

Big Events & Ideas

God returns exiled Jews to the promised land.

In 538 B.C., King Cyrus of Persia decreed that the Jews could return home from all the places they had been exiled (Ezra 1). Soon after, a group of Jews return to the promised land under the leadership of Zerubbabel, a descendant of David, and Jeshua, a priest (Ezra 2:2). In 458 B.C., Ezra leads another group of exiles back to the promised land (Ezra 7:6–9). After seventy years in exile, God's people are returning to God's place.

The Jews rebuild the temple, but the glory of God does not return.

One of the first actions of the returned exiles is to reestablish the worship of God at the site of the destroyed temple. They rebuild the altar and lay the temple's foundation (Ezra 3). Despite opposition, the temple is finally rebuilt in 516 B.C.

After Moses completed the tabernacle, God's glory filled it (Exod 40:34–38). After Solomon completed the first temple, God's glory filled it (1 Kgs 8:10–11; 2 Chron 5:13–14). But when the second temple's foundation is laid there is joyful worship but God's glory never comes. Those who had seen the first temple can tell a difference, even as early as the laying of the foundation:

> But many of the older priests, Levites, and family heads, who had seen the first temple, wept loudly when they saw the foundation of this temple, but many others shouted joyfully. The people could not distinguish the sound of the joyful shouting from that of the weeping, because the people were shouting so loudly. And the sound was heard far away (Ezra 3:12–13).

God's people have returned to God's place, and they have rebuilt the temple. But God's glory has not returned. Their exile is not yet over.

Nehemiah rebuilds Jerusalem's walls.

When Nehemiah hears that the walls of Jerusalem remain in ruins, it grieves him. During fasting and prayer, Nehemiah repents for his people's sins and appeals to God's character and promises. God is "the great and awe-inspiring God who keeps his gracious covenant with those who love him and keep his commands" (Neh 1:5). God had exiled Israel for their sins, but God had also promised to regather Israel if they would return to him (Neh 1:9; see Deut 30:1–6).

God intervenes by moving King Artaxerxes of Persia to commission Nehemiah to return to Jerusalem and rebuild its walls (Neh 2:1–8). The gentiles who had inhabited the land during the exile oppose Nehemiah and accuse him of rebuilding the city as a way to establish himself as king in Judah (Neh 6:6–7). While Nehemiah does not desire to make himself king, there is some truth in their accusation. Jerusalem is the city of David, and rebuilding Jerusalem's walls is necessary to reestablish the city of the king. By doing so, Nehemiah expresses his faith that the exile is ending and the kingdom of God will come.

Ezra renews God's covenant with the Jews.

Ezra comes to the promised land as a new Moses who will reestablish God's covenant with Israel and teach the people God's law. When Ezra arrives, he finds that the Jews have intermarried with idol worshipers from other nations. The sin of idolatry, which caused the exile, continues, and the people must repent (Ezra 9–10).

Ezra reads and explains the law of Moses to the people, and the people respond by confessing their sins (Neh 8). Under Ezra's leadership, they renew their commitment to God's covenant with Israel (Neh 10).

The Jews return from exile, but remain slaves in their land.

Despite all this progress toward reestablishing God's kingdom, the kingdom has not yet come. In their prayer of confession, the people say,

> Here we are today, slaves in the land you gave our ancestors so that they could enjoy its fruit and its goodness. Here we are—slaves in it!
>
> Its abundant harvest goes to the kings you have set over us, because of our sins. They rule over our bodies and our livestock as they please. We are in great distress (Neh 9:36–37).

The Persian King Cyrus had decreed the return of the exiles. His successors support the rebuilding of the temple and of Jerusalem's walls. But as long as these foreign kings rule over the Jews, the kingdom of God remains in the future. They wait for the day when they will live freely under a king from the family of David. But the problem is not political or military. They confess that they are slaves "because of our sins" (Neh 9:37).

Seeing Jesus

Ezra-Nehemiah begins with hope, but ends with disappointment. After seventy years in exile, God's people had finally returned to God's place. Over the years, they began to reestablish all the important aspects of the kingdom. The temple was rebuilt. The walls of Jerusalem were rebuilt, and Ezra renewed God's covenant with the people. But three things were missing: (1) God's presence never filled the temple like it had before. (2) No king descended from David ruled on the throne. Instead, the people continued to be ruled by foreigners. (3) God's people continued to sin. Their hearts needed to change.

Only Jesus could establish God's perfect kingdom. In Jesus, God's presence would return to God's people (John 1:14). Jesus was the king from the family of David who would reign forever. Jesus would pay the penalty for his people's sin and would send his Spirit to give his people new hearts.

Esther

Basic Facts
Author: unknown, possibly Mordecai or Ezra.
Original Audience: the nation of Israel
Place Written: either Persia or Canaan
Date Written: about 470 B.C.

The Main Idea
God controls all things for the salvation of his people.

Structure
- 1–2. God exalts Esther as Queen of Persia.
- 3–4. Haman plans evil against the Jews.
- 5–10. God uses Esther to save the Jews.

Big Events & Ideas
God uses Esther to save the Jews.

God is never mentioned directly in the book of Esther, but those who know the God of Abraham will see his hand everywhere. Queen Vashti dishonors the

Persian King Ahasuerus (known by his Greek name Xerxes to modern history) and is removed as queen. Then a Jewish girl named Hadassah (Hebrew) or Esther (Persian) is chosen as Queen of Persia at the exact point in history when a man named Haman plots to destroy the Jewish people.

Who can explain these events? Mordecai tells Esther that her exaltation as queen had a greater purpose when he says, "Who knows, perhaps you have come to your royal position for such a time as this" (Est 4:14)? While Esther certainly acts in courage, the reason the Jews are saved is God's protective hand as he directs those in power for the salvation of his people.

Seeing Jesus

What would have happened if Haman's plan had succeeded? He would have destroyed the Jewish people, and the promises made to Abraham would have been extinguished. God promised to bless all the peoples on earth through the family of Abraham (Gen 12:3). Because the Jewish people were the way that God was going to bless all peoples, God promised Abraham, "I will curse anyone who treats you with contempt" (Gen 12:3). God preserved and protected the family of Abraham so that the Messiah Jesus Christ would come and redeem all nations. No one, no matter how powerful, could stop God's plan.

Job

Basic Facts
Author: unknown
Original Audience: the nation of Israel
Place Written: unknown
Date Written: unknown

Is Job history? We know almost nothing about the author or the writing of Job. According to both Ezekiel and James, Job was a real person (Ezek 14:14, 20; Jas 5:11). But we do not know the location of "the country of Uz" in 1:1 or how Job, who seems to be a non-Israelite, had a relationship with God. The lifestyle of Job is similar to that of Abraham, Isaac, and Jacob, so it seems that the story occurred around 2000 B.C.–1800 B.C. But we do not know when the story was written down. For everything that remains unknown about Job, the Holy Spirit inspired someone to write down his story in order to give God's people wisdom for suffering.

The Main Idea
God controls our suffering for his glory.

Structure
- 1–2. God allows Satan to test Job.
- 3–31. Three friends accuse Job of doing wrong.
- 32–37. Elihu accuses Job of doing wrong.
- 38–41. God speaks to Job.
- 42. Job trusts God and is restored.

Big Events & Ideas
God allows Satan to test Job.
God himself draws Satan's attention to Job (Job 1:8). While Satan seeks to dishonor God by enticing Job to curse God, God controls Job's suffering for his own purposes (Job 1:9; 2:4–5). God even limits the degree of Job's suffering (Job 1:12; 2:6). In his suffering, Job continues to praise God (Job 1:21; 2:10). Job does not understand the reasons for his suffering. He does not know the events in heaven. Even though he does not know God's purposes, he continues to trust and praise God.

Friends accuse Job of doing wrong.
At first, Job is visited by three friends: Eliphaz, Bildad, and Zophar (Job 3–31). Later, a young man, Elihu, speaks up (Job 32–37). While Job's friends speak some truth, their main point is absolutely wrong. They claim that Job must be suffering for doing wrong. Job repeatedly defends himself. We know that Job has done nothing wrong because we know what God has said about him (Job 1:8; 2:3). The speech of Elihu begins also by accusing Job (Job 32–35), but he ends by focusing on God's character (Job 36–37). Elihu's speech prepares the reader for the voice of God in 38–41.

God speaks to Job, and Job trusts God.
When God speaks to Job in chapters 38–41, he never explains to Job the reasons for his suffering. Instead, God displays his own power to Job. God's

primary message is that he is God, and he does whatever he pleases. Job learns this lesson and says, "I know that you can do anything and no plan of yours can be thwarted" (Job 42:2). He humbles himself before God, and God restores to Job the things he lost.

Seeing Jesus

Job gives us an example of a righteous man who suffers. The Bible does teach that good things generally happen to the righteous and sin brings sorrow to a person's life (see Deut 28; Prov 3:13–26). In the book of Job, Job's friends could only understand Job's suffering as a punishment for his sin. But both God and Job himself maintained that Job was righteous. The reader of Job knows that Job was suffering as a test of his integrity (Job 1–2), but Job never learned God's purposes for his suffering. Even when God spoke, he did not explain Job's suffering. He instead revealed himself in order to deepen Job's faith.

The book of Job prepares us to understand Jesus. Jesus was perfectly righteous. Yet, he still suffered. God had greater purposes in the suffering of Jesus: the salvation of the world. Like Job, after Jesus suffered God restored Jesus and gave him new life. Like Job, Jesus never rejected God. He continued to trust the Father even as he died on the cross.

Job was confident that his "Redeemer lives" (Job 19:25). The Christian shares this confidence, and because of this hope, Christians can suffer like Job and like Jesus (see Jas 1:2–4; 1 Pet 1:6).

The Old Testament

Psalms

Basic Facts
Author: David (73 psalms), Asaph (12), the sons of Korah (9), Solomon (2), Heman, Ethan, Moses, and others
Original Audience: the nation of Israel
Place Written: The Sinai wilderness, Canaan, Babylon
Date Written: 1440 B.C.–500 B.C.

The Main Idea
Praise God! He will reign forever through a righteous king.

Structure
- 1–2. Beginning: God will reign forever through a righteous king.
- 3–41. Book 1: Prayers of the King
- 42–72. Book 2: More prayers of the King
- 73–89. Book 3: Prayers in days of Trouble
- 90–106. Book 4: God reigns!
- 107–145. Book 5: The king will come.
- 146–150. Ending: Praise Yahweh!

Big Events & Ideas

God will reign forever through a righteous king.

Psalms 1–2 are the introduction to the entire book of Psalms. Psalm 1 observes the happiness of a man who does not walk in the way of sinners, but instead delights in God's instruction. Psalm 2 declares the futility of human rebellion against God. God will establish his anointed king forever in Jerusalem. These two psalms are placed beside each other in order to speak with one voice. God will give Israel the king in Psalm 2, and he will be the righteous man of Psalm 1.

This is the hope of the people of Israel: God will reign forever through a righteous king. These two psalms are like the two lenses of a pair of eyeglasses, and through them we should read the other 148 psalms. Each psalm is a prayer that is sung to God. The book of Psalms speaks to every human emotion: happiness, worry, sorrow, anger, and more. But through every high and low, the hope of Israel remains the same. No matter what circumstance we face, we are encouraged by the Psalms to live by faith in this hope: God will reign forever through a righteous king!

God's people will live through days of trouble.

Many of the psalms are laments, or songs that express sorrow. Laments are scattered throughout the book. Many of the prayers of David are laments that came from the hardships he faced in his life. Book 3 of the Psalms (Pss 73–89) focuses on days of trouble. Many of these psalms were written after Babylon destroyed Jerusalem and sent the people into exile. In the Psalms, God's people suffer. But even in the midst of our suffering, we find our hope in God's coming kingdom.

Praise Yahweh!

The Psalms are prayers that were sung to God. Many of them command people to worship God. "Rejoice in the LORD, you righteous ones; praise from the upright is beautiful" (Ps 33:1). "Let the whole earth shout joyfully to God" (Ps

66:1)! "Hallelujah! Praise the name of the LORD. Give praise, you servants of the LORD" (Ps 135:1). The Psalms guide us in worship today. They teach us to sing praises to God in every circumstance of life — amidst both joys and sorrows. Paul even commands us to sing psalms with thankfulness in our hearts (Eph 5:19; Col 3:16).

Seeing Jesus

Jesus is the righteous king that Psalms awaited. He is the man who does not walk in the way of sinners and delights in God's instruction (Ps 1). He is God's anointed king who will reign from Jerusalem (Ps 2). He is the hope of God's people that guides us through both happiness and sorrow.

Since Jesus is the greater David, the psalms of David can be read as the prayers of Jesus. In fact, Jesus did this on the cross when he quoted Psalm 22:1, "My God, my God, why have you abandoned me?" Just as God rescued David and established his kingdom, God rescued the greater David and will establish Jesus' kingdom forever!

The Old Testament

Proverbs

Basic Facts
Author: mainly Solomon, also Agur, Lemuel, and others.
Original Audience: the nation of Israel
Place Written: Canaan
Date Written: Solomon's Proverbs, 970–931 B.C.

The Main Idea
If you fear God, then you will know how to live in God's world.

Structure
- 1–9. A Father's Instructions.
- 10–22:16. Proverbs of Solomon.
- 22:17–24:22. The Words of the Wise.
- 25–29. Proverbs of Solomon collected by Hezekiah
- 30. The Words of Agur
- 31. The Words of King Lemuel

Big Events & Ideas

Learn to live in God's world.

The book of Proverbs is very down to earth. It's about wisdom. It's about making right choices and avoiding wrong choices. "The fear of the LORD is the beginning of knowledge" (Prov 1:7; see 9:10). Why does wisdom and knowledge begin with the fear of Yahweh? God is the creator of this world. Since he designed it, he knows how life works best in his world. To be wise, we must learn from the creator how life works best in his world.

Get wisdom. Avoid foolishness.

The opposite of wisdom is foolishness. To do what is right, we must learn to avoid what is wrong. To be wise, we must learn not to be a fool. Sin is foolishness. As sinners, we try to justify our sin. We tell ourselves that sin isn't really that bad or that in our particular circumstances sin is the best choice. Proverbs seeks to destroy our self-delusion and shine the light of the truth on our sin. Sin is like the forbidden woman in Proverbs. Her lips "drip honey" but "in the end she's as bitter as wormwood" (Prov 5:3–4).

Seeing Jesus

Proverbs gives us royal wisdom. Most of the book was written by Solomon, the son of David. God promised David that one of his sons would reign on his throne forever (2 Sam 7:13). Early in his reign, it looks like Solomon is that king. He is a wise king who brings peace and prosperity to Israel. Proverbs is a record of Solomon's wisdom. But later in his life, Solomon foolishly worshiped false gods (1 Kings 11:4). Solomon was not the wise king who would reign forever.

Jesus is "the wisdom of God" (1 Cor 1:24, 30). Jesus lived according to God's wisdom in this world and never sinned. He is the wise king who will reign forever and teaches God's people wisdom. Jesus is "greater than Solomon" (Matt 12:42).

Ecclesiastes

Basic Facts
Author: Solomon
Original Audience: the nation of Israel
Place Written: Canaan
Date Written: about 935 B.C.

The Main Idea
Life without God is meaningless.

Structure
- 1–3. Everything is meaningless, but God put eternity in the human heart.
- 4–10. Everyone dies, so enjoy the life God gives.
- 11–12. Fear God and keep his commands.

Big Events & Ideas
Everything is meaningless. Everything dies.

    Ecclesiastes starts from a human perspective on the world. Time keeps passing. People attempt to accomplish great works in this world, but in the end time makes them meaningless. As sad as this sounds, we must admit that it is true. Without God, life is meaningless. We live our lives and try to accomplish many things. But then we die, and everything is forgotten.

God gives meaning to life.

While life without God is meaningless, this is not true of life with God. Our relationship to God is what gives meaning to our lives. God put eternity in human hearts (Eccl 3:11). He made us to desire to live for something that will outlast time. That desire should point us to our need to God. God has given us life to enjoy (Eccl 9:7–10), and we can enjoy life if we remember our creator, fear him, and obey him (Eccl 12:1, 13).

Seeing Jesus

Death makes life meaningless. We all die, and everything we have done will be forgotten (Eccl 1:2–4; 9:3). But God has made the human heart to desire the eternal (Eccl 3:11). Jesus entered this meaningless world in order to destroy death. "Death no longer rules over him" because he has been resurrected (Rom 6:9). By defeating death, Jesus has made eternal life available to anyone who would repent and believe. We have been given "new birth into a living hope through the resurrection of Jesus Christ from the dead" (1 Pet 1:3). Our lives are meaningful because our lives are eternal and can be used for God's purposes.

Song of Songs

Basic Facts
Author: either written by Solomon or for Solomon
Original Audience: the nation of Israel
Place Written: Canaan
Date Written: about 960–930 B.C.

The Main Idea
God gives the gift of sex to be enjoyed by a husband and wife.

Structure
- 1–2. The lovers desire one another.
- 3–5. The woman dreams about marriage and love.
- 6–7. The lovers desire one another again.
- 8. The lovers marry.

Big Events & Ideas
God gives the gift of sex.

God is never mentioned in the Song of Songs. Song of Songs celebrates the marriage of King Solomon to a young woman. We know that Solomon married many women. The Bible condemns Solomon's polygamy, not only because it went against God's design for marriage in Genesis 2, but also because it turned his heart away from God (1 Kings 11:1–6). Either Song of Songs was written early in Solomon's reign to celebrate his first marriage, or Song of Songs is a poem that celebrates marriage the way it should be and shouldn't be read as a historical description of Solomon's life.

God created the woman and brought her to the man in Genesis 2. Genesis 2:24 says that "a man leaves his father and mother and bonds with his wife, and they become one flesh." God created both marriage and sex to be enjoyed by a husband and wife before sin ever entered the world. Song of Songs celebrates God's gifts of marriage and sex.

Because sex is a gift of God, it isn't shameful. A husband and wife should enjoy God's gift. In the Song of Songs, we see a man and woman desiring one another (Song 1–2, 6–7). The woman even dreams about the man (Song 3–5), and ultimately they marry and enjoy God's gift of sex in chapter 8. These lovers give us an example to follow in our own marriages.

The gift of sex is powerful and dangerous if misused.

The gift of sex is powerful: "For love is as strong as death; jealousy is as unrelenting as Sheol. Love's flames are fiery flames — an almighty flame" (Song 8:6). Because it is powerful, it should not be misused. Repeatedly, the woman warns other young women, "Young women of Jerusalem, I charge you, do not stir up or awaken love until the appropriate time" (Song 8:4; see also 2:7; 3:5). The young woman is made beautiful by her virginity, which she preserves for her wedding night. She is a "locked garden and a sealed spring" (Song 4:12). She is a wall that blocks entry rather than a door that invites entry (Song 8:9–10). She saves herself for her husband, and the two belong exclusively to one another: "I am my love's and my love is mine" (Song 6:3; see also 7:9).

Seeing Jesus

Song of Songs is about the sexual love of a husband and wife, but the love of marriage points to the love of Christ for his church. In Ephesians, Paul quotes Genesis 2:24, and then explains that the passage speaks about Jesus: "For this reason a man will leave his father and mother and be joined to his wife, and the two will become one flesh. This mystery is profound, but I am talking about Christ and the church" (Eph 5:31–32).

Song of Songs shows how beautiful the love of marriage should be when we enjoy it as a gift from God, and we protect it by obeying God's commands against sexual immorality. But as beautiful and joyful as marriage is, it points forward to something eternal: the love of Christ for his bride, the Church. Our marriages are temporary since they end with death, but the love of Christ for us will never end. We will enjoy his love forever.

The Old Testament

About the Prophets

God sent prophets throughout Israel's history to remind the people of their covenant obligations to God, and to warn them of the covenant curses that would come for disobedience. The earliest prophets did not write down their prophecies, although we read about the ministries of prophets like Elijah and Elisha in 1–2 Kings. In the 700s B.C., prophets began to write down their messages to God's people, resulting in the 18 prophetic books in our Bibles today.

The prophets divide into 3 groups based on their relationship to the Babylonian exile of the southern kingdom of Judah. Most of the prophets wrote in the 700s B.C. before the exile. Three prophets ministered directly before or during the exile: Jeremiah, Ezekiel, and Daniel. Three other prophets prophesied after the Jews returned to the promised land beginning in 520 B.C.: Haggai, Zechariah, and Malachi.

The prophets spent much of their time warning God's people about the consequences of disobedience, but these books are also filled with beautiful pictures of hope that God would one day come and make all things new.

The Old Testament

Three Periods of Prophetic Activity

Before Exile	During Exile	After Exile
800s B.C.	**600–536 B.C.**	**After 520 B.C.**
Elijah (did not write)	Jeremiah (also wrote	Haggai
Elisha (did not write)	Lamentations)	Zechariah
	Ezekiel	Malachi
700s B.C.	Daniel	
Isaiah		
Hosea		
Joel		
Amos		
Obadiah		
Jonah		
Micah		
Nahum		
Habakkuk		
Zephaniah		

Isaiah

Basic Facts
Author: Isaiah
Original Audience: the southern kingdom of Judah
Place Written: Canaan
Date Written: about 700 B.C.

The Main Idea
God will judge Judah and the nations, but he will send a Servant who will save all nations.

Structure
- **1–35. God will judge the sin of Judah and the nations.**
  - 1–12. God will judge Judah's sin.
  - 13–23. God will judge the nations.
  - 24–27. God will save his people.
  - 28–35. God's people should trust in him.
- **36–39. God saves Judah from Assyria, but will judge them through Babylon.**
  - 36–37. God saves Judah from the Assyrians.
  - 38. God saves Hezekiah's life.

- 39. God will judge Judah through the Babylonians.
- **40–66. God will redeem his people and the world.**
  - 40–55. God will redeem the exiled nation through his Servant.
  - 56–66. God will establish his perfect kingdom in a new creation.

Big Events & Ideas

God is sovereign over all things.

Isaiah discusses the activities of great nations like Assyria, Egypt, and Babylon, but it also makes clear that God is the one in control of human history. God reveals himself to Isaiah as an enthroned king, and the angels declare that "his glory fills the whole earth" (Isa 6:3). God declares about himself, "I am God, and no one is like me. I declare the end from the beginning, and from long ago what is not yet done, saying: my plan will take place and I will do all my will" (Isa 46:9–10).

God's sovereign power is exercised in judgment upon the sins of Judah and the nations. He will not allow human rebellion to continue forever. But his sovereign power will also be exercised for the salvation of his people. So God's people should trust in him rather than the nations. God will accomplish his plan and establish his forever kingdom.

God will redeem his people through his Servant.

To save his people, God must solve the problem of his people's sin. Isaiah foresees that God will do this through his Servant. The Servant will be anointed with the Spirit of God (Isa 42:1; 61:1). He will be righteous, but he will die for the sins of the nation as a sacrifice (Isa 52:13–53:12). Isaiah 53 is one of the most important chapters of the Old Testament, since it so clearly predicts the suffering and death of Jesus. Isaiah foresees that God's servant will be "rejected by men" and will be "a man of suffering" (Isa 53:3), but his death would not be for his own sins. He would die in the place of the people: "But he was pierced because of our rebellion, crushed because of our iniquities; punishment for our peace was on him, and we are healed by his wounds" (Isa 53:5). We are like sheep who have run away, but God has punished his servant for our iniquities (Isa 53:6).

God will bring about a new David, a new exodus, and a new creation.

When God brings about salvation through the sacrificial death of the Servant, God will establish his kingdom. God will raise up a new David as king over his people. God promises that even though his judgment will chop down the family tree of David, "a shoot will grow from the stump of Jesse and a branch from his roots will bear fruit" (Isa 11:1). He will "reign on the throne of David and over his kingdom," but his kingdom will extend to the ends of the earth (Isa 9:7).

When the new David comes, God will bring about a new exodus. Like the original exodus, in the new exodus God will free his people from their captivity and gather them to himself (Isa 11:11–16). Judah will be exiled from Canaan by the Babylonians, but God will bring them back (Isa 40).

God will give his people a new home: a new Jerusalem in a new creation where the new David will reign over God's redeemed people (Isa 62, 66). Isaiah prophesies the destruction of Jerusalem because of Judah's sin, but he also prophesies Jerusalem's restoration. The new Jerusalem will be holy and will be "called Cared For, A City Not Deserted" (Isa 62:12). But Isaiah also sees that the restoration of Jerusalem will expand to all of creation. The coming of the new creation gives hope that God will also transform his people through his faithful covenant love: "'For just as the new heavens and the new earth, which I will make will remain before me' — this is the LORD's declaration — 'so your offspring and your name will remain'" (Isa 66:22).

Seeing Jesus

Just as Isaiah prophesied, the Babylonians came and took Judah into exile. God judged Judah's sin. God also brought Judah back from exile according to his promise. But the physical return of Judah from exile did not fulfill God's promise to free Judah from sin and bring about his forever kingdom.

God accomplished his sovereign plan through Jesus. Jesus is the Servant who suffered for the sins of his people. He was righteous, but he died as a sacrifice for sin. Jesus is also the new David whom Isaiah foresaw. Through Jesus, God fulfills all his promises of salvation to Judah. Jesus' life, death, and resurrection has started God's forever kingdom, and the day will come when God will bring about the new creation, putting a final end to sin (Rev 21).

Jeremiah

Basic Facts
Author: Jeremiah
Original Audience: the southern kingdom of Judah
Place Written: Canaan
Date Written: about 600–550 B.C.

The Main Idea
God will judge Judah now, but he will establish a new covenant in the future.

Structure
- 1. God calls Jeremiah to serve as a prophet.
- 2–45. God will judge the sin of Judah.
  - 1–29. God condemns the sin of Judah.
  - 30–33. God will establish a new covenant with his people.
  - 34–45. God judges Judah with Babylon.
- 46–51. God will judge the sin of the nations.
- 52. God destroys Jerusalem and exiles Judah.

The Old Testament

Big Events & Ideas

God calls Jeremiah to serve as a prophet.

God told Jeremiah, "I chose you before I formed you in the womb; I set you apart before you were born. I appointed you a prophet to the nations" (Jer 1:5). God called Jeremiah to a simple task: "speak whatever I tell you" (Jer 1:7). As Jeremiah spoke God's word, he would face resistance, but God instructed him, "Do not be afraid of anyone, for I will be with you to rescue you" (Jer 1:8). Jeremiah demonstrates the qualities of a true prophet from God: God chose him. He spoke only what God told him to speak, and all his predictions came to pass. But at the same time, he suffered. True prophets are marked by the suffering and rejection they experience.

God fulfills his threat of judgment.

Jeremiah prophesied in the final days before God judged Judah by sending the Babylonians. He warned Judah to repent before God's judgment came, but his message was rejected by the leaders in Jerusalem. Because Jeremiah proclaimed the truth, King Zedekiah imprisoned Jeremiah (Jer 37–38). Judah's leaders should have acted like shepherds. Instead of caring for God's sheep, they scattered the flock (Jer 23:1–2).

Jeremiah is sometimes called the weeping prophet because he experienced the disaster that he prophesied. The Babylonians destroyed Jerusalem and took Judah into exile just as God had foretold through his prophet.

God will establish a new covenant.

Judgement will not be the end of Judah's story. God promises Judah that he has "plans for your well-being, not for disaster, to give you a future and a hope" (Jer 29:11). He will bring them back from exile after seventy years (Jer 25:11, 12; 29:10). He will send fishers of men who will bring his people back to him (Jer 16:16; see Matt 4:19; Mark 1:17).

God reveals that his plans for a future and a hope center on the establishment of a new covenant with his people (Jer 31:31). The old covenant had been given to Israel at Sinai, and people became members of the covenant people by being born into the nation of Israel. The old covenant promised blessing if Israel would obey God's law, but Israel could never obey God's law, so they received God's curse instead of his blessing (see Deut 28).

Under the new covenant, God would guarantee the obedience of his people by changing their hearts. Instead of giving a prophet tablets of stone as he did with Moses, God promises, "I will put my teaching within them and write on their hearts" (Jer 31:33). God will forgive the sin of his people, and each member of the covenant people will know their God personally (Jer 31:34).

God will raise up a new David.

This new covenant will be accompanied by a new David who will reign over God's redeemed people. Unlike the unrighteous kings in David's line who ruled in the time of Jeremiah, God says, "In those days and at that time I will cause a Righteous Branch to sprout up for David, and he will administer justice and righteousness in the land" (Jer 33:15). This kingdom will last forever and will no longer be able to be destroyed by the people's sin. God promises, "In those days Judah will be saved, and Jerusalem will dwell securely, and this is what she will be named: The LORD is Our Righteousness" (Jer 33:16).

Seeing Jesus

Jesus taught that his death was the sacrifice that established the new covenant foretold by Jeremiah. When he took the cup at the last supper, he said, "This cup is the new covenant in my blood" (Luke 22:20; 1 Cor 11:25). Hebrews says that Jesus is "the mediator of a new covenant" (Heb 9:15; 12:24). Jesus' sacrifice of his own blood inaugurated the new covenant and began a new age in which God will renew all creation (Heb 9:15–28).

God's renewal begins with the hearts of his people. The church is the new covenant people of God predicted by Jeremiah. Unlike under the old covenant, people do not become part of God's new covenant people through physical birth. God's people are those whose sins are forgiven and whose hearts now love God and his ways.

One day, God will renew all of creation as well, and Jesus, the new David, will reign over his new covenant people forever from the new Jerusalem.

Lamentations

Basic Facts
Author: Jeremiah
Original Audience: the exiled nation of Judah
Place Written: Canaan
Date Written: about 586 B.C.

The Main Idea
God has poured out his anger against Jerusalem, but his faithful love will bring about the city's restoration.

Structure
- 1. Jeremiah laments the destruction of Jerusalem.
- 2. God has poured out his anger against Jerusalem's sin.
- 3. Jeremiah finds hope in God's faithful love.
- 4. God's anger has been satisfied.
- 5. Jeremiah prays for the restoration of Jerusalem.

Big Events & Ideas

Jeremiah laments the destruction of Jerusalem.

Lamentations is a collection of five poems. Four of the poems (Lam 1–4) are acrostic poems and follow the pattern of the Hebrew alphabet with each line or group of lines starting with a different letter. Jeremiah wrote these poems to express his sorrow over the destruction of Jerusalem.

As Jeremiah attempts to understand this disaster, he freely expresses his sorrowful emotions to God. Jeremiah says that he continually remembers his affliction and has "become depressed" (Lam 3:20). But the expression of his sorrow before God also brings him to greater understanding. He finds hope in God's faithful love (Lam 3:21–22).

God has poured out his anger against Jerusalem.

God's anger against the sin of Jerusalem is righteous. Jerusalem deserves God's judgment. The descriptions of God's anger in the book are intense. "Without compassion the LORD has swallowed up all the dwellings of Jacob" (Lam 2:2). In the seige of Jerusalem, women ate their own children (Lam 2:20). After the battle, "both young and old are lying on the ground in the streets" (Lam 2:21).

Even though Jerusalem deserved God's judgment, Jeremiah mourns the city's destruction. He demonstrates for the reader the proper response to God's wrath. He is not angry with God. God's actions are right. But he is nevertheless sorrowful for those who have suffered because of their lack of repentance.

Jeremiah finds hope in God's faithful love.

The key to understanding the book is in 3:19–24. Jeremiah is sorrowful, but he finds hope. His hope is in the faithful love and mercies of God. Jeremiah remembers all the promises that God has made to his people, and he trusts in the promises of God. Even though Israel has rejected God, God will not finally reject Israel. They are experiencing God's justice in the moment, but God will be faithful to his promises and show them mercy. In the character of God, Jeremiah finds hope. God makes promises, and God keeps promises.

Seeing Jesus

Jesus is the fulfillment of Jeremiah's hope. Through Jesus, God has shown love and mercy to his people. All people deserve to suffer under the intense anger of God. God is just to punish our rebellion in ways that far exceed the suffering of the city of Jerusalem.

But God has demonstrated his love for us by sending his own Son to die for our sins. On the cross, Jesus suffered the intense and just anger of God against sin and sinners in our place. Through faith in Jesus, we can escape the coming wrath and possess an eternal and unfading hope. Since we have found shelter from God's wrath in the sacrifice of Jesus, we can truly say with Jeremiah, "Because of the LORD's faithful love we do not perish, for his mercies never end. They are new every morning; great is your faithfulness" (Lam 3:22–23)!

The Old Testament

Ezekiel

Basic Facts
Author: Ezekiel
Original Audience: the exiled nation of Judah
Place Written: Babylon
Date Written: 593–571 B.C.

The Main Idea
God has abandoned Judah and the temple, but he will one day restore his people and place.

Structure
- **1–24. God will judge Judah.**
  - 1–3. God calls and prepares Ezekiel.
  - 4–24. Ezekiel proclaims the judgment of Judah.
- **25–32. God will judge the nations.**
- **33–48. God will restore his people and his place.**
  - 33–39. God will restore his people.
  - 40–48. God will restore his place.

Big Events & Ideas

God abandons his people and place.

Judah had rejected God to worship idols, and had even brought idols into the temple complex itself (Ezek 8). In a vision, Ezekiel sees the glory of God depart the temple (Ezek 10). In the time of Solomon, God's glory had filled the temple (2 Chron 5:13–14). The temple was God's place where God's people could worship him and experience his blessing. When God departed the temple, he was withdrawing his blessing from the people. They would now receive his wrath through the Babylonians.

God will restore his people.

God promises to cleanse his people of their sins, give them hearts of flesh, and send his Spirit to dwell in them (Ezek 36:25–27). Judah did not fulfill its purpose as God's people because of their sin. In the future, God will correct the problem of sin. He promises to make his people new so they will want to obey him. Under God's judgment, the nation of Judah is like a valley filled with dry bones, but through God's word, they will be brought back to life and be filled with God's Spirit (Ezek 37:1–14).

This restoration of God's people will come through the establishment of God's kingdom. David will once again be the king of God's people, but the new David will reign forever (Ezek 37:24–28).

God will restore his place.

In chapters 40–48, Ezekiel receives a detailed vision of the future temple in the new Jerusalem. The description of the temple in these chapters is not an exact plan to be followed to rebuild the temple in the end-times. Instead, it is a symbolic description of God's holiness and his care for his people. God wants Judah to know that even though he has abandoned Solomon's temple, he will one day dwell again with his people (Ezek 43:4–5). The temple is not only a building. It is a garden, a new Eden. Like Eden, a river will flow from it with the trees of life growing on its banks (Ezek 47; see Gen 2:9–14). Ezekiel also describes God's place as a new promised land to be divided among the tribes of Israel (Ezek 48). Ezekiel sees a new Jerusalem inhabited by God himself: "The name of the city from that day on will be, The LORD Is There" (Ezek 48:35).

Seeing Jesus

Jesus is the new David who will shepherd God's people and reign forever (Ezek 37:24–28). The rulers of Judah in Ezekiel's day were like shepherds "who have been feeding themselves" instead of feeding the flock (Ezek 34:2). They took advantage of the sheep instead of caring for them. But Jesus tells us that he is the good shepherd, who "lays down his life for the sheep" (John 10:15).

Through what Jesus has done, God is restoring a people for himself. Jesus said that "unless someone is born of water and the Spirit, he cannot enter the kingdom of God" (John 3:5). When Jesus refers to water and the Spirit, he is referencing Ezekiel 36:25–27. To enter God's forever kingdom, people need to be cleansed from their sins and indwelt by the Holy Spirit. They must be born again. Those who are born again will enter into God's presence and enjoy God's blessing in the new Jerusalem.

The Old Testament

Daniel

Basic Facts
Author: Daniel
Original Audience: the exiled nation of Judah
Place Written: Babylon, Persia
Date Written: about 605–536 B.C.
Languages Written: Chapters 1, 8–12 are written in Hebrew. Chapters 2–7 are written in Aramaic.

The Main Idea
God will deliver his people from this wicked world through the Son of Man.

Structure
- **1–6. God delivers Daniel and his friends from wicked kings.**
  - 1. God rules over kings.
  - 2. A rock destroys four kingdoms and fills the earth.
  - 3. God delivers his three servants.
  - 4–5. God humbles Nebuchadnezzar and Belshazzar.
  - 6. God delivers his servant Daniel.
- **7–12. God will deliver his people through the Son of Man.**
  - 7. The Son of Man destroys four beasts and rules the earth.

- 8–11. God's people and place will suffer, but Daniel prays for them.
- 12. God will resurrect his people.

Big Events & Ideas

God delivers his people and humbles kings.

The book of Daniel splits into two sections. In the first section, we read about how God repeatedly delivered Daniel and his friends from wicked kings (Dan 1–6). In the second section, Daniel records visions that foretell the future suffering and salvation of God's people (Dan 7–12). The stories about Daniel and his friends serve as an example of how God saves his people from suffering. By looking at the past, we should trust God's perfect care in the future.

Daniel and his friends were taken from their families and forced into service for the Babylonian empire. Because they wanted to remain faithful to their God while serving a wicked king, they often found themselves in conflict. The wicked kings repeatedly attempt to put themselves in the place of God, but God repeatedly shows that he is in control. In chapters 1–6, God repeatedly rescues Daniel and his friends from certain death, and the mightiest kings on the earth are humbled before a sovereign God.

The Son of Man will rule all nations.

Daniel's vision in chapter 7 contains the central message of the book. It repeats the earlier dream of Nebuchadnezzar in chapter 2. Nebuchadnezzar saw a rock destroy an image that represented four kingdoms. Then the rock grew into a mountain that filled the entire earth. In chapter 7, Daniel sees four beasts that represent four kingdoms. Then Daniel sees God himself seated on his heavenly throne. God gives his kingdom to "one like a son of man" who "was coming with the clouds of heaven" (Dan 7:13). To this Son of Man, God gave "dominion and glory and a kingdom so that those of every people, nation, and language should serve him" (Dan 7:14). Unlike the temporary human kingdoms of the four beasts, the kingdom of the Son of Man "is an everlasting dominion that will not pass away and his kingdom is one that will not be destroyed" (Dan 7:14). God's people are directed to trust in God's plan to establish his kingdom through the Son of Man no matter what happens in human history.

God will resurrect his people.

Before the perfect establishment of God's kingdom, God's people will suffer. But their suffering will not last forever. God will deliver his people by resurrecting them from the dead (Dan 12:1–2). In fact, all people will be resurrected at the end of history, "some to eternal life, and some to disgrace and eternal contempt" (Dan 12:2). Those who belong to God "will shine like the bright expanse of the heavens" (Dan 12:3). God's people will be resurrected to share God's glory in a new creation forever.

Seeing Jesus

Jesus called himself the Son of Man (see Matt 9:6; 10:23; 13:41). By doing this, he was clearly identifying himself as the one whom Daniel saw. Jesus claimed to be God's appointed king who will rule forever over the entire earth. The Great Commission is a command to extend the kingdom of the Son of Man in this world. Jesus says, "All authority has been given to me in heaven and on earth" (Matt 28:18). Since "every people, nation, and language should serve him" (Dan 7:14), Jesus commands us to "make disciples of all nations" (Matt 28:19).

This kingdom that will fill the entire world will be a kingdom of resurrected and glorified believers. Jesus' resurrection guarantees the end time resurrection foreseen by Daniel. Jesus is "the firstfruits of those who have fallen asleep" (1 Cor 15:20). At his return, those who belong to Christ from all nations will be resurrected and enjoy God's kingdom forever (1 Cor 15:23).

The Old Testament

The Twelve (The Minor Prophets)

When the Bible was still written on a collection of scrolls, the twelve prophets who wrote shorter books, which we often call the Minor Prophets today, were contained on a single scroll called The Book of the Twelve. While each of the books have important things to say independent of the others, as a collection they speak together about God's character and his interactions with his people.

The Twelve prophets are ordered roughly according to the time period in which they prophesied:

Before and During the Exile of Judah: Hosea, Joel, Amos, Obadiah, Jonah, Micah, Nahum, Habakkuk, Zephaniah

During the Return from the Exile: Haggai, Zechariah, Malachi

But this ordering also follows the themes of sin, punishment, and restoration. The first six books, written during the times of the kings of Judah and Israel, focus on the sinfulness of God's people. The next three, written shortly before the exile of Judah, focus on the punishment that Judah will receive for their sin, and the final three books, written after the exiles began returning, focus on the restoration of God's people.[5]

Sin: Hosea, Joel, Amos, Obadiah, Jonah, Micah
Punishment: Nahum, Habakkuk, Zephaniah

Restoration: Haggai, Zechariah, Malachi

As we read The Twelve, we must read them in two ways: (1) We must read them as individual books, which have truth to teach us independent from the others. (2) We must read them as a collection that summarizes Israel's history from a prophetic point-of-view. Together, they tell the story of Israel's sin and punishment, but they also give us the hope of the restorations of God's kingdom.

Hosea

Basic Facts
Author: Hosea
Original Audience: the northern kingdom of Israel
Place Written: Canaan
Date Written: about 715 B.C.

The Main Idea
Even though Israel has been unfaithful, God loves and will restore Israel.

Structure
- 1–3. God's love for Israel is shown in the marriage of Hosea.
- 4–14. Israel has been unfaithful, but God will restore the nation.
  - 4–10. Israel will be judged for unfaithfulness.
  - 11–14. God will restore Israel.

Big Events & Ideas

Israel has been unfaithful.

God commands Hosea to "marry a woman of promiscuity" (Hos 1:2). Predictably, this leads to heartbreak for Hosea as his promiscuous wife, Gomer, commits adultery against him. Hosea's marriage is a living illustration of the relationship between God and Israel. Like a marriage, God made a covenant with Israel, but Israel did not remain faithful to him. The Israelites have turned to other gods (Hos 3:1).

As a result, God will judge the nation. Hosea declares to the northern kingdom of Israel that "the days of punishment have come" (Hos 9:7). The Assyrians will come and take the nation into exile.

God loves and will restore Israel.

Judgement is not the end of the story. God commands Hosea to redeem his unfaithful wife to illustrate God's continuing love for Israel: "Go again; show love to a woman who is loved by another man and is an adulteress, just as the LORD loves the Israelites though they turn to other gods and love raisin cakes" (Hos 3:1).

God's love changes those he loves. God will restore Israel, and their hearts will turn toward him. He proclaims, "Afterward, the people of Israel will return and seek the LORD their God and David their king. They will come with awe to the LORD and to his goodness in the last days" (Hos 3:5).

Seeing Jesus

God demonstrated his love for sinners through the death of his Son, Jesus Christ (John 3:16; Rom 5:8). Jesus paid the redemption price of Israel with his own blood, and through his death, sinners have been changed and seek after God.

In Hosea's love for his wife Gomer, we see an illustration of the love of Christ for his church. "Christ loved the church and gave himself for her to make her holy, cleansing her with the washing of water by the word" (Eph 5:25–26). Christian husbands are commanded to love their wives in the same way Christ loved the church and Hosea loved Gomer (Eph 5:25).

Joel

Basic Facts
Author: Joel
Original Audience: the southern kingdom of Judah
Place Written: Canaan
Date Written: about 835–796 B.C.

The Main Idea
God will judge Judah on the day of the Lord, but then he will pour out his Spirit on his people.

Structure
- 1–2:17. God will judge Judah on the day of the Lord.
    - 1:1–20. God will send an invasion of locusts as a warning.
    - 2:1–17. God will send an invading army on the day of the Lord.
- 2:18–3:21. God will pour out his Spirit on his people and judge the nations.

Big Events & Ideas

God will judge Judah on the day of the Lord.

Joel first warns Judah about an invasion of locusts, which will devour their fields and bring devastation upon the nation (Joel 1). But this invasion of locusts is only a warning. God will send an invading army to bring his judgment upon Judah's sin.

Joel calls this day of judgment the day of the Lord, or the day that God will act in judgment (Joel 1:15; 2:1, 11, 31; 3:14). The invasion of locusts is a lesser day of the Lord that points forward to the greater day of the Lord when the invading army will come. But both point forward to the final day of the Lord when God will judge all people everywhere at the end of time. People can only avoid the suffering that is coming on the final day of the Lord by repenting of their sin (Joel 2:12–17).

God will pour out his Spirit on his people.

Even though God will judge their sin, God refuses to abandon his people completely. He will restore them (Joel 2:25). He promises, "After this, I will pour out my Spirit on all humanity" (Joel 2:28). In the Old Testament, God's Spirit only came upon people for specific purposes, such as kings, prophets, and craftsmen. But Joel foresees a day when all of God's people will be filled with God's Spirit — "Jew or Greek, slave or free, male and female" (Gal 3:28). These people will be saved from God's judgment because they will call upon the name of the Lord (Joel 2:32).

Seeing Jesus

On the day of Pentecost, Peter quotes Joel 2:28–32 and claims that the prophecy has been fulfilled when God poured his Spirit out upon his church (Acts 2:18–21). Peter explains to the crowd that Jesus was killed, but rose on the third day. He then was exalted to the right hand of God, where he "received from the Father the promised Holy Spirit" (Acts 2:33). Jesus later poured out his Spirit upon his church. The day of judgment is coming, but anyone from all the nations of the earth who calls on the name of Jesus can be saved from God's judgment and will receive the Holy Spirit. In the last days, God's people are all those who have called on the name of Jesus for salvation and received the Holy Spirit.

The Old Testament

Amos

Basic Facts
Author: Amos
Original Audience: the northern kingdom of Israel
Place Written: Canaan
Date Written: about 760–750 B.C.

The Main Idea
God will judge Israel for its idolatry and injustice.

Structure
- 1–2. God will judge Israel.
- 3–6. Israel has sinned by commiting idolatry and injustice.
- 7–9. Amos sees visions of God's judgment.
  - 7:1–6. Amos sees visions of locusts and fire.
  - 7:7–17. Amos sees a vision of a plumb line.
  - 8. Amos sees a vision of a fruit basket.
  - 9:1–10. Amos sees a vision of the altar.
  - 9:11–15. God will restore Israel.

Big Events & Ideas

Israel has sinned by commiting idolatry and injustice.

Through Amos, God accuses Israel of sins of injustice. They "oppress the poor and crush the needy" (Amos 4:1). They take bribes and deprive the poor of justice (Amos 5:12). Injustice arises from people who have rejected God and committed idolatry (Amos 4:1–5). The only way to be saved from the coming judgment is to "seek the LORD and live" (Amos 5:6).

God will restore Israel.

After judgment, God will restore the kingdom of David, and he will even bring gentiles into his kingdom (Amos 9:11–12). Amos says that "all the nations," not just Israel, will bear his name (Amos 9:12). At that time, the earth will become exceedingly fruitful, and God's people will experience joy and security (Amos 9:13–15).

Seeing Jesus

After some gentiles become followers of Christ, James quotes Amos 9:11–12 to show that such an event had been foretold (Acts 15:15–18). Jesus is the king in the line of David. Through him, God has restored his kingdom, and through the preaching of the gospel of Jesus Christ, Jews and gentiles are being brought into the perfect kingdom of the last days. When Jesus returns, he will transform creation and bring about the frutifulness foretold in Amos 9:11–14. "Look, the days are coming — this is the LORD's declaration — when the plowman will overtake the reaper and the one who treads grapes, the sower of the seed. The mountains will drip with sweet wine, and all the hills will flow with it" (Amos 9:13).

Obadiah

Basic Facts
Author: Obadiah
Original Audience: the southern kingdom of Judah and the nation of Edom
Place Written: Canaan
Date Written: about 580–550 B.C.

The Main Idea
God will judge the nations who oppose his people.

Structure
- 1–16. God will judge Edom.
- 17–21. God will restore Israel

Big Events & Ideas
God will judge the nations who oppose his people.

When the Babylonians destroyed Jerusalem, the nation of Edom, who descended from Esau, joined forces with the conquering Babylonians instead of seeking to help their brothers in the nation of Judah. Even though God planned the destruction of Jerusalem, he will not forget the wickedness of those who opposed his people. He will fulfill his promise to Abraham: "I will curse anyone who treats you with contempt" (Gen 12:3).

God will judge all nations (Obad 15), and he will establish his kingdom, which will have dominion over all kingdoms (Obad 17–21).

Seeing Jesus

God is establishing his kingdom through Jesus Christ. While the gospel is being proclaimed to all nations, the day will come when God will judge all nations. Paul explained to the Greeks in Athens that God "has set a day when he is going to judge the world in righteousness by the man he has appointed" (Acts 17:31). This man is Jesus. Through Jesus, all the rebellious nations of the earth will be defeated, and the kingdom of God will be established forever.

Jonah

Basic Facts
Author: Jonah
Original Audience: the nation of Israel
Place Written: Canaan
Date Written: about 770–750 B.C.

The Main Idea
God controls everything and will give mercy to whomever he chooses.

Structure
- 1. Jonah runs from God, but God pursues him.
- 2. Jonah repents, and God forgives him.
- 3. Jonah obeys, Ninevah repents, and God forgives them.
- 4. Jonah is displeased with God's mercy.

Big Events & Ideas

God controls everything.

God commands Jonah to proclaim judgment against Nineveh, the capital city of the Assyrians (Jonah 1:2). Jonah knows that the preaching of judgment will

The Old Testament

give the people an opportunity to repent, and since the Assyrians are the enemies of Israel, he decides to flee in the opposite direction (Jonah 1:3; 4:2).

But God pursues Jonah. The events that follow show God's control over everything. God sends a storm (Jonah 1:4). He controls the casting of lots (Jonah 1:7), and God eventually sends a great fish to swallow Jonah (Jonah 1:17). God prepared the events of Jonah's life in order to bring Jonah to a place of repentance so that he could use Jonah to preach to the people of Nineveh. Jonah recognizes this when he says that he worships "the God of the heavens, who made the sea and the dry land" (Jonah 1:9). God controls everything for his own purposes.

God will give mercy to whomever he chooses.

God desires to give mercy to the people of Nineveh. That is why he sends Jonah to Nineveh. The preaching of judgment gives the people an opportunity to repent, and when they repent, God turns away from the disaster that had been proclaimed (Jonah 3:10).

God's mercy angers Jonah. He says, "Please, LORD, isn't this what I thought while I was still in my own country? That's why I fled toward Tarshish in the first place. I knew that you are a gracious and compassionate God, slow to anger, abounding in faithful love, and one who relents from sending disaster" (Jonah 4:2). Jonah lacks the compassion for sinners that God has, and he fails to understand that God had shown him the same mercy. God rules over all things and all people, and he has the right to show mercy to whomever he chooses (see Exod 33:19).

Seeing Jesus

The book of Jonah gives a preview of the abounding mercy that God will show the world through his Son Jesus Christ. Just as Jonah was rescued from death after three days in the fish, Jesus will be resurrected from the dead after three days (Matt 12:39–40). After this, God's mercy in Christ will be proclaimed to gentiles all around the world. Like the people of Nineveh, peoples from every nation and language will repent and receive God's free mercy that he gives to whomever he chooses.

The Old Testament

Micah

Basic Facts
Author: Micah
Original Audience: the northern kingdom of Israel and the southern kingdom of Judah
Place Written: Canaan
Date Written: about 750–730 B.C.

The Main Idea
God will judge his people, but he will always remain faithful to his covenant.

Structure
- 1–2. God will exile but then regather his people.
- 3–5. God will judge wicked leaders but then send a righteous king.
- 6–7. God will punish but then forgive his people's sin.

Big Events & Ideas
God will judge wicked leaders.

Leaders have greater responsibility before God for the sins of the nation. The rulers of Israel had perverted justice, taken bribes, and promoted sin (Mic 3:8–

10). The prophets had prophesied only what people desired to hear in order to make money (Mic 3:5–7, 11). God promises to judge these leaders, but he also promises to send a righteous leader. God will bring peace to his people through this king born in Bethlehem, the city of David (Mic 5:2).

God will forgive his people's sin.

Micah says that God's mercy will be shocking to the world. God will glorify himself by demonstrating his great mercy toward sinners. Micah says, "Who is a God like you, forgiving iniquity and passing over rebellion for the remnant of his inheritance? He does not hold on to his anger forever because he delights in faithful love" (Mic 7:18). This mercy is founded upon God's covenant promises to Abraham, and he will not fail to fulfill these promises (Mic 7:20).

Seeing Jesus

Micah prophecies the birth of Jesus in Bethlehem (Mic 5:2–5; Matt 2:1–6). Jesus is the righteous ruler who will bring peace to God's people. Through Jesus' sacrificial death, God will be able to forgive his people without neglecting the justice their sin deserves. In Jesus, Micah's prophecy will be fulfilled, "He will again have compassion on us; he will vanquish our iniquities. You will cast all our sins into the depths of the sea" (Mic 7:19).

Nahum

Basic Facts
Author: Nahum
Original Audience: the southern kingdom of Judah and the people of Nineveh
Place Written: Canaan
Date Written: about 663–612 B.C.

The Main Idea
God will punish and destroy wicked nations.

Structure
- 1. God will punish Nineveh.
- 2. Nineveh will be attacked.
- 3. Nineveh will fall to its enemies.

Big Events & Ideas

God is slow to anger but great in power.

Nahum begins with a psalm that praises God's power and righteous anger. Nahum says, "The LORD is slow to anger but great in power; the LORD will never leave the guilty unpunished" (Nah 1:3). While the wicked like the Assyrians seem to prosper for a time, God will punish them. He has the power to destroy them, and he is only waiting for the perfect time. But judgment will come.

God uses the same power to protect his people. Nahum explains, "The LORD is good, a stronghold in a day of distress; he cares for those who take refuge in him. But he will completely destroy Nineveh with an overwhelming flood, and he will chase his enemies into darkness" (Nah 1:7–8).

Seeing Jesus

Nahum demonstrates the certainty of God's justice against sin. Sinners will not escape his judgment. Even though he is "slow to anger," he "will never leave the guilty unpunished" (Nah 1:3; see Exod 34:6–7). Therefore, God cannot forgive sinners by overlooking their sin. Sin must be punished, or God no longer remains just. In Jesus, God offered the solution to his desire to be both just and merciful.

Paul explains, "God presented [Jesus] to demonstrate his righteousness at the present time, so that he would be righteous and declare righteous the one who has faith in Jesus" (Rom 3:26). God wanted to declare sinners righteous, but to remain righteous himself he had to punish sin. So God offered his own Son as the atoning sacrifice for sin. He punished Jesus for our sin so that he could declare sinners righteous and forgive us.

Habakkuk

Basic Facts
Author: Habakkuk
Original Audience: the southern kingdom of Judah
Place Written: Canaan
Date Written: about 620–605 B.C.

The Main Idea
God will certainly judge the wicked and rescue the righteous.

Structure
- 1:1–11. Habakkuk's Question and God's Answer
  - 1:1–4. When will God punish the wicked?
  - 1:5–11. God will send the Babylonians to punish the wicked.
- 1:12–2:20. Habakkuk's Complaint and God's Response
  - 1:12–2:1. How can God use wicked Babylon to punish his people?
  - 2:2–20. God rules all nations and will punish Babylon too.
- 3. Habakkuk's Psalm: God will judge the wicked and rescue the righteous.

Big Events & Ideas

God rules over all nations and will judge the wicked.

Habakkuk begins with the prophet's desire to know when God will punish the sin of Judah. God tells Habakkuk that he will soon use the Babylonians to judge Judah. This disturbs Habakkuk. He cannot understand how God can use a nation that is more wicked than Judah to punish Judah's sins. God explains to the prophet that Babylon will one day be punished as well.

The Babylonians have become prideful. "They are guilty; their strength is their god" (Hab 1:11). They seek to build an empire, but only God's plan will succeed. He promises, "For the earth will be filled with the knowledge of the LORD's glory as the water covers the sea" (Hab 2:14).

The righteous one will live by his faith.

God will judge all the wicked. Only the righteous will live. But who is righteous? The righteous is the one who has faith in God's promised victory. "But the righteous one will live by his faith" (Hab 2:4). Circumstances often seem to contradict God's promises, but faith continues to trust in God. Habakkuk writes, "Though the fig tree does not bud and there is no fruit on the vines, though the olive crop fails and the fields produce no food, though the flocks disappear from the pen and there are no herds in the stalls, yet I will celebrate in the LORD; I will rejoice in the God of my salvation" (Hab 3:17–18)!

Seeing Jesus

Habakkuk 2:4 is quoted three times in the New Testament: Romans 1:17, Galatians 3:11, and Hebrews 10:38. Habakkuk teaches that salvation from God's judgment doesn't come through obedience to the law. Instead, it comes through faith in the promises of God. The person whom God regards as righteous is the person who trusts in God's promises. Those promises point forward to Jesus Christ. So for Paul and Hebrews, saving faith is faith in Jesus Christ. God declares everyone who believes in Jesus to be righteous. Believers in Jesus will live and will not endure God's judgment. "The righteous one will live by his faith" (Hab 2:4).

The Old Testament

Zephaniah

Basic Facts
Author: Zephaniah
Original Audience: the southern kingdom of Judah
Place Written: Canaan
Date Written: about 630–620 B.C.

The Main Idea
God will judge Judah and all nations, but then he will bless all nations.

Structure
- 1:1–3:8. God will judge Judah and all nations.
- 3:9–20. God will bless Judah and all nations.

Big Events & Ideas

God will judge all nations.

Zephaniah prophesies about God's universal judgment at the end of time. God says, "I will completely sweep away everything from the face of the earth" (Zeph 1:2). God promises to judge Judah for its idolatry (Zeph 1:4–7), but God will also judge other nations. He says that "the whole earth will be consumed by the fire of my jealousy" (Zeph 3:8). God is the God of the entire earth, and so all people are accountable to him as the judge of all nations.

God will bless all nations.

While God's judgment will certainly come on all the earth, his blessing will also be universal. God promises to "restore pure speech to the peoples so that all of them may call on the name of the LORD and serve him with a single purpose" (Zeph 3:9). He will make both Jews and gentiles righteous, and they will worship him forever (Zeph 3:11–20).

Seeing Jesus

God promises, "The LORD has removed your punishment; he has turned back your enemy. The king of Israel, the LORD, is among you; you need no longer fear harm" (Zeph 3:15). God has fulfilled this promise through Jesus. By punishing Jesus for sin, he has removed the punishment we deserve and defeated the enemies of sin, death, and Satan. In King Jesus, God dwells with his people and gives them security. When Jesus returns, then these promises will be fulfilled perfectly, and God will dwell with his people forever in the New Jerusalem.

Haggai

Basic Facts
Author: Haggai
Original Audience: Jewish people returning to Jerusalem from exile
Place Written: Canaan
Date Written: 520 B.C.

The Main Idea
God commands the Jews returning from the exile to rebuild the temple.

Structure
- 1. God commands the rebuilding of the temple.
- 2. God encourages the work.

Big Events & Ideas
God should be loved more than anything else.

The Jews who had returned from the exile were claiming that it was not yet time to rebuild the temple (Hag 1:2), but they still found time and resources to build nice homes for themselves. Even though they were no longer worshiping idols like their forefathers before the exile, they continued to love other things more than God. The worship of God should take priority in our lives over everything else.

Seeing Jesus

The temple rebuilt by the exiles seemed like nothing in comparison to the glory of the first temple built by Solomon (Hag 2:3). In fact, at the dedication of the foundation, the old men who had seen the first temple mourned because the second temple was so inferior to the first (Ezra 3:12). But God promises, "The final glory of this house will be greater than the first" (Hag 2:9). This points forward to the glory of the New Jerusalem, where God the Father and God the Son will dwell with their people and their glory will fill the earth (Rev 21–22).

Zechariah

Basic Facts
Author: Zechariah
Original Audience: Jewish people returning to Jerusalem from exile
Place Written: Canaan
Date Written: about 520–480 B.C.

The Main Idea
God's people should find hope in the promise that God's king will come.

Structure
- 1–8. God's people must return to God to prepare for God's return to them.
  - 1–6. Zechariah has eight visions.
  - 7–8. Zechariah rebukes and encourages the people.
- 9–14. God's king will come to his people.

Big Events & Ideas

God will return to his people.

Zechariah focuses on the future fulfillment of God's promises to his people. God had exiled the Jews for their sin (Zech 1:2). Now the Jews had returned to the promised land, but they had not whole-heartedly returned to God (Zech 1:3). They had not completed the temple (Zech 6:9–15). They focused on religious observance like fasting instead of righteous actions like caring for the oppressed (Zech 7).

God promises to come and bring prosperity to his people (Zech 1:17; 2:10–13). But the people must prepare themselves by turning from their evil ways and returning to God (Zech 1:4).

God's king will come to his people.

God reveals to Zechariah many promises concerning both the first and the second coming of the promised king. God declares that he will come in peace upon a donkey's colt (Zech 9:9). Yet, this king will also be pierced and mourned over (Zech 12:10). This Shepherd will be struck, and the sheep will scatter (Zech 13:7). But after this piercing, God will "wash away sin and impurity" (Zech 13:1). Then the king will defeat God's enemies and establish his eternal kingdom, which will be holy and free from sin (Zech 14).

Seeing Jesus

Jesus fulfilled Zechariah 9:9 when he entered Jerusalem on a donkey's colt (Matt 21:1–9). After Jesus' arrest, the disciples scattered like sheep, fulfilling Zechariah 13:7. On the cross, a Roman soldier pierced Jesus' side with a spear fulfilling Zechariah 12:10. Other prophecies remain to be fulfilled. Zechariah's visions of the defeat of God's enemies, prosperity for his people, and a holy kingdom free from sin have begun to be fulfilled in believers but remain to be fulfilled perfectly at the return of Christ.

Malachi

Basic Facts
Author: Malachi
Original Audience: Jewish people returning to Jerusalem from exile
Place Written: Canaan
Date Written: about 430 B.C.

The Main Idea
God will judge his people's sin, and then he will return to his people.

Structure
- 1:1–2:16. God condemns sinful priests and husbands.
- 2:17–4:6. God will send a messenger before his coming.

Big Events & Ideas
God deserves the best from his people.

Malachi condemns the priests because they offered lame and sick animals as sacrifices (Mal 1:8). God refuses to accept such offerings. The priests profane God's name, but he promises, "My name will be great among the nations" (Mal 1:11). God does not accept all worship. He deserves only the very best from his people. Similarly, Malachi condemns Jewish men for divorcing their Jewish wives and marrying foreign women who worship idols. By marrying women who worship idols, they have brought impurity to the people of God. God will not accept people with this kind of half-hearted devotion to him.

God will send a messenger before his coming.

God says, "See, I am going to send my messenger, and he will clear the way before me" (Mal 3:1). This messenger is "the prophet Elijah" who will come "before the great and terrible day of the LORD comes" (Mal 4:5). When he comes, "he will turn the hearts of the fathers to their children and the hearts of children to their fathers" (Mal 4:6). This messenger who will be similar to Elijah is the final prophet before God begins to fulfill all of his promises of judgment and of salvation.

Seeing Jesus

Jesus identified John the Baptist as the messenger foretold by Malachi (Matt 11:1–15). John came preaching against the sin of the Jewish people, and he baptized those who responded for the repentance of their sins. In this way, he prepared the way for the coming of Jesus. While John was the greatest born of women (Matt 11:11), Jesus was still greater. John explained, "I am not the Messiah, but I've been sent ahead of him ... He must increase, but I must decrease" (John 3:28, 30). God's coming kingdom would come through King Jesus, but John prepared the way for the king.

About the Apocrypha and Other Books

Maybe you've heard that other churches, like the Roman Catholic Church, have more books in their Bibles, or maybe you've heard about other gospels that weren't included in the Bible. Hearing about these books may have confused you. The truth is that there were many other books written by Jews and Christians during the same time the Bible was written, but these books were not included in the Bible because it was recognized by believers that they were not inspired by God.

The Apocrypha

In addition to the 39 books of the Old Testament and 27 books of the New Testament, Roman Catholics believe 7 other books, as well as additions to the books of Esther and Daniel, should be included in the Bible. Eastern Orthodox (like Greek and Russian Orthodox) Bibles include 4 more books than the Catholics, as well as an additional psalm. Ethiopian Orthodox Bibles include even more books.

The Old Testament

The Apocrypha according to Different Churches

Roman Catholic	Eastern Orthodox	Ethiopian Orthodox
Tobit	Tobit	Tobit
Judith	Judith	Judith
1 Maccabees	1 Maccabees	1 Maccabees (Ethiopic Version)
2 Maccabees	2 Maccabees	2 Maccabees (Ethiopic Version)
Wisdom of Solomon	Wisdom of Solomon	Wisdom of Solomon
Ecclesiasticus (or Sirach)	Ecclesiasticus (or Sirach)	Ecclesiasticus (or Sirach)
Baruch and Letter of Jeremiah	Baruch and Letter of Jeremiah	Baruch and Letter of Jeremiah
Additions to Esther	*Additions to Esther*	*Additions to Esther*
Additions to Daniel	*Additions to Daniel*	*Additions to Daniel*
Prayer of Azariah	*Prayer of Azariah*	*Prayer of Azariah*
Susanna	*Susanna*	*Susanna*
Bel and the Dragon	*Bel and the Dragon*	*Bel and the Dragon*
	1 Esdras (or 3 Ezra)	1 Esdras (or 3 Ezra)
	Prayer of Manasseh	Prayer of Manasseh
	3 Maccabees	3 Maccabees (Ethiopic Version)
	4 Maccabees	
	Addition to Psalms: Psalm 151	*Addition to Psalms: Psalm 151*
		2 Esdras (or 4 Ezra)
		1 Enoch
		Jubilees
		Additions to Lamentations
		Rest of the Words of Baruch (or 4 Baruch)

These additional books are often called the Apocrypha, which is a name that means "hidden away" in Greek. Some prefer to call these books Deuterocanonical, which means "Second Canon." Protestant Christians rejected these books for three primary reasons. First, it is clear that some of these books, like Bel and the Dragon, contain stories that are more like fairy tales than historical stories about God working in the world. Second, many of these books could not have been written by the people who supposedly wrote them. These first two points mean the books could not be inspired by God, because they simply aren't true. The final reason Protestant Christians rejected these books is because it is clearly evident from reading them that they are not inspired by the Holy Spirit. They do not posses the clear power evident in the inspired books, and this is why the books were not universally accepted by all Christians everywhere.

Nevertheless, these books continue to have value for students of the Bible. Some of the books, like 1–2 Maccabees, give us reliable historical information about the time between the Old and New Testaments. All of them give us a glimpse into the way some Jews thought about God and the world around the time of Jesus. For this reason, Protestant confessions of faith have said, "The books commonly called Apocrypha, not being of divine inspiration, are no part of the canon of the Scripture, and therefore are of no authority in the church of God, nor to be any otherwise approved, or made use of, than other human writings."[6] They are not Scripture, but they can be read like other human writings.

Since you may encounter these books when sharing the gospel with people who go to other churches, it may be helpful to be familiar with the contents of some of the most important of these books.

Tobit. Tobit tells the story of a man named Tobit and Anna, his wife, as well as their son Tobias. Tobias goes on a journey to collect money that belongs to his father Tobit, who has become blind. He is joined by a man who is actually the angel Raphael. Raphael helps Tobias marry a woman named Sarah, who had married seven men previously. Each of her husbands were killed by a demon on their wedding night. Tobias, however, drives away the demon, marries Sarah, and helps cure Tobit of his blindness. While an entertaining story, the book does not appear historical or relate directly to the big story of the Bible.

Judith. Judith is a widow in the unhistorical Jewish city of Bethulia. When King Nebuchadnezzar of Babylon sends his general Holofernes to attack the city, Judith goes out to the general, befriends him, gets him drunk, and then cuts off his head. Like Tobit, Judith shares an entertaining story, but it is not historically accurate.

1 Maccabees. This book tells of the rebellion of an old priest named Mattathias and his sons against the Greek ruler of Syria, Antiochus IV. When Mattathias dies, his son Judas Maccabeus, a nickname that means "the Hammer," led the Jews to overthrow their Greek rulers and gain independence. The book covers historical events from 180–134 B.C. and is generally believed to be historically accurate. However, it is not recognized as inspired by the Holy Spirit.

2 Maccabees. This book is another retelling of the Maccabean revolt, covering events from 180–161 B.C. It focuses more on the cleansing of the temple after it had been defiled with idols by Antiochus IV. It is not considered to be as historically accurate as 1 Maccabees.

Wisdom of Solomon. This book contains various psalms and teachings emphasizing the importance of wisdom. The book was written around the year 100 B.C. and therefore could not have been written by Solomon who lived 800 years earlier.

Ecclesiasticus (or Sirach). Ecclesiasticus is also known by the longer name the Wisdom of Jesus the Son of Sirach, or simply Sirach or ben Sira. The book contains teachings on the importance of pursing wisdom and obeying the law. It demonstrates the false belief that someone can be saved by works of the law (compare with Romans 3:19–20). It was written around 180 B.C. in Hebrew, and was translated into Greek in 132 B.C. Since it contradicts the New Testament teachings on salvation, it is rejected as not inspired by the Holy Spirit.

Baruch and Letter of Jeremiah. The book of Baruch claims to be a history written down by Jeremiah's scribe Baruch. The final sections of the book containssongs of praise. The Letter of Jeremiah is added as chapter 6 of Baruch, and claims to be a letter written by Jeremiah to the Jewish exiles, similar to Jeremiah 29. Baruch and the Letter of Jeremiah contradict the history recorded in the biblical book of Jeremiah on several points, and were written long after Jeremiah and Baruch had died.

Additions to Esther. Some Bibles add sections to the book of Esther (usually at the end of the book) that relate a dream received by Esther's relative Mordecai, as well as prayers from Esther and Mordecai. These additions can be found in Greek versions of the book, but they do not occur in any of the Hebrew copies of the book, demonstrating that they were added later and were not inspired by the Holy Spirit.

Additions to Daniel. Bibles containing the Apocrypha include 3 additions to the book of Daniel. In Daniel 3, the Prayer of Azariah, or the Song of the Three Young Men, adds a song of praise that Daniel's friends give to God for their deliverance from the fiery furnace.

At the end of the book is added two more sections: Susanna and Bel and the Dragon. Susanna tells of a young woman who is falsely accused of sexual immorality. Susanna is cleverly able to demonstrate that her accusers are telling lies, saving her life.

In Bel and the Dragon, King Cyrus commands Daniel to worship the false god Bel. Daniel claims that Bel is not a living god, but Cyrus asks why the food offered to him each day disappears if Bel is not alive. To prove that Bel is not a true god, Daniel secretly sprinkles the floor of his temple with ashes. The next morning reveals that it was the priests who were eating the food. Then Daniel kills a dragon worshiped by the Babylonians. Outraged, the Babylonians throw Daniel in the den of lions for a week, but Daniel is not harmed. In addition to being only entertaining stories, these additions appear only in Greek versions of the book and not in any of the Hebrew/Aramaic copies of Daniel.

1 Esdras (or 3 Ezra). 1 Esdras is also known as 3 Ezra, depending on what books you begin counting as belonging to Ezra or Esdras. The Old Testament books of Ezra and Nehemiah are sometimes counted as 1 and 2 Ezra. In the book called either 1 Esdras, or 3 Ezra, the author retells many of the events from 2 Chronicles, Ezra, and Nehemiah while adding other entertaining stories. The book is recent and was probably written even after the New Testament had been completed. Therefore, it was not truly written by the priest Ezra.

Prayer of Manasseh. This book claims to be a prayer of repentance from the wicked king of Judah Manasseh based on the statements in 2 Chronicles 33:11–13, 18–19 that he repented at the end of his life. The book only comes to us in Greek and was written long after the death of Manasseh.

The Jewish Pseudepigrapha

Another group of books we do not recognize as inspired is the Jewish Pseudepigrapha, which comes from Greek words meaning "false writings." Some of these books are included in the Bibles of the Eastern and Ethiopian Orthodox churches, while there are many others that are not included in any Bibles at all.

Some simply retell sections of the Bible, adding additional stories or explaining things from a certain perspective. *Jubilees* for example records an angel retelling many of the stories of Genesis and Exodus to Moses. *Jubilees* may have been written originally in Hebrew but only comes to us today in the ancient Ethiopian language of Ge'ez. Since it was written long after Genesis and Exodus, it is not recognized as inspired by any church except the Ethiopian Orthodox.

Others claim to relate wisdom like the *Psalms of Solomon* or final words of famous men like *The Testament of Moses* or *The Testament of Abraham*. Even others claim to record apocalyptic visions such as *1 Enoch* or *4 Ezra*.

These books were written long after the deaths of the people that supposedly wrote them, and therefore they cannot be genuine. There are too many of these books to list. Reading these books can help us understand the way many of the Jews were thinking during the time of the New Testament, but they do not give us spiritual benefit because they are not inspired.

About the Apocrypha and Other Books

The Dead Sea Scrolls

In 1946, an Arab shepherd boy threw a stone into a cave near the Dead Sea in southern Israel and heard the sound of breaking pottery. When archaeologists investigated, they found numerous caves with ancient jars filled with scrolls written around the time of Jesus. Some of these scrolls contain Old Testament books in Hebrew, and have confirmed the accuracy of our copies of the Old Testament books.

Other books like *The Community Rule* or *The War Scroll* contain the writings of a Jewish group called the Essenes, who had left their communities to live a life committed to God in the town of Qumran in the desert. Their writings teach that all the other Jewish groups, including groups we meet in the New Testament like the Pharisees and Sadducees, had abandoned God. The Essenes believed they were the only true people of God, and awaited the coming of the Messiah in the dessert. When the Messiah came, he would conquer the world and reign forever with the Essenes at his side.

Like the Pseudepigrapha, these writings give us an idea of some of the teachings embraced by groups of Jews during the time of Jesus and the apostles. But they are not inspired and give no spiritual benefit.

The Apostolic Fathers

After the death of the apostles, Christians continued writing books and letters. These writings are often called the Apostolic Fathers because they come from the generations immediately following the apostles. Some of these writings, like *The Letter of Barnabas* and *The Shepherd of Hermas*, were almost included in the New Testament. However, they were never recognized by the entire church as inspired by the Holy Spirit.

The Apostolic Fathers include letters from early Christians like *The Letter of Barnabas, 1 Clement, 2 Clement, The Letter of Ignatius*, and *The Letter of Polycarp*. *The Martyrdom of Polycarp* tells the story of how one early pastor gave his life for the gospel. *The Didache* or *The Teachings of the Twelve* is a church manual that gives instructions about church practice. *The Shepherd of Hermas* records an apocalyptic vision of an unknown shepherd, which teaches spiritual lessons.

While some of these books are historically accurate, such as *1 Clement*, others are not. These writings have important historical value when studying what early Christians believed after biblical times, but they are not inspired by the Holy Spirit.

The Gnostic Gospels

Other writings arose from a group that rejected the true teachings of the apostles. This group was called Gnostics, a name that comes from the Greek word for "knowledge." They claimed to possess secret knowledge, which Jesus had passed down to his followers. To record this knowledge, they wrote alternative records of Jesus' life, such as *The Gospel of Peter* and *The Gospel of Thomas*. These other gospels are not historically accurate, and were rejected by early Christians because they contradicted the true teachings passed down from the apostles and recorded in the New Testament.

The New Testament

The New Testament

The Time between the Old and New Testaments

Paul writes, "When the time came to completion, God sent his Son" (Gal 4:4). God's plan for the sending of his Son was precise. Jesus came exactly when God had ordained and arranged all the events of human history for his coming.

Between Malachi and Matthew, there is 400 years of history. While this history is not directly recorded in the Bible, it is nevertheless important to understand. This period, often called the Intertestamental Period because it is the time between the Old and New Testaments, saw the fulfillment of many Old Testament prophecies and the preparation for the coming of Jesus in the New Testament.

In the book of Daniel, King Nebuchadnezzar dreams of a statue made of four different materials—gold, silver, bronze, and iron—that is then crushed by a stone that grows into a mountain, which fills the entire earth (Dan 2:31–35). Daniel explains to Nebuchadnezzar that the four materials represent four kingdoms, beginning with his own kingdom, that will later be replaced by the kingdom of God, which will fill the entire earth (Dan 2:36–45).

This dream gives us a basic overview of the history between the two testaments. Four kingdoms come and go: Babylon, Persia, Greece, and Rome.

The Old Testament ends with the fall of Babylon and the emergence of the Persian Empire. The New Testament is written in the Greek language under the rule of the Roman Emperor.

Human Kingdoms

Daniel prophesies that human kingdoms would come and go in the time leading up to God sending the Messiah. In the book of Daniel, we read about the fall of the Babylonian Empire under Belshazzar (Dan 5). At the end of the Old Testament, the Jewish people live under the rule of the Persians.

The Persians

The Persians (sometimes called the Medo-Persians because of the alliance between two people groups, the Medes and Persians) arose from their homeland in modern Iran and conquered the Babylonian Empire to their east. Two Persian kings are prominent in the Old Testament: (1) Cyrus the Great, who conquered Babylon and allowed the Jewish people to return to the promised land (Isa 44:28; 45:1; Ezra 1:1), and (2) Ahasuerus, who married Esther and is called Xerxes outside the Bible (Est 1:1).

The Persians sowed the seeds of their own destruction by attempting to invade Greece. Darius the Great attempted to invade first, but he was defeated by the Greeks at the Battle of Marathon in 490 B.C. Ten years later, Xerxes attempted to invade Greece a second time, but was defeated at the Battle of Thermopylae, retreating in 479 B.C. While the Persian Empire would continue for another fifty years, the Greeks never forgot what they had done and looked forward to taking their revenge upon Persia.

The Greeks

Alexander the Great united the various city-states of Greece into a single kingdom and led his army to inflict revenge on the Persian Empire. From 334–323 B.C., he created the largest empire to that point in history, stretching from Greece and Egypt in the west to Afghanistan and India in the east.

The Time Between the Old and New Testaments

After Alexander's early death at 32 years-old, his empire was divided among his four most powerful generals. The promised land became a buffer zone between General Ptolemy in Egypt, and General Seleucius in Syria. These two Greek kingdoms—the Ptolemies and the Seleucids—fought continuously over dominance in the land of Canaan.

Jewish Independence

The Jews would eventually rebel against Seleucid rule when King Antiochus IV attempted to force the Jews to conform to Greek culture and to worship the Greek gods. In 167 B.C., the Jews revolted under the leadership of Judas Maccabeus. For a period of almost 100 years, the Jews enjoyed independent rule under high priests who acted like kings.

The Romans

The Romans conquered the Jews in 63 B.C. under General Pompey. The Romans installed Herod as king of Judea in 37 B.C. to rule under Roman authority. As the New Testament opens, the rule of Rome and Herod represented foreign oppression to most of the Jewish people. They longed for God to defeat the Romans and establish his promised, eternal kingdom.

Three Influences on the New Testament

The world that Jesus was born into was a world dominated by three major influences: Greek culture, Roman rule, and Jewish religion. All three of these influences took shape during the time between the testaments.

Greek Culture

Alexander and his successors believed in unifying their kingdoms through forcing all peoples to adopt Greek culture. The Greeks believed their culture was more enlightened and superior to the cultures of other peoples, whom they called barbarians.

Eventually, most of the lands around the eastern portion of the Mediterranean Sea adopted Greek as their primary trade language. While local languages remained important within communities and families, Greek was spoken when interacting with others. This is why the New Testament is written in Greek.

The Greeks were great city builders, and wherever their influence went, they built cities following the pattern of cities in their homeland. Greek cities consisted of temples to their gods, usually on higher mountains or hills above the city. The life of the city centered around the marketplace, which was a place where both goods and ideas were traded. The Greeks also emphasized theater and athletics. For this reason, they built amphitheaters, stadiums, and race courses.

The Greek city of Athens is known as the birthplace of democracy because before the city was conquered by Alexander's father Phillip, the citizens had ruled themselves through an assembly where citizens voted. This influenced the city of Rome, which was ruled as a republic by the Roman Senate for about 500 years before the establishment of the empire. In the New Testament, we encounter an assembly called the Sanhedrin. Although based on the idea of the elders of Israel in the Old Testament, the Sanhedrin we read about in the Gospels and Acts was convened by the Romans in 57 B.C. as a republican body to oversee the religious and cultural aspects of the Jewish nation.

Roman Rule

In addition to the Sanhedrin, Roman rule exercised great influence on the New Testament in several ways. Augustus Caesar had established what was known as the *Pax Romana*, or Roman Peace. By defeating pirates and thieves on the seas and roads, and by establishing Roman armies to guard the border regions of the empire, the central areas of the empire experienced a unique period of peace and prosperity. This peace, along with the construction of Roman roads, allowed people like the Apostle Paul to travel easily and safely across the empire. Because of this connectivity, the gospel of Jesus was taken throughout the Roman Empire very quickly after the resurrection of Jesus.

While Roman rule was helpful for early Christians in many ways, it also posed dangers. The Romans were tolerant of different people who practiced their indigenous religions and cultures as long as they lived peacefully and worshiped (or in the case of the Jews, offered sacrifices on behalf of) the emperor. The Romans persecuted Christianity for four primary reasons: (1) Christians came from every people group, and therefore it was seen as a new superstition rather than an established religion. (2) While the Jews were seen as an odd people group who had always worshiped only one God, many Christians were former worshipers of other gods who now believed that all people should worship the one, true God. This put the empire at risk of the gods' wrath. (3) Christians declared a crucified man named Jesus to be their Lord and Savior, which were titles that belonged to the emperor. This made them seem like political rebels. (4) Christians refused to offer worship to the emperor. Roman authorities saw this as another sign that they sought to overthrow the empire.

Jewish Religion

The Jewish people at the time of the New Testament faced a dilemma. God had promised to establish his kingdom forever under a descendant of David, but right now, they were dominated by the Romans.

Sects. Different Jewish people responded to this crisis in different ways, resulting in the development of various sects. In the New Testament, we encounter three: Pharisees, Sadducees, and Zealots. Another important sect that isn't mentioned in the New Testament was the Essenes.

The Pharisees believed that if the Jewish people would live precisely according the law of Moses, then they could prepare the way for God to establish his kingdom. This is why the Pharisees we encounter in the Gospels are so concerned about keeping the Sabbath and not interacting with people who are ceremonially unclean. The Pharisees exercised a lot of influence over the lives of regular people in Judea and Galilee.

By contrast, most of the Sadducees came from the ruling, priestly class. They only believed that God had inspired the five books of Moses (Gen–Deut) and did not believe in angels or the resurrection, because they did not see those things in those five books. Their primary objective, however, was to maintain peace under Roman rule in order to keep their positions of power (see John 11:48).

The Zealots believed that the way to bring about the kingdom of God was to fight like the Israelites did so often in the Old Testament, or like Judas Maccabeus had done a century earlier. Some of them lived as rebels in wilderness areas and funded their operations through crime like theft. Apparently, one of Jesus' disciples was a former Zealot (Matt 10:4).

The Essenes believed that the Jewish people as a whole had been rejected by God and needed a fresh start. They left their families and communities to form a new people of Israel in their own Essene communities. Once they had truly separated themselves from the wicked, then God would bring about his kingdom. Some of these communities lived within cities like Jerusalem, but others dwelled in wilderness areas like Qumran, where the Dead Sea Scrolls were produced.

Institutions and Identity Markers. With the Greeks seeking to force their culture on everyone and the Romans dominating them politically, it was a difficult time for the Jews to maintain their unique identity as descendants of Abraham and the nation chosen by God. Two institutions and three identity markers helped the Jewish people maintain their distinct identity, beginning in the Intertestamental Period and continuing into the time of the New Testament.

The two institutions were the temple and the synagogue. The temple in Jerusalem was the institution that united Jews from every sect. It was the place that represented God's presence among them and where they could obey the commands of the law of Moses to offer sacrifices. When the Romans destroyed the temple in A.D. 70, it was devastating to the nation.

But most Jews rarely went to the temple. To them, the synagogue played a more important role in their daily lives. Most synagogues were established by Pharisees as a place for Jews to study the law and the prophets. Many held schools that taught children to read Hebrew and recite the Bible, and all of them held services on the Sabbath (Saturday) where the Old Testament was read and explained. The weekly church meetings established by the apostles on the day of Jesus' resurrection (Sunday) were based on the services of the synagogues — prayer, singing, reading, and preaching.

Through these institutions, especially the synagogue, Jews passed on three identity markers from generation to generation: the kosher diet, Sabbath observance, and circumcision. Jews who lived in pagan cities throughout the Roman Empire were radically different from their pagan neighbors. They didn't eat like their neighbors. They honored one day as holier than the others and used that day for worship and rest, and finally they circumcised their children so every Jew bore a physical mark identifying them as belonging to the family of Abraham.

As the gospel went to the non-Jewish nations, the apostles, who were Jews themselves, were led by the Holy Spirit to recognize that non-Jews did not have to become Jews to become part of the people of God. We become part of God's people through faith in Jesus. Therefore, it isn't necessary for us to eat a Jewish diet, observe Saturday as the Sabbath, or be circumcised. This stance caused great controversy during the New Testament and is the focus of books like Galatians and Romans.

Messianic Hope. The Jewish people looked forward to the day when God would fulfill his promises to Abraham and David by sending the Messiah, the promised anointed king who would bring about God's eternal kingdom. Most envisioned this kingdom as being a repetition of the kingdoms of David and Solomon. God's chosen king would rise, cast out the foreign oppressors, and rule the world from Jerusalem. The only difference between the Messiah's kingdom and the Old Testament kingdom would be that the Messiah's kingdom would never end.

Various men arose during the 200 year period between 100 B.C. and A.D. 100 who claimed to be the Messiah. But all of their movements eventually fell apart. In Acts 5, the Jewish teacher Gamaliel mentions one named Judas the Galilean who arose, but he was killed and his followers scattered.

It's obvious throughout the Gospels and Acts that Jesus' disciples were thinking about Jesus in this same earthly way. Peter rebuked Jesus for saying he would be crucified because he couldn't imagine a crucified Messiah (Mark 8:32). The disciples argued with one another about who would be the greatest once Jesus established himself as king (Mark 8:33–34). Even after the resurrection, they asked Jesus, "Lord, are you restoring the kingdom to Israel at this time" (Acts 1:6)?

Jesus was the fulfillment of the Jewish hope for a Messiah. That's why we call him Christ, which is the Greek word for Messiah. But his kingdom is not what the Jewish people expected. He was a Messiah, crucified for the sins of the world. He is a Messiah seated at God's right hand in heaven. His kingdom is a kingdom that must now be proclaimed to all the world, and it is only after this time of proclamation that God will establish Jesus' messianic kingdom forever in the new creation.

About the New Testament

Basic Facts
Number of Books: 27
Language: Greek
Places Written: across the Roman Empire — Judah, Syria, Asia Minor, Greece, Italy
Dates Written: about A.D. 40–96

The Big Idea of the New Testament
The big idea of the Old Testament was:
THROUGH HIS COVENANTS, GOD PROMISES HIS KINGDOM.
The Old Testament focuses on God's promises, while the New Testament demonstrates the fulfillment of those promises:
Old Testament: PROMISE → New Testament: FULFILLMENT
The big idea of the New Testament is:
THROUGH THE NEW COVENANT, GOD IS ESTABLISHING HIS KINGDOM IN JESUS.
Jesus is God who became man and was born in fulfillment of all the prophesies in the Old Testament predicting the coming of the Messiah. As an adult, Jesus proclaimed the coming of God's kingdom and demonstrated the

advance of God's kingdom through the miracles he performed. Jesus overcame temptation and lived a life without sin. But then Jesus died on the cross for our sins. Three days later, he rose from the dead, victorious over sin, death, and Satan. He ascended into heaven, and is seated now at the right hand of God, ruling as Messiah and Lord.

From heaven, Jesus sent the Holy Spirit to his followers, empowering them to bear witness to the good news about him to all nations of the earth. The apostles and other Christians went out from Jerusalem to all nations, preaching the good news, baptizing believers, and planting churches throughout the world. Since these churches faced various problems, including false teaching, misunderstanding, and persecution, the apostles wrote letters to the churches in order to teach and correct them.

Soon God's plan for history will come to a close. Jesus will return in all his glory. All people will be resurrected and judged. Those who have not believed the gospel will be thrown in the lake of fire forever, while those who belong to Jesus will enter into eternal life with Jesus in the new creation. Finally, God's great purpose will be fulfilled. God will dwell with his people as their God.

The Order of the Books

Christians were some of the first people to adopt the new technology of books over scrolls. The book allowed Christians to collect many pages of different holy books and sew them together into a single volume, which could be easily carried or stored. When gathering the different books of the Bible into one volume, the order of the books became more important.

Christians chose to organize the books based on the big story of the New Testament. First comes the Gospels, which tell the story of Jesus' life, followed by Acts, which tells of the early church after Jesus ascended into heaven. The letters of the apostles to Christians come next with Revelation, which reveals how Jesus will return and establish a new creation, coming at the end of the New Testament.

About the New Testament

Among the Gospels, Matthew was put first because of his focus on Jesus' fulfillment of the Old Testament. Mathew, Mark, and Luke go together because they share many of the same stories and words. John was the last gospel written and tells many different things about Jesus, so it was placed last among the Gospels.

Among the letters, Paul's 13 letters come first. They are divided first between letters written to churches and letters written to individuals. Then they are ordered generally based on length. Hebrews–Jude come next because they were written by other apostles. They are also ordered generally by length.

Divisions of the New Testament

Gospels and Acts	Paul's Letters	General Letters and Revelation
Matthew	*Letters to Churches*	Hebrews
Mark	Romans	James
Luke	1 Corinthians	1 Peter
John	2 Corinthians	2 Peter
	Galatians	1 John
Acts	Ephesians	2 John
	Philippians	3 John
	Colossians	Jude
	1 Thessalonians	
	2 Thessalonians	Revelation
	Letters to Individuals	
	1 Timothy	
	2 Timothy	
	Titus	
	Philemon	

The New Testament

Matthew

Basic Facts
Author: Matthew, a former tax collector
Original Audience: possibly non-Christian Jews, to reach them with the gospel
Place Written: possibly Judah or Galilee
Date Written: about A.D. 60–65

The Main Idea
God's kingdom has come through Jesus the Messiah.

Structure
- **1–4. The kingdom of heaven comes to earth.**
- **5–25. Jesus proclaims the kingdom of heaven.**
  - 5–7. Teaching 1: Life in the kingdom of heaven (Sermon on the Mount)
  - 8–9:34. Jesus demonstrates his authority as king in Galilee.
  - 9:35–10:42. Teaching 2: Jesus sends out his disciples with authority.
  - 11–12. People oppose King Jesus.
  - 13:1–52. Teaching 3: Jesus reveals the kingdom in parables.
  - 13:53–17:27. Jesus reveals that the Messiah must suffer.

- 18. Teaching 4: Life Together in the Kingdom of Heaven
- 19–23. Jesus demonstrates his authority as king in Jerusalem.
- 24–25. Teaching 5: The Coming of the Kingdom in Power (The Olivet Discourse)
- **26–28. King Jesus receives all authority.**
  - 26:1–28:15. King Jesus is crucified and raised.
  - 28:16–20. King Jesus will extend his reign to all nations.

Big Events & Ideas

Jesus fulfills the Old Testament.

Jesus says that "every teacher of the law who has become a disciple in the kingdom of heaven is like the owner of a house who brings out of his storeroom treasures new and old" (Matt 13:52). Matthew is this disciple. His gospel comes first in the New Testament because he focuses on how the Old and the New Testaments fit together. In his gospel, Matthew is bringing out of his storeroom his old and new treasures to show us the beauty of both.[7]

Twelve times Matthew says Jesus fulfilled the Old Testament (Matt 1:22; 2:15, 23; 3:15; 4:14; 5:17; 8:17; 12:17; 13:14, 35; 21:4; 27:9). Jesus' birth, life, death, and resurrection were predicted by the Old Testament. But even more than that, Matthew says Jesus "fulfills" the Old Testament itself (Matt 5:17). The purpose of the Old Testament was to point to Jesus, and Jesus fulfills that purpose.

Jesus is the king of God's People.

Matthew begins with Jesus' family tree to show that Jesus has descended from the line of Abraham and King David (Matt 1:1–17). Wise men from the east visit Jesus as a child in order to honor him as the king of the Jews (Matt 2:2), and when Jesus begins his public ministry, he preaches, "Repent, because the kingdom of heaven has come near" (Matt 4:12). Jesus identifies himself as the Son of Man whom Daniel saw in a vision receiving "dominion, and glory, and a kingdom" (Dan 7:14; see Matt 9:6). Even in his suffering, the truth is declared about him: He is mocked by Roman soldiers with a crown of thorns, and the sign above his head on the cross declares him king of the Jews (Matt 27:27–37). After his resurrection, Jesus declares, "All authority has been given to me in heaven and on earth" (Matt 28:18). Jesus is the king, and he has inaugurated God's kingdom on earth.

Jesus is a wise teacher of God's word.

Matthew records five examples of Jesus' teaching: (1) Life in the Kingdom of Heaven (The Sermon on the Mount; Matt 5–7), (2) Jesus sends out the disciples with authority (Matt 9:35–10:42), (3) Jesus reveals the kingdom in parables (Matt 13:1–52), (4) Life Together in the Kingdom of Heaven (Matt 18); (5) The Coming of the Kingdom in Power (The Olivet Discourse; Matt 24-25).

By emphasizing Jesus' teaching like this, Matthew identifies Jesus as a wise teacher and a new Moses for God's people. In the Sermon on the Mount (Matt 5–7), Jesus even ascends a mountain like Moses and begins to teach God's law (Matt 5:1–2). To enter God's kingdom, we must become disciples or students of Jesus. Jesus tells his disciples that they must make disciples of all nations by "teaching them to observe everything I have commanded you" (Matt 28:20).

Make disciples of all nations.

Matthew ends his gospel with Jesus' final command to his disciples. We call this command the Great Commission because it is the task that Jesus gave his followers to do until he returns:

> All authority has been given to me in heaven and on earth. Go, therefore, and make disciples of all nations, baptizing them in the name of the Father and of the Son and of the Holy Spirit, teaching them to observe everything I have commanded you. And remember, I am with you always, to the end of the age (Matt 28:18–20).

Jesus wants his kingdom to spread through the entire world to every people group and every language. The task of the church is to make disciples. We do this through proclaiming the gospel so people believe and are baptized. Then we teach those who believe the teachings of Jesus, and those believers become a new generation of disciple-makers to reach others with the gospel of Jesus Christ. "This good news of the kingdom will be proclaimed in all the world as a testimony to all nations, and then the end will come" (Matt 24:14).

Mark

Basic Facts
Author: Mark, Peter's assistant
Original Audience: Gentile Christians, possibly the churches in Rome
Place Written: probably Rome
Date Written: about A.D. 55–60

The Main Idea
Jesus is the Messiah and the Son of God who came to die for sin.

Structure
- 1–8:26. Who is Jesus? The Messiah.
  - 1:1–13. The gospel begins.
  - 1:14–8:26. Jesus reveals himself in Galilee.
- 8:27–16. Why Did Jesus Come? To Die.
  - 8:27–10:52. Jesus reveals himself to his disciples.
  - 11:1–13:37. Jesus reveals himself in Jerusalem.
  - 14:1–16:20. Jesus is revealed as sacrifice.

Big Events & Ideas

Jesus is the Messiah and the Son of God.

In Mark 8:27–30, Jesus asks his disciples, "Who people say that I am" (Mark 8:27)? They answer that people believe he is John the Baptist, Elijah, or another prophet. Then Jesus asks, "But you, who do you say that I am" (Mark 8:29)?

Who is Jesus? Mark writes to answer this question, especially in the first 8 chapters of his gospel. But he gives the answer at the very beginning: "The beginning of the gospel of Jesus Christ, the Son of God" (Mark 1:1). Jesus is the Christ, or Messiah, the anointed King whom God promised to send in the Old Testament. When Jesus asks his disciples who they say he is in chapter 8, Peter says, "You are the Messiah" (Mark 8:29). Jesus is the anointed king who has invaded a world that is broken by sin in order to establish the kingdom of God (Mark 1:15).

But he is also the Son of God. After Jesus' crucifixion, a Roman centurion said, "Truly this man was the Son of God" (Mark 15:39). Jesus does things that only God can do. He forgives sin (Mark 2:1–12). He calms storms (Mark 4:35–40). Jesus is superior to Moses and Elijah (Mark 9:2–8). He is the son in the parable of the vineyard owner who is sent and killed by the farmers (Mark 12:1–12). Now he is seated "at the right hand of God" (Mark 16:19).

Jesus came to die for sin.

After Peter identifies Jesus as the Messiah in Mark 8:29, Jesus begins to teach his disciples about the purpose of his coming. The disciples, like the other Jews, expected the Messiah to initiate a war against their enemies and establish an earthly kingdom. But Jesus taught "that it was necessary for the Son of Man to suffer many things and be rejected by the elders, chief priests, and scribes, be killed, and rise after three days" (Mark 8:31). Three times Jesus teaches his disciples that he came to die, and three times his disciples fail to understand (Mark 8:31–9:1; 9:30–50; 10:32–45). Even at Jesus' death, the crowd taunted him, "Let the Messiah, the king of Israel, come down now from the cross that we may see and believe" (Mark 15:32). They failed to understand that God's plan was for the king of Israel to be crucified, and seeing him die for sin we should believe in him.

Follow Jesus.

Mark enables his readers to become witnesses of Jesus' life and ministry. By telling what Jesus did and said, he helps his readers discover who Jesus is and why he came. As we grow in our understanding of Jesus, we are challenged by Mark to become Jesus' disciple. He says to us, "Follow me" (Mark 1:17; 2:14). Jesus calls us to deny ourselves, take up our cross, and follow him (Mark 8:34). He demands that we value him more than family or possessions (Mark 10:29–31).

The New Testament

Luke

Basic Facts
Author: Luke, physician and co-laborer with Paul
Original Audience: Theophilus (a wealthy sponsor) and other gentile Christians
Place Written: possibly Rome or Greece
Date Written: about A.D. 60–62

The Main Idea
Jesus is the Spirit-filled man who saves all nations through his death and resurrection.

Structure
- 1:1–4:13. Jesus comes into the world.
- 4:14–9:50. Jesus ministers in Galilee by the Spirit's power.
- 9:51–19:27. Jesus determines to journey to Jerusalem.
- 19:28–21:38. Jesus judges the powerful in Jerusalem.
- 22:1–24:53. Jesus is crucified and resurrected.

Big Events & Ideas

Jesus' life, death, and resurrection are historical facts.

Luke writes to a man named Theophilus (a name that means "lover of God," and is possibly a fake name to protect him from persecution). Theophilus probably gave Luke the money needed to research and write both the Gospel of Luke and the book of Acts (Luke 1:3; Acts 1:1).

Luke, like a good historian, "carefully investigated everything" in order to write an accurate account of Jesus' life, death, and resurrection (Luke 1:1–4). He wants people to know that the stories about Jesus are true. He adds the details of when events took place: An angel appeared to Zechariah "in the days of King Herod of Judea" (Luke 1:5). Jesus was born after "a decree went out from Caesar Augustus that the whole empire should be registered" (Luke 2:1), and this took place "while Quirinius was governing Syria" (Luke 1:2). John the Baptist's ministry began "in the fifteenth year of the reign of Tiberius Caesar" (Luke 3:1). The gospel of Jesus Christ is historical fact.

Jesus is the Son of Adam and the Son of God.

Luke traces Jesus' family tree all the way back to the first man. Jesus is "the son of Adam, the son of God" (Luke 3:38). In Luke, Jesus is a new Adam or a new kind of man who can stand as a representative for all humans. He is tempted like Adam, but unlike Adam, he doesn't sin (Luke 4:1–13). While Adam was cast out of paradise, Jesus tells the thief on the cross beside him, "Truly I tell you, today you will be with me in paradise" (Luke 23:43).

Jesus is filled with the Spirit.

As the new representative of all humans, Jesus is filled with the Holy Spirit. He is conceived by the power of the Holy Spirit (Luke 1:34–35). At his baptism, the Spirit anointed him with the result that he was "full of the Holy Spirit and was led by the Spirit" (Luke 3:22; 4:1). He began his ministry "in the power of the Spirit" (Luke 4:14, 18). He "rejoiced in the Holy Spirit" and gave praise to God the Father (Luke 10:21). Jesus is a new kind of person: a person in whom the Holy Spirit dwells. He promises that the Father will "give the Holy Spirit to those who ask him" (Luke 11:13). In the book of Acts, God pours out his Holy Spirit on those who have believed in the gospel of Jesus Christ. To believe in Jesus is to be transformed into the pattern of Jesus: to become a person in whom the Spirit dwells.

You cannot serve God and money.

Luke writes down more of Jesus' teachings about money than any other gospel. Jesus teaches that you cannot serve both God and money (Luke 16:10–13). To the poor belongs the kingdom of God, but the rich receive their reward in this life only (Luke 6:20–26). Riches choke out the seed of the gospel in the human heart (Luke 8:14). Our life is not measured by the worth of our possessions (Luke 12:13–21). Luke gives us a choice: If we are like the rich man who refused to sell all that he had in order to follow Jesus, we will go away sad (Luke 18:22–23). But if we give all we have like the poor widow, then we will receive Jesus' approval (Luke 21:1–4).

Jesus determines to journey to Jerusalem.

Luke writes, "When the days were coming to a close for him to be taken up, he determined to journey to Jerusalem" (Luke 9:51). Luke then spends 10 chapters describing Jesus' journey from Galilee to Jerusalem. Luke wants his readers to know that Jesus' death was not an accident. It was God's plan, and Jesus set forth to obey his Father by voluntarily going to his sacrificial death.

Jesus came to save sinners.

Jesus came "to seek and to save the lost" (Luke 19:10). He is like the shepherd who seeks out the lost sheep, the woman who searches for a lost coin, and the father who welcomes home a lost son (Luke 15). Jesus said, "I have not come to call the righteous, but sinners to repentance" (Luke 5:32). He came for Jews like Zacchaeus, who were notorious sinners (Luke 19:1–10). But he also came to save the gentiles. When Jesus was a child, Simeon prophesied that he was "a light for revelation to the gentiles" (Luke 2:32). After his resurrection, Jesus explains to his disciples, "This is what is written: The Messiah would suffer and rise from the dead the third day, and repentance for the forgiveness of sins would be proclaimed in his name to all the nations, beginning at Jerusalem" (Luke 24:46–47).

John

Basic Facts
Author: John, the former fisherman and disciple
Original Audience: Jews and gentiles, both Christians and non-Christians
Place Written: Ephesus
Date Written: about A.D. 80–90

The Main Idea
Jesus is the Messiah and the Son of God, and everyone who believes in him will have eternal life.

Structure
- 1:1–18. The Word became flesh and dwelled among us.
- 1:19–12:50. Signs bear witness to Jesus.
  - 1:19–51. John the Baptist and the disciples bear witness to Jesus.
  - 2:1–4:54. Jesus begins a new age.
  - 5:1–10:21. The Jewish festivals bear witness to Jesus.
  - 11:1–12:50. Jesus is the resurrection and the life.
- 13:1–20:31. Jesus' death and resurrection bear witness to Jesus.
  - 13:1–17:26. Jesus loves his disciples to the end.

- 18:1–20:31. Jesus is glorified by his death and resurrection.
- 21:1–25. Jesus gives clarity to the roles of Peter and John.

Big Events & Ideas

Jesus is the Word.

John starts his gospel "in the beginning," a deliberate imitation of Genesis 1:1. John explains that his gospel is about the Word. The Word has always existed, and the Word is at the same time fully God and yet distinct from God (John 1:1). "All things were created through him" (John 1:2). John's gospel tells the story about how "the Word became flesh and dwelt among us" (John 1:14).

While Matthew, Mark, and Luke put us in the shoes of the disciples and allow us to slowly realize that Jesus is God, John gives us the answer at the beginning: Jesus is God the Son who became a man in order to reveal God to us. "No one has ever seen God. The one and only Son who is himself God and is at the Father's side — he has revealed him" (John 1:18).

Jesus is life.

"In him was life, and that life was the light of men" (John 1:4). John writes about Jesus' life "so that you may believe that Jesus is the Messiah, the Son of God, and that believing you may have life in his name" (John 20:31). Everyone will die because of sin. But "God loved the world in this way: He gave his one and only Son, so that everyone who believes in him will not perish but have eternal life" (John 3:16). Resurrection and life is available to everyone who believes in Jesus because Jesus himself is "the resurrection and the life." He says, "The one who believes in me, even if he dies, will live. Everyone who lives and believes in me will never die" (John 11:25–26). He is like a vine, and we are like branches that derive their life by remaining in the vine (John 15:1–8). Jesus is "the way, the truth, and the life" through whom we come to the Father (John 14:6).

Signs bear witness to Jesus.

In his gospel, John identifies seven signs, which testify to Jesus' identity as God's Son: (1) Jesus turns water into wine (John 2:1–11). (2) Jesus heals a man's son (John 4:46–54). (3) Jesus heals the sick (John 5:1–15). (4) Jesus feeds 5,000 people (John 6:5–13). (5) Jesus walks on water (John 6:16–21). (6) Jesus heals a man who was born blind (John 9:1–7). (7) Jesus raises Lazarus from the dead (John 11:1–44).

These signs serve to condemn the Jewish leaders because they witness them, but still refuse to believe (John 12:37). But John records these signs "so that you may believe ... and that by believing you may have life in his name" (John 20:31).

Jesus begins a new age.

Jesus' signs demonstrate that he has begun a new age, a new period in history where God's kingdom becomes reality. When Jesus turns water into wine, he brings to mind prophecies from Isaiah and Amos that speak about the abundance of wine in the new creation (Isa 25:6–8; Amos 9:11–15). Jesus heals sickness, brings sight to the blind, and raises the dead. All of these miracles demonstrate that God is renewing the world through Jesus (see Isa 25:7–8; 29:18; 35:5).

Jesus is...

Jesus uses the phrase "I am" seven times to describe his unique identity as the God-man who reveals the Father to the world. Jesus says, "I am the bread of life" (John 6:35, 48, 51). "I am the light of the world" (John 8:12; 9:5). "I am the gate for the sheep" (John 10:7, 9). "I am the good shepherd" (John 10:11, 14). "I am the resurrection and the life" (John 11:25). "I am the way, the truth, and the life" (John 14:6). "I am the true vine" (John 15:1).

Jesus uses the phrase "I am" five more times to identify himself as the God of the Old Testament who revealed his name as "I am who I am" or Yahweh (Exod 3:14; John 6:20; 8:24, 28, 58; 18:5). The Jews clearly understand that Jesus identifies himself with God because at one point they attempt to stone him for using the phrase (John 8:59). Jesus does not reveal himself merely as a good teacher, but as the creator and ruler of the universe. To him, everyone owes faith and allegiance.

Acts

Basic Facts
Author: Luke, physician and co-laborer with Paul
Original Audience: Theophilus (a wealthy sponsor) and other gentile Christians
Place Written: possibly Rome or Greece
Date Written: about A.D. 62

The Main Idea
The Holy Spirit empowers the church to bear witness to Jesus from Jerusalem to the end of the earth.

Structure
- **1:1–8:3. The church bears witness in Jerusalem.**
  - 1:1–2:13. The Holy Spirit prepares the church for witness.
  - 2:14–8:3. The Holy Spirit acts in Jerusalem.
- **8:4–11:18. The church bears witness in Samaria and Judea.**
  - 8:4–40. The Holy Spirit speaks through Philip to Samaritans and an Ethiopian.
  - 9:1–31. The Holy Spirit prepares Paul for witness.
  - 9:32–11:18. The Holy Spirit leads Peter to preach to gentiles.

- **11:19–28:31. Churches bear witness to the end of the earth.**
  - 11:19–30. The Holy Spirit acts in Antioch.
  - 12:1–24. The Holy Spirit leads the Jerusalem Church through persecution.
  - 12:25–16:5. The Holy Spirit sends Paul to Asia Minor.
  - 16:6–19:20. The Holy Spirit sends Paul to Europe also.
  - 19:21–28:31. The Holy Spirit sends Paul to Rome.

Big Events & Ideas

Jesus sends the Holy Spirit to empower the church.

Before ascending into heaven, Jesus made a prediction: The disciples would become his witnesses from Jerusalem to the end of the earth. But before this would happen, first they would "receive power when the Holy Spirit has come on you" (Acts 1:8). The book of Acts is about how Jesus sends the Holy Spirit and how the Holy Spirit empowers the church to bear witness to Jesus to the end of the earth.

In Acts 1:1, Luke says that his gospel records "all that Jesus began to do and teach," which means that Acts records what Jesus *continued* to do and teach. But in the book of Acts, Jesus acts through the Holy Spirit, who works through churches. While the book of Acts records the actions of many important men like Peter, Philip, and Paul, the main actor is the Holy Spirit. He is the one who works first in Jerusalem, then in Judea and Samaria, and then to the end of the earth when he guides Paul to Rome.

People are saved through the preaching of the gospel.

When the Holy Spirit comes upon the church on Pentecost, Peter begins to preach the gospel of Jesus Christ (Acts 2:14–36). Through Peter's preaching, those who hear are "pierced to the heart" and desire to be saved from their sin (Acts 2:37). Wherever the Holy Spirit leads God's people, God's kingdom spreads through the preaching of the gospel. Peter preaches in the temple (Acts

3:11–26). Stephen preaches to the Sanhedrin (Acts 7). After Stephen's death, persecution scatters the Jerusalem Church. "So those who were scattered went on their way preaching the word" (Acts 8:4). When Peter visits a gentile's home, he preaches the gospel (Acts 10:34–46). Wherever Paul goes from Asia Minor to Europe, he preaches the gospel, and people believe in Jesus (see Acts 13:13–41; 17:22–34; 28:23–24).

Those who are saved form local churches.

Wherever the Holy Spirit leads the disciples to preach the gospel, those who are saved and baptized begin to form local churches. This begins in Jerusalem, when those baptized on Pentecost "devoted themselves to the apostles' teaching, to the fellowship, to the breaking of bread, and to prayer" (Acts 2:42). After persecution scatters the Jerusalem Church, those who flee to Antioch quickly form a local church there (Acts 11:19–26). As Paul travels preaching the gospel, wherever he goes he forms those baptized into local churches (see Acts 14:21–23).

God saves the gentiles through the gospel.

Beginning with Cornelius, the Holy Spirit starts saving gentiles as well as Jews (Acts 10). The Old Testament had pointed forward to the day when all the families of the earth would be blessed through Abraham, and the kingdom of God would expand to the entire world (see Gen 12:3). Jesus had commanded the disciples to "make disciples of all nations" (Matt 28:19). Even so, the salvation of gentiles is surprising to the apostles and early Christians.

One group objects to the full acceptance of gentiles into the church. They believe that gentiles must first be circumcised and become Jews before they can become followers of Jesus, but the Holy Spirit comes upon the uncircumcised gentiles who believe just as he had Jewish people (Acts 10:47–11:3). While the apostles decide that the gentiles should avoid meat offered to idols, the eating of blood, and sexual immorality, they are led by the Holy Spirit to recognize that gentiles are full-members of God's covenant family on the basis of faith, not circumcision (Acts 15).

About Paul and His Letters

After Jesus himself, the Apostle Paul is the most influential leader to arise among early Christians. Through his letters, he continues to shape our understanding of Jesus' death and resurrection. Paul's letters, which are some of the first Christian testimony to Jesus, teach us how the gospel changes our lives.

Paul's Early Life and Call

Paul was born around A.D. 5–10 in the city of Tarsus, which was in the southeastern corner of Asia Minor (modern Turkey). We know very little about his early life. He was born into a Jewish family from the tribe of Benjamin (Phil 3:5). His family was likely influential or wealthy because he was born a Roman citizen. The privilege of citizenship did not belong to everyone born in the empire, but was usually granted as a gift for service to the empire or bought for a large amount of money (Acts 22:25–29).

His names are another clue to his early identity, both as a Jew and a Roman citizen. We initially meet him in Acts under the name Saul, which would have been his Jewish name after King Saul (Acts 8:1). When he began proclaiming the gospel among gentiles in Cyprus, Luke begins to use his Roman name, Paul (Acts 13:9). Since Paul was born a Roman citizen, he would have had his Roman name from birth. He did not change his name because of his salvation, as some people mistakenly teach, but in order to reach gentiles with the gospel.

At some point as a child or young man (about A.D. 15–20), Paul moved to Jerusalem to study the Bible and become a teacher among the Pharisees. Paul studied under the greatest teacher of his time, Gamaliel (Acts 22:3). Paul's letters demonstrate his immense knowledge of the Old Testament, which he had from his early training.

Paul was zealous to keep the Jewish people pure and prepared for the Messiah's kingdom. Therefore, following the resurrection of Jesus in A.D. 30, he began persecuting Christians (Acts 8:1–3; Gal 1:13–14; Phil 3:6). He probably thought it was blasphemous to teach that the Messiah had been crucified. But while he was on a trip to Damascus in A.D. 33/34 to arrest Christians, Jesus appeared to him and called him to be his chosen instrument to proclaim the gospel among the gentiles (Acts 8). After meeting Jesus, Paul would never be the same.

Paul's Ministry and Death

After becoming a Christian, Paul initially began teaching in Damascus, where many of the local Christians slowly began to trust him (Acts 9:19–20). For a period, he went into the Arabian Dessert in modern Jordan where he probably preached the gospel and planted churches among the Nabataean Arab people (Gal 1:17). After returning to Damascus, probably in A.D. 36/37, government officials attempted to arrest him, but he escaped by being lowered through the city wall (Acts 9:23–24; 2 Cor 11:32–33). He then went to Jerusalem, where he met the other apostles (Acts 9:28–30; Gal 1:21).

In A.D. 37–45, he ministered further in the regions of Syria and Cilicia, perhaps in the prominent cities of Damascus, Antioch, and his hometown of Tarsus (2 Cor 11:22–27). He seems to have eventually settled in Antioch, where he ministered alongside Barnabas and visited Jerusalem a second time to provide famine relief to the Judean churches (Acts 11:25–30; Gal 2:1–10).

About Paul and His Letters

Around A.D. 46, the Holy Spirit led the Antioch Church to set Paul and Barnabas apart for missionary service. With their church's support, Paul and Barnabas set out on what would become known as Paul's first missionary journey, although Paul had already been involved in missions from the time of his calling. The missionary team traveled to the island of Cyprus, which was Barnabas' homeland, and then to the region of Galatia in southern Asia Minor (modern Turkey). About one and a half years after departing, Paul and Barnabas returned to Antioch (Acts 13–14). Because of their work of planting churches among gentiles, the two then went on to Jerusalem, where church leaders decided that gentiles did not have to take on Jewish identity through circumcision to become Christians (Acts 15).

In A.D. 48/49, Paul and Barnabas prepared to set out on a second missionary journey, but due to a disagreement, they parted ways. Paul instead took Silas as his missionary partner. This new team began by visiting churches in Galatia before the Holy Spirit led them to cross over to Greece. During this journey, which lasted for about two and a half years, Paul and Silas planted the churches in Philippi, Thessalonica, and Corinth (Acts 16–18).

After visiting Jerusalem and Antioch, Paul set out again for his third missionary journey in A.D. 52. Most of the next three years were spent planting the church in Ephesus, although he also visited the churches in Greece. After being chased out of Ephesus due to a riot, he returned to Greece for the next few years (Acts 19–20).

In A.D. 57, he returned to Jerusalem, where he was arrested in the temple. He was then transferred to Caesarea, where he remained imprisoned for two years. As a Roman citizen, he appealed his case to Caesar and was transferred to Rome, although he was shipwrecked on the way. The book of Acts ends with Paul under house arrest in Rome, awaiting his trial before Caesar. Probably around A.D. 62, he was released from his imprisonment (Acts 21–28).

We know very little about Paul's life after the book of Acts ends. But information from 1 Timothy and Titus suggests that he returned to ministry in

Greece and Crete. Perhaps, Paul even traveled to preach the gospel in Spain in the western Roman Empire (Rom 15:24). But he was eventually arrested again and executed under Emperor Nero, who began persecuting the Christians in Rome. Paul probably died by beheading around A.D. 67.

Paul's Letters

Paul wrote letters to the churches he planted in order to solve problems and correct false teaching, as well as to encourage. Paul also wrote letters to individuals like his disciples, Timothy and Titus, or his friend, Philemon. Writing letters during Paul's time could be expensive. For this reason, Paul would have carefully planned what he was going to say in order to not waste expensive ink and paper. He also apparently used professional scribes so that the letters would be written beautifully and efficiently. While Paul spoke the letter, the scribe would carefully write it down. Tertius, who wrote down Romans, even sends his greetings in Romans 16:22.

While we possess 13 of Paul's letters in our Bibles, Paul mentions other letters that we do not have. In Colossians 4:16, Paul explains that he also sent a letter to the Laodicea Church, which the Colossae Church should read also. Paul refers to another letter he wrote to the Corinth Church in 1 Corinthians 5:9, which means that what we call 1 Corinthians is actually at least Paul's second letter to Corinth. In 2 Corinthians 2:3-4, Paul mentions another letter he sent to Corinth between 1 and 2 Corinthians, which means 2 Corinthians is at least the fourth letter Paul wrote to Corinth.

Why do we only possess 13 of Paul's letters, and not these other letters we know he wrote? Apparently, the other letters to Corinth and Laodicea were not recognized by Paul and the early Christians as being inspired by the Holy Spirit in the same way as the 13 that we now possess. As early as when 2 Peter was written in A.D. 64-67, Christians recognized Paul's letters as being God's word in the same way as the books of the Old Testament (1 Pet 3:16).

Because Paul's letters were treated as Scripture, churches would have made their own copies, as well as passing on copies to other churches. It's also possible that Paul kept his own authoritative copies of those letters the Holy Spirit had inspired, and these may be the scrolls and parchments he refers to in 2 Timothy 4:13.

Paul's Ministry and Letters

Letter	Date	Place Written	Original Audience
A.D. 46–47, The First Missionary Journey			
Galatians	A.D. 48–52	possibly Antioch	Churches in Galatia
A.D. 48/49–51, The Second Missionary Journey			
1 Thessalonians	A.D. 50–51	Corinth	Thessalonica Church
2 Thessalonians	A.D. 50–51	Corinth	Thessalonica Church
A.D. 52–57, The Third Missionary Journey			
1 Corinthians	A.D. 54	Ephesus	Corinth Church
Romans	A.D. 55–58	Corinth	Churches in Rome
2 Corinthians	A.D. 56	Macedonia	Corinth Church
A.D. 57–62, Imprisonment in Caesarea, Voyage to Rome, Imprisonment in Rome			
Ephesians	about A.D. 62	Rome	Churches in Ephesus and surrounding region
Philippians	about A.D. 62	Rome	Philippi Church
Colossians	about A.D. 62	Rome	Colossae Church
Philemon	about A.D. 62	Rome	Philemon in Colossae
A.D. 62–67, Release, Further Ministry, Arrest, Execution			
1 Timothy	A.D. 62–64	Macedonia	Timothy in Ephesus
Titus	A.D. 62–64	Macedonia	Titus on Crete
2 Timothy	A.D. 66–67	Rome	Timothy in Ephesus

Romans

Basic Facts
Author: Paul
Original Audience: churches in Rome
Place Written: Corinth
Date Written: about A.D. 55–58

The Main Idea
The gospel is the power of God for salvation because it reveals that God gives righteousness as a gift to everyone who believes.

Structure
- 1–11. God gives righteousness as a gift to everyone who believes.
  - 1:1–17. Opening and Main Idea: The gospel reveals God's gift of righteousness.
  - 1:18–3:20. All have sinned and are under God's wrath.
  - 3:21–4:25. Jesus is God's sacrifice for sin, and is received by faith.
  - 5:1–8:39. God's gift of righteousness also gives us peace and hope.
  - 9:1–11:36. The gospel is only believed by God's chosen children.
- 12–16. Therefore, give yourself as a living sacrifice.

- 12:1–15:13. The gospel transforms the lives of those who believe.
- 15:14–16:27. The gospel must be preached to every nation.

Big Events & Ideas

All have sinned and are under God's wrath.

"For all have sinned and fall short of the glory of God" (Rom 3:23). In the first three chapters of Romans, Paul is building toward this conclusion. First, he argues that the gentiles have sinned and are under the wrath of God (Rom 1:18–32). The Jews listening to the letter would be in happy agreement with this point, but then Paul argues that the Jews also have sinned and are under the wrath of God. Even though they have the law of Moses and circumcision, they are not exempt from God's judgment against sin (Rom 2). All people — both gentiles and Jews — are in the same position before God. All have sinned and are under God's wrath.

Jesus is God's sacrifice for sin.

God offered up Jesus Christ as his atoning sacrifice for human sin (Rom 3:21–26). God cannot simply forgive human sin because that would make him unjust. Sin must be punished. For God to simply overlook sin would make him an unrighteous God who is complicit in human sin by allowing it. But God also wanted to have mercy upon sinners. Therefore, he poured out his wrath upon Jesus Christ, who became "an atoning sacrifice in his blood" (Rom 3:25). By punishing Jesus for human sin, God was able to remain just — he punished sin — but also he became the justifier—he declared sinners to be righteous (Rom 3:26).

Through Christ, God gives the gift of righteousness to everyone who believes.

Through the blood of Christ, God offers the gift of righteousness to sinners. This gift is "received through faith" (Rom 3:25). God will declare everyone who believes to be righteous before him. This means two things: First, God will forgive every sin the believer has committed. Second, God will credit Jesus' own perfect righteousness to the believer. As a result, the believer has peace with God (Rom 5:1). Those who believe no longer fear God's judgment because their sin is forgiven (Rom 8:1). But they also have the joy of being adopted into God's family because God treats them as he treats his righteous Son, Jesus Christ (Rom 8:14–17).

The gospel is only believed by God's chosen children.

In Romans 1–3, Paul argues that all have sinned, but anyone can receive the gift of righteousness by faith in Christ. But sinners love their sin. Paul quotes the Old Testament, "There is no one righteous, not even one. There is no one who understands; there is no one who seeks God" (Rom 3:10–11; Pss 14:1–3; 53:1–3). So if people love sin and hate God, how will they ever believe? How would anyone turn from sin they love in order to embrace a God they hate? The prime example of this problem comes from Paul's own nation. The Jewish people have largely rejected the Messiah and are therefore under God's judgment (Rom 9:1–5).

The answer to this dilemma is found in God's choice. Before individuals had done anything right or wrong, God chose those he would save (Rom 9:6–13). His choice was not based on any decision that he foresaw individuals making in the future, or any good works that he foreknew they would do. He made his decision as a free act of his grace toward people who had done nothing to deserve it.

God personally and lovingly foreknew the people that he would save and made the predetermined decision (predestined) to conform these sinners into the image of Christ (Rom 8:29). In his perfect timing, he calls those that he has chosen to faith in Jesus Christ by the miraculous work of the Spirit, and when they respond in faith, he justifies them. Because God's plan for those that he chose was predetermined, he will certainly glorify them, or make them perfectly like Jesus Christ, in the future (Rom 8:30).

The truth of God's free choice gives believers two incredible gifts. First, it causes us to marvel at the undeserved grace of God and to boast in God instead of in anything we are or anything we could do. Second, it strengthens us to face every trial of life because we know God's plan for us will never fail. As Paul writes, "We know that all things work together for the good of those who love God, who are called according to his purpose" (Rom 8:28).

The gospel must be preached to every nation.

Because the gospel is the power of salvation, Paul emphasizes that it must be preached to every nation. It's the mission of his call as an apostle to preach the gospel so that it might be believed among all nations (Rom 1:5). He says, "My aim is to preach the gospel where Christ has not been named" (Rom 15:20). He is eager to get this good news to all the world.

1 Corinthians

Basic Facts
Author: Paul
Original Audience: the Corinth Church
Place Written: Ephesus
Date Written: about A.D. 54

The Main Idea
The people of God should live according to God's wisdom and power in Christ rather than according to the false wisdom of the world.

Structure
- 1:1–9. The Corinth Church is made holy and enriched in Christ.
- 1:10–4:21. But the Corinth Church is divided.
- 5:1–6:20. The Corinth Church also tolerates immorality.
- 7:1–15:58. Paul confronts difficult issues in the church.
  - 7:1–40. Marriage and Singleness: Live according to God's call.
  - 8:1–11:1. Food offered to Idols: Flee from idolatry.
  - 11:2–14:40. Problems in Worship: Men and Women, the Lord's supper, Spiritual Gifts

- 15:1–58. The church is built upon the gospel of the resurrection.
- 16:1–25. Do everything in love.

Big Events & Ideas

God's church must live according to God's wisdom and power.

The crucified Christ is a stumbling block to the Jews and foolishness to the gentiles, but "to those who are called, both Jews and Greeks, Christ is the power of God and the wisdom of God" (1 Cor 1:24). God's wisdom is not recognized by the wisdom of the world. Paul confesses that his preaching was "not with persuasive words of wisdom but with a demonstration of the Spirit's power" (1 Cor 2:4). Faith in Christ is a rejection of the wisdom of the world and an acceptance of the wisdom of God that is revealed in Christ (1 Cor 2:10–16). Therefore, God's people live fundamentally different lives from the people around them.

God's church shouldn't allow division and immorality.

But the Corinth Church has failed to live according to the wisdom of God. Instead, they have continued to operate according to the world's wisdom, even though they belong to God. Because of this, the church has been infected with division and immorality. They have imitated worldly politics by dividing into parties that claim to follow different personalities (1 Cor 3:4), and they have accepted levels of immorality that are "not even tolerated among the gentiles" (1 Cor 5:1). Paul, therefore, exhorts the Corinth Church to abandon worldly thinking and embrace godly wisdom, which will bring unity to the church and will lead them to holy living.

God's church is one body with many parts.

God's church is one body with many diverse parts (1 Cor 12:12). Every disciple of Jesus is united with every other disciple through faith in the gospel and the experience of the Holy Spirit. But this unity does not make everyone identical. The Holy Spirit has given different gifts to different believers for the common good of the church: a message of wisdom, a message of knowledge, faith, healing, miracles, prophecy, distinguishing spirits, tongues, and interpretation of tongues (1 Cor 12:7–11).

These various gifts are meant for the common good of the church, not for the self-promotion of the person with the gift. Paul accuses the Corinth Church of desiring miraculous gifts, like tongues, over gifts that are more beneficial to the church, like prophetic teaching (1 Cor 14:3–5). Every spiritual gift must be used out of love, which seeks the good of others (1 Cor 13). Love unifies the diverse body of Christ. So Paul closes his letter with the command, "Do everything in love" (1 Cor 16:14).

The worship of God's church must be orderly and unified.

In Corinth, the weekly worship gathering had become a competition for each person to display their superior spiritual gifts. Everyone wants to contribute, which results in people talking simultaneously and causing confusion (1 Cor 14:25–22). Similarly, when they gather for the Lord's supper, the rich arrive first and leave no food for the poorer brothers and sisters (1 Cor 11:17–26). By eating the Lord's supper in this divisive way, they actually contradict the meaning of the Lord's supper, which shows the unity of the church in faith in Christ. The worship of God's church must be orderly and unified because this reflects the character of God himself and the true character of God's church.

What were the gifts of prophecy and tongues, and do they continue in the church today?

The prophecies in 1 Corinthians are revelations communicated to God's people through the Holy Spirit (1 Cor 14:29–30; see also Acts 11:27–28; 13:2; 21:10–11). In the New Testament period, these prophecies are essential to protect the church from false teachers and to guide the church to godly action while the New Testament is still being written. Today, there is no group of people who can offer authoritative prophecies without error. Sometimes the Holy Spirit gives churches impressions of his leadership, but this should not be confused with the authoritative prophecy without error that was received in New Testament times.

Like in Acts 2:4–11, 10:46, and 19:6, the gift of speaking in tongues in 1 Corinthians 12–14 is speaking in a human language the speaker has never learned, but while in Acts 2 there were people present who could hear and understand the different languages, in 1 Corinthians, translation is necessary because the people present could not understand the different languages. The gift of speaking in tongues in the New Testament is very different from what is seen in many churches today. It was speaking earthly languages that were able to be interpreted instead of the wild jabbering that occurs in many churches today.

Why have these gifts ceased? Ephesians 2:20 says that the church is "built on the foundation of the apostles and prophets with Jesus himself as the cornerstone." The apostles who had witnessed Jesus' resurrection and the New Testament prophets were both special groups of people who were used by God to build the foundation of the church. With the completion of the foundation, these gifts began to be less prevalent. Similarly, gifts like tongues, healing, and miracles were more prominent at the foundation of the church in order to demonstrate the power of the gospel. Today these gifts have all but ceased (except possibly in pioneer missionary work) because they were not meant to be a normal part of worship in churches.

2 Corinthians

Basic Facts
Author: Paul
Original Audience: the Corinth Church
Place Written: the Province of Macedonia, possibly from the city of Philippi
Date Written: about A.D. 56

The Main Idea
The people of God demonstrate God's glory and power through weakness and affliction.

Structure
- **1:1–7:16. Paul the Apostle shows God's glory through affliction.**
  - 1:1–2:11. Paul explains his change in travel plans.
  - 2:12–6:13. Paul is a minister of the new covenant.
  - 6:14–7:16. Paul begs the Corinth Church to reject the super-apostles.
- **8:1–9:15. Give because of God's gift!**
- **10:1–13:14. Paul the Apostle is made strong through weakness.**
  - 10:1–12:13. Paul defends his weakness as an apostle.

- 12:14–13:14. Paul appeals to the Corinth church to become mature in faith.

Big Events & Ideas

Super-Apostles operate according to the world's wisdom.

In 2 Corinthians, Paul is defending himself. False teachers, whom Paul calls "super-apostles," have infiltrated the church (2 Cor 11:5; 12:11). These men boasted that their speaking skills and knowledge made them superior to Paul, and therefore the Corinth church should follow them. But Paul says that these men offer a different Jesus, a different spirit, and a different gospel (2 Cor 11:4). These men are obsessed with glory and power, which contradicts the gospel of a suffering Christ.

True apostleship is seen in affliction and weakness.

Paul compares gospel ministers to simple clay jars that surprisingly hold treasure (2 Cor 4:7). Paul's suffering as an apostle demonstrates visibly the beautiful gospel of Christ (2 Cor 4:8–10). The super-apostles wrongly seek their glory in this life. Paul explains that his afflictions are only "momentary" and are producing for him "an absolutely incomparable eternal weight of glory" (2 Cor 4:17). In the same way, Paul has learned to boast in his weakness because God manifests his power through Paul's weakness (2 Cor 12:9). Paul says, "For when I am weak, then I am strong" (2 Cor 12:10).

Gospel ministry is the ministry of the new covenant.

Paul says that God "has made us competent to be ministers of a new covenant, not of the letter, but of the Spirit" (2 Cor 3:6). The new covenant was foretold in Jeremiah 31 and Ezekiel 36. God promised through the prophets to transform his people, and by changing their hearts, God would cause his people to obey him. God would truly be their God, and they would be his people. Paul explicitly identifies his ministry as bringing this end-time prophecy to pass.

Under the old covenant, the people of Israel saw the reflected and fading glory of God on Moses' face, but under the new covenant, "we all, with unveiled faces, are looking as in a mirror at the glory of the Lord and are being transformed into the same image from glory to glory" (2 Cor 3:18). Through this superior revelation of God in Christ, we also have experienced a superior fellowship with God. Under the old covenant, God dwelled with Israel in an earthly tent, but under the new covenant, we will dwell with God forever (2 Cor 5:1–10). This is possible because through the new covenant sacrifice of Jesus Christ God has reconciled us to himself (2 Cor 5:16–21).

The New Testament

Galatians

Basic Facts
Author: Paul
Original Audience: churches in Galatia (south-central Turkey today)
Place Written: possibly Antioch
Date Written: about A.D. 48–52

The Main Idea
Do not turn away from God's gospel, which proclaims adoption into Abraham's family through faith in Christ!

Structure
- 1:1–2:21. Paul preaches God's gospel, not a human gospel.
- 3:1–4:11. God's gospel proclaims adoption into Abraham's family through faith in Christ.
- 4:12–6:10. Through God's gospel, we are free to live by the Spirit.
- 6:11–18. Summary: Paul boasts in the cross, not circumcision.

Big Events & Ideas

Do not accept a different gospel!

Paul writes to the Galatians because he has heard they are turning to a different gospel, which is not the true gospel of God, and he wants to warn them not to abandon the gospel he preached (Gal 1:6–9). The different gospel of the false teachers claims that gentiles must be circumcised to belong to the family of Abraham. Paul identifies this as a misunderstanding of what Jesus accomplished on the cross.

The requirements of the law, like circumcision, were never meant to bring salvation. Instead, they brought humanity under God's curse because people can never perfectly obey the law (Gal 3:10). Christ fulfilled the requirements of the law for us by bearing the curse of the law on our behalf. God declares people righteous on the basis of their faith in Christ alone. If anyone tries to add a human requirement to the gospel of salvation by faith, they create a completely different gospel that does not have the power to save.

God's people are adopted into Abraham's family through faith in Christ.

The false gospel claims that people become part of Abraham's family by circumcision. Paul demonstrates from the Old Testament that Abraham was justified by faith, not through circumcision. He writes, "You know, then, that those who have faith, these are Abraham's sons" (Gal 3:7). We belong to Abraham's covenant family when we believe in Abraham's offspring, Jesus Christ (Gal 3:25–26), and God has given us his Spirit, which testifies to our adoption as sons and heirs of God (Gal 4:1–7).

God's people have been freed from the present, evil age and belong to the new creation.

Jesus' death and resurrection has not only made a way for the gentiles to come to God. Christ has fundamentally changed the universe. Through his death, Christ has rescued us "from this present evil age" (Gal 1:4). We were formerly enslaved to sin, and were therefore condemned under God's law (Gal 4:3). But now we belong to the new creation through faith in Christ, and we are already experiencing the freedom of the new creation through the Spirit that dwells within us (Gal 4:1–7; 5:1; 6:15). As believers, we must stand firm in this freedom by living according to the Spirit instead of following the ways of our flesh, which belong to the present, evil age from which we have been freed (Gal 5).

Live by the Spirit and bear the fruit of the Spirit.

We have been freed from this age and belong to the new creation, but we continue to live in this fallen world. Therefore, we experience conflict between the desires of our flesh and the leadership of the Holy Spirit within us (Gal 5:17). We must resist the habits that come naturally to us, which belong to our flesh or our old, earthly way of life in the world. We must instead follow the leadership of the Spirit, and he will produce in us the fruit of the Spirit. The fruit of the Spirit consists of godly character traits. The most important of these is love. The Spirit leads us to live in a way that pleases God, and therefore, "the law is not against such things" (Gal 5:21).

The New Testament

Ephesians

Basic Facts
Author: Paul
Original Audience: churches in Ephesus and the surrounding region
Place Written: Rome
Date Written: about A.D. 62

The Main Idea
God has richly lavished grace on his people through Jesus Christ, who is greater than any power.

Structure
- **1:1–3:21. God has richly lavished grace on his people in Christ.**
  - 1:1–2:10. God has shown his people grace in Christ.
  - 2:11–3:13. In his people, God has revealed his mysterious wisdom.
  - 3:14–21. Paul responds to grace with prayer and praise.
- **4:1–6:20. Live worthy of this calling by the Spirit.**
  - 4:1–3. The Principle: Live worthy of the calling.
  - 4:4–16. Every church member has a gift to use to build up the body.
  - 4:17–5:21. Live the new life that God has given.

- 5:22–6:9. Live this new life in your family relationships.
- 6:10–24. Engage in the spiritual battle by prayer.

Big Events & Ideas

God has richly lavished grace on his people through Jesus Christ.

Paul begins this letter by praising God, "who has blessed us with every spiritual blessing in the heavens in Christ" (Eph 1:3). God began his work of showing grace towards believers by choosing them before the creation of the world and predestining them to become part of his family. To accomplish these plans, God paid the redemption price of his people with the blood of his Son, made us his children and heirs, and caused this good news to be proclaimed.

From the human point of view, the story begins with death. Paul writes, "And you were dead in your trespasses and sins" (Eph 2:1). We were under the wrath of God. "But God, who is rich in mercy, because of his great love that he had for us, made us alive with Christ even though we were dead in trespasses" (Eph 2:4–5). But not only has the believer been raised from spiritual death, God also "seated us with him in the heavens in Christ Jesus" (Eph 2:6). Paul summarizes, "For you are saved by grace through faith, and this is not from yourselves; it is God's gift" (Eph 2:8).

Christ is greater than any power on earth.

Our unity with Christ through faith frees us from the powers on earth we might fear. Ephesus was a center of powerful witchcraft. When Paul was in Ephesus, many people confessed their demonic practices, and "many of those who had practiced magic collected their books and burned them in front of everyone" (Acts 19:18–19). The value of these books was calculated as fifty thousand pieces of silver (Acts 19:19). So its not surprising that in his letter to the same people he emphasizes the superior power of Jesus Christ. God has exercised his power through the resurrection of Christ, and has seated Christ "far above every ruler and authority, power and dominion, and every title given"

(Eph 1:20–21). And it is this power of God that strengthens believers "through his Spirit" (Eph 3:16). Paul praises God because he "is able to do above and beyond all that we ask or think according to the power that works in us" (Eph 3:20).

God has a specific design for his church that reveals his wisdom.

In Ephesians, Paul focuses on how God's power is seen through his specific design of the church. God has created one people from Jews and gentiles, who were once enemies, and by doing this, "God's multi-faceted wisdom may now be made known through the church to the rulers and authorities in the heavens" (Eph 3:11). But the members of God's united church remain unique and different according to God's design. The church is unified, but God has given to each individual in the church different gifts (Eph 4:4–7). He has given the church leaders, like pastor-teachers, who have the task of "equipping the saints for the work of ministry, to build up the body of Christ" (Eph 4:10–12). The church works well when each individual part is working properly to support the entire body in love (Eph 4:16).

God's grace changes our family relationships.

As we live out the new life we have received through faith in Christ, we begin to see our lives change. Nowhere do we see more clear change than in our family relationships. Paul explains that God has a specific design for the family, and we experience joy when we live according to his design. Wives are to submit to their husbands like the church does to Christ (Eph 5:22–24), and husbands are to love their wives sacrificially like Christ loved the church (Eph 5:25–33). Children should obey their parents (Eph 6:1–3). Parents should be careful not to stir up anger in their children, but instead should "bring them up in the training and instruction of the Lord" (Eph 6:4–5).

We engage in the spiritual battle around us through prayer.

As we live our new life in Christ, we must remember that "our struggle is not against flesh and blood but against the rulers, against the authorities, against the cosmic powers of this darkness, against evil, spiritual forces in the heavens" (Eph 6:12). The temptations we face and the conflicts we find ourselves in are part of a spiritual battle that is being waged all around us. Yet the demonic forces aligned against us should not fill us with fear. God has given us everything we need to enjoy the victory he has won in Christ. Paul describes these gifts as armor — truth, righteousness, the gospel, faith, salvation, and the word of God (Eph 6:13–17). We utilize these gifts in the battle through prayer. He commands, "Pray at all times in the Spirit" (Eph 6:18). By making our needs known to God, God will give us the victory we need over every demonic power.

Philippians

Basic Facts
Author: Paul
Original Audience: the Philippi Church
Place Written: Rome
Date Written: about A.D. 62

The Main Idea
Followers of Jesus should live their life worthy of the gospel.

Structure
- 1:1–30. Live worthy of the gospel.
- 2:1–30. Christ gives the example of how to live worthy of the gospel.
- 3:1–4:1. Knowing Christ is the goal of living worthy of the gospel.
- 4:2–20. Christ supplies what we need to live worthy of the gospel.

Big Events & Ideas
To live is Christ. To die is gain.

Paul writes from prison as he awaits the verdict that will determine if he lives or dies. But Paul is not afraid. If he lives, he will work for Christ among the churches he has planted, but if he dies, he actually gets to be in the presence of Christ, "which is far better" (Phil 1:21–26). Paul commands the Philippi church to follow his example: "As citizens of heaven, live your life worthy of the gospel of Christ" (Phil 1:27). They should dedicate themselves to serving Jesus, and like Paul, they shouldn't be afraid. If they suffer for Christ, it is a gift that God has given to them (Phil 1:29).

Christ gives us the example of humility.

If we are going to live worthy of the gospel, then we must become like Christ himself. Paul says, "Adopt the same attitude as that of Christ Jesus" (Phil 2:5). Jesus was God the Son and equal with God the Father, but he "emptied himself by assuming the form of a servant," becoming a man (Phil 2:7). He humbled himself to the point of dying on the cross. Because of his humility, God raised him up and "highly exalted him" to the highest place in the universe (Phil 2:9–10). If Christ could humble himself in such an incredible way, then we, as his people, should also be known for our humility.

Timothy and Epaphroditus serve as real life examples of Christ-like humility. Paul's co-laborer Timothy has served the Philippi church faithfully and put their interests before his own (Phil 2:19–24). Epaphroditus was a member of the Philippi church who brought a gift from the church to Paul in prison. On the journey, he became so sick that he nearly died, demonstrating his commitment to the work of Jesus (Phil 2:25–30).

Knowing Christ is our goal.

To live worthy of the gospel, we must live lives focused on knowing Jesus Christ. Paul explains that everything he believed to be valuable before he knew Christ became worthless to him once he met Jesus (Phil 3:7). He writes, "More than that, I also consider everything to be a loss in view of the surpassing value of knowing Christ Jesus, my Lord" (Phil 3:8). Paul's goal is "to know him and the power of his resurrection and the fellowship of his sufferings" (Phil 3:10). Following Christ is not about knowing the right answers about Jesus or doing the right things. Following Christ is about knowing and loving Jesus Christ himself.

Christ supplies what we need in every situation.

As we live worthy of the gospel, we depend upon Christ to supply every need. Paul instructs the church to not worry about anything, but to take their needs before God through prayer. When we do this, God will give us "the peace of God, which surpasses all understanding" (Phil 4:7). Paul explains that because of Christ, he has learned to be content in every circumstance — "whether well-fed or hungry, whether in abundance or in need" (Phil 4:12). Jesus is enough. While he may not save us from every trial, he will strengthen us to endure our trials in a way that glorifies him (Phil 4:13).

The New Testament

Colossians

Basic Facts
Author: Paul
Original Audience: the Colossae Church
Place Written: Rome
Date Written: about A.D. 62

The Main Idea
We have hope because Christ is above all things and our life is secure with him.

Structure
- **1:1–2:23. Christ is above all things.**
  - 1:1–14. Paul thanks God for what he has done in the Colossae church.
  - 1:15–2:3. Christ is above all things and believers are united with him.
  - 2:4–23. Christ is better than human religion.
- **3:1–4:18. Live the life that is secured in Christ above.**
  - 3:1–17. Christ has secured a life that is above.
  - 3:18–4:18. The life above gives us wisdom in every area of life.

The New Testament

Big Events & Ideas

Christ is above all things.

Christ "is the image of the invisible God" and "the firstborn over all creation" (Col 1:15). This means that he is superior to every created thing, which makes sense because he created all things. "He is before all things and by him all things hold together" (Col 1:17). There is no higher power or authority than Christ. No spirit or magical skill even comes close to his sovereign power. Therefore, we must not seek any other power but Christ. By his death, Christ paid for our sins and "disarmed the rulers and authorities and disgraced them publicly" (Col 2:15).

Our life is secure in him.

Christ is in us, and he gives us "the hope of glory" (Col 1:27). Our relationship with Christ guarantees to us eternal life and our future glorification with him. We should not fear anything because Christ is seated at the right hand of God in heaven, and our life "is hidden with Christ in God" (Col 3:3). So Paul commands, "Set your minds on things above, not on earthly things" (Col 3:2). This means killing our sinful desires such as "sexual immorality, impurity, lust, evil desire, and greed" (Col 3:5), and putting on godly character — "compassion, kindness, humility, gentleness, and patience" (Col 3:12).

Sing to God

One way we set our minds on things above is by singing. Paul writes, "Let the word of Christ dwell richly among you, in all wisdom teaching and admonishing one another through psalms, hymns, and spiritual songs, singing to God with gratitude in your hearts" (Col 3:16). Paul teaches here that singing is an important part of worship in the church. When we sing, we sing both as a way to give thanks to God and as a way to teach and admonish one another. Therefore, the songs we choose are important. The songs we sing should contain the truth of the Bible set to music so we are truly obeying the command to "let the word of Christ dwell richly among you" (Col 3:16).

The New Testament

1 Thessalonians

Basic Facts
Author: Paul
Original Audience: the Thessalonica Church
Place Written: Corinth
Date Written: about A.D. 50–51

The Main Idea
God will continue to work in his people through his powerful word until he perfects them.

Structure
- 1:1–3:13. God continues to work in the Thessalonians through his word.
- 4:1–5:22. Live according to God's word.
- 5:23–28. God will continue and complete his work among the Thessalonians.

Big Events & Ideas

God accomplishes his work through his powerful word.

Paul was forced to leave the Thessalonica church only a short time after planting it due to persecution (1 Thess 2:17; see Acts 17:1–9). Because Paul did not have the extended time needed to teach and firmly established the church, they have a lot of misunderstandings about Paul's teachings, especially concerning the second coming of Christ. Paul tries to provide for them the teaching they need through his two letters to the Thessalonica church.

He also wants to reassure them that persecution, which had forced Paul out of the city and which the church is still enduring, will not stop God's work. God does his work through the power of his word. When Paul first preached in Thessalonica, he says, "Our gospel did not come to you in word only, but also in power, in the Holy Spirit, and with full assurance" (1 Thess 1:5). Even though there was opposition and persecution, the church "received the word of God" not as a human message but "as it truly is, the word of God" (1 Thess 2:13).

God has planned the persecution of his people.

Persecution could not stop the power of God's word. But even more than that, God planned the persecution of his people for his good purposes. Paul writes, "For you yourselves know that we are appointed to this" (1 Thess 3:3). Paul warned them in person that this would be the case (1 Thess 3:4). This doesn't mean that the human persecutors (1 Thess 2:14–16), or Satan who inspires such persecution (1 Thess 2:18), are free from guilt for their actions against God's churches. It does mean that God even uses their evil actions to accomplish his good plans for his people.

Jesus will return for his people and God will perfect them.

God's ultimate plan for his people is their perfection. Paul prays that God will make the church "blameless in holiness before our God and Father at the coming of our Lord Jesus with all his saints" (1 Thess 3:13; 5:23). Paul prays this prayer with absolute confidence: "He who calls you is faithful; he will do it" (1 Thess 5:24). God has begun his work in the church, and he will absolutely finish it!

God will finish his work when Jesus returns from heaven. At that time, followers of Jesus who have died will be resurrected, and those who remain alive will also meet Jesus in glory (1 Thess 4:13–18). This gives us hope. We will not experience God's wrath against sin, because we have salvation through Jesus! Nevertheless, we must remain alert and always ready for Christ's return (1 Thess 5:1–11).

The New Testament

2 Thessalonians

Basic Facts
Author: Paul
Original Audience: the Thessalonica Church
Place Written: Corinth
Date Written: about A.D. 50–51

The Main Idea
We must live in expectation of Jesus' return.

Structure
- 1:1–12. God will judge justly on the day of the Lord.
- 2:1–17. The day of the Lord has not come yet.
- 3:1–18. Live in expectation of Jesus' return.

Big Events & Ideas

Live in expectation of Jesus' return.

Jesus' return should transform the way believers live in the world. First, it enables believers to endure persecution. When Jesus returns, God will reward his suffering people, but he will also "repay with affliction those who afflict you" (2

Thess 1:5–6). "They will pay the penalty of eternal destruction from the Lord's presence and from his glorious strength" (2 Thess 1:9).

Second, Jesus' return informs how believers should work. Some in Thessalonica thought that since Jesus' return was coming soon, they didn't need to work and provide for their families (2 Thess 3:6–11). Paul warns against this idleness, and says that the Lord Jesus commands them "to work quietly and provide for themselves" (2 Thess 3:12).

The man of lawlessness will come before Jesus' return.

Some believers in Thessalonica had heard that the day of the Lord had already come (2 Thess 2:2), and so they were confused about the second coming of Christ. Paul explains that certain events must take place before Jesus' return. There will be an "apostasy," or a falling away from the truth (2 Thess 2:3). This will happen because a "man of lawlessness" will be revealed. This mysterious individual will oppose God and exalt himself as a god (2 Thess 2:4). This person, called the antichrist in the writings of the apostle John (see 1 John 2:18, 22; 4:3; 2 John 7), will be empowered by Satan to do false miracles, and will be allowed to deceive the world (2 Thess 2:5–10). But even this is part of God's plan. This apostasy will give further evidence of the justice of God's wrath against the world (2 Thess 2:11–12), and thus the man of lawlessness and the apostasy are necessary to prepare the way for Christ's return.

1 Timothy

Basic Facts
Author: Paul
Original Audience: Timothy, located in Ephesus
Place Written: the region of Macedonia, possibly the city of Philippi
Date Written: about A.D. 62–64

The Main Idea
Leaders must fight for the faith by defending it from false teaching and guarding themselves from worldly motives.

Structure
- 1:1–20. Defend the faith from false teaching.
- 2:1–3:16. The godly church protects the truth of the gospel.
- 4:1–16. Defending the faith starts with guarding yourself.
- 5:1–6:2. Defending the faith happens by honoring everyone in the church.
- 6:3–21. Defending the faith starts with guarding yourself from worldly motives.

Big Events & Ideas

Leaders must fight against false teaching.

Paul had left Timothy in Macedonia in order to "instruct certain people not to teach false doctrine" (1 Tim 3:3). The Ephesus church had suffered greatly from false teaching, which turned people away from the truth of the gospel. Paul had warned the Ephesian pastors that this would happen (see Acts 20:29–31). Paul emphasizes that the power and unity of the church comes from the truth of its teaching, and when we depart this teaching, then we depart from God himself.

A godly church is made up of godly men and women.

A godly church loves true teaching. False doctrine infiltrates the church through people with evil motives, such as desire for power or money. A godly church is made up of godly men and women. Paul recognizes that men and women have unique temptations. Men tend to be tempted to anger and conflict, but the way to resist the temptation to anger is by praying constantly and expressing our frustrations to God (1 Tim 2:8).

Women are tempted to find their worth through their bodies, and so they dress in ways that draw attention to their beauty. Paul tells them to find their beauty in godliness and good works (1 Tim 2:9–10). Women are also tempted to seek to exercise authority in the church. Paul says, "I do not allow a woman to teach or to have authority over a man" (1 Tim 2:12). Even though women are not called by God to be pastors, women have a beautiful role to play in the family and the church. Paul says they "will be saved through childbearing, if they continue in faith, love, and holiness, with good sense" (1 Tim 2:15). This does not mean that women are actually saved by having babies, but by living faithfully for God by embracing their calling as mothers, both as physical mothers to their own children and as spiritual mothers to orphans, younger women in the church, and those in need.

A godly church is led by godly pastors and deacons.

Paul gives Timothy qualifications for godly pastors (which he calls overseers in this instance) and deacons. When the leadership of the church is not godly, then the church itself will be corrupted. Paul requires pastors to "be above reproach" (1 Tim 3:2). He then lists characteristics of a man who is above reproach (1 Tim 3:2–7). Similarly, deacons must "be worthy of respect" (1 Tim 3:8–12). Without leaders of good character, the church tarnishes its witness to the world and threatens its devotion to the truth.

The New Testament

2 Timothy

Basic Facts
Author: Paul
Original Audience: Timothy, located in Ephesus
Place Written: Rome
Date Written: about A.D. 66–67

The Main Idea
Leaders must guard the faith against false teaching with the powerful word of God, even while suffering.

Structure
- 1:1–2:13. Guard the faith without fear.
- 2:14–3:9. Guard the faith against false teaching.
- 3:10–4:22. Guard the faith with the powerful word of God.

Big Events & Ideas
Do not fear suffering.

Timothy was tempted to allow fear to compromise his ministry. Paul reminds Timothy, "For God has not given us a spirit of fear, but one of power, love, and sound judgment" (2 Tim 1:7). Timothy should imitate Paul's fearlessness and should even "share in suffering for the gospel, relying on the power of God" (2 Tim 1:9). Even when we suffer in this world for the gospel, God's purposes can never fail. He will save and establish his people forever.

All Scripture is inspired by God, so preach the word.

Paul reminds Timothy that "all Scripture is inspired by God" (2 Tim 3:16a). This means that it is "profitable for teaching, for rebuking, for correcting, for training in righteousness" (2 Tim 3:16b). The power of Timothy's ministry comes from the power of the word of God to work in God's people. Therefore, Paul commands Timothy to "preach the word" (2 Tim 4:2). By preaching the word, Timothy will "rebuke, correct, and encourage" God's people (2 Tim 4:2). Sometimes the preaching of the word is "in season" and sometimes we preach and do not see a harvest (2 Tim 4:2). But even when people refuse to listen to God's word, and instead seek teachers who will tell them what they want to hear, the preaching of God's word must never be abandoned. The preaching of God's word is the primary task of the pastor, no matter how the world responds.

Finish the race.

This was the last letter Paul wrote before he was beheaded around A.D. 67. Paul tells Timothy, "I have fought the good fight, I have finished the race, I have kept the faith" (2 Tim 4:7). While this is a clear expression of Paul's commitment to Christ until death, it also stood as an example for Timothy. Timothy and every other Christian should seek to remain faithful to Christ until the end. The reward for our faithfulness should keep us focused on Christ. Paul writes, "There is reserved for me the crown of righteousness, which the Lord, the righteous judge, will give me on that day, and not only to me, but to all those who have loved his appearing" (2 Tim 4:8).

Titus

Basic Facts
Author: Paul
Original Audience: Titus, located in Crete
Place Written: the region of Macedonia, possibly the city of Nicopolis
Date Written: about A.D. 62–64

The Main Idea
Leaders must teach sound teaching because it leads to godly living.

Structure
- 1:1–16. Godly leaders protect the church from false teaching.
- 2:1–15. Godly leaders should teach all kinds of people because God saves them all.
- 3:1–15. Godly leaders never forget their own salvation.

Big Events & Ideas
Godly pastors teach and protect the church.

Paul left Titus on the island of Crete to appoint pastors (also called overseers and elders) in each church. Paul describes the task of these pastors: They must "be able both to encourage with sound teaching and to refute those who contradict it" (Tit 1:9). Because of this, these men must be "blameless" (Tit 1:6). Their lives must reflect the truth they teach. Paul explains that the false teachers on Crete do not posses such blamelessness. "They claim to know God, but they deny him by their works" (Tit 1:16). Why do such wicked people seek to teach in the church? They do it "in order to get money dishonestly" (Tit 1:11). Godly pastors, however, live the message they teach.

Teach all kinds of people because God saves them all.

Even though Titus must appoint leaders, Paul tells him to teach all kinds of people. He gives him specific instruction for men and women, young and old, slave and free (Tit 2:1–10). Paul explains that Titus must teach all kinds of people because "the grace of God has appeared, bringing salvation for all people" (Tit 2:11). God's salvation is not only for men, or for the old, or for the wealthy. It's for every type of person. Through God's grace, everyone who believes learns "to deny godlessness and worldly lusts" and to live a godly life (Tit 2:12). The sound teaching of the gospel should lead every type of person to live a godly life.

Never forget your own salvation.

The Cretans had a reputation for wickedness (Tit 1:12). But Paul challenges Titus to avoid seeing himself as superior to the people to whom he ministered. He writes, "For we too were once foolish, disobedient, deceived, enslaved to various passions and pleasures" (Tit 3:3). Even though Paul and Titus were once sinners, God saved them, and in the same way he can save and transform the Cretans. God can save anyone, and this truth of salvation should cause us all to devote ourselves to good works (Tit 3:8).

Philemon

Basic Facts
Author: Paul
Original Audience: Philemon along with Apphia, Archippus, and the Colossae Church
Place Written: Rome
Date Written: about A.D. 62

The Main Idea
Our relationship to Christ transforms every other relationship we have.

Structure
- 1–7. Philemon is a dear friend and coworker in the gospel.
- 8–20. In Christ, the slave becomes a brother.
- 21–25. Paul is confident that Philemon will obey his wish for the slave's freedom.

The New Testament

Big Events & Ideas

Our relationship to Christ transforms every other relationship we have.

Philemon is a personal letter from Paul to a dear friend in Colossae, but the truth of the letter applies to every Christian. Philemon's slave, Onesimus, ran away, but when Onesimus came to Rome, Paul shared the gospel with him. Onesimus became a follower of Jesus. Paul explains the situation to Philemon, "For perhaps this is why he was separated from you for a brief time, so that you might get him back permanently, no longer as a slave, but more than a slave—as a dearly loved brother" (Phm 15–16). Since Onesimus and Philemon were now brothers in Christ, Paul insists that Philemon free Onesimus from slavery, and asks him to consider sending Onesimus back to Paul to assist him. We, too, must treat fellow believers as brothers in Christ, and this will transform our relationships within our family, workplace, and community.

Hebrews

Basic Facts
Author: Unknown
Original Audience: Jewish Christians in the churches in Rome
Place Written: Unknown
Date Written: about A.D. 60–70

The Main Idea
Continue in faith and don't turn back to the old covenant because Jesus is better.

Structure
- 1:1–2:18. Jesus is greater than the angels.
- 3:1–4:13. Jesus is greater than Moses.
- 4:14–7:28. Jesus is the greater high priest.
- 8:1–10:18. Jesus mediates a greater covenant.
- 10:19–13:25. Continue in faith and don't turn back.

Big Events & Ideas

Jesus is better.

The book of Hebrews is a written sermon that explains how Jesus fulfilled the promises of the Old Testament. Due to persecution, some of the Jewish Christians in the churches in and around Rome have been tempted to turn away from Jesus as the Messiah, and to go back to the sacrifices instructed in the Old Testament. Hebrews encourages them to remain faithful to Jesus because he is vastly superior to the old covenant. Jesus is greater than angels (Heb 1:4) and greater than Moses (Heb 3:3). He is our "great high priest" (Heb 4:14) who offers a greater sacrifice (Heb 9:14) and mediates a greater covenant (Heb 8:6). All these things were only shadows of what God sent in Jesus Christ (Heb 8:5; 10:1).

Jesus sympathizes with our weaknesses.

Even though Jesus is a superior Savior and sacrifice, he is also sympathetic to our weaknesses. To become our Savior, Jesus "had to be like his brothers and sisters in every way, so that he could become a merciful and faithful high priest in matters pertaining to God, to make atonement for the sins of the people" (Heb 2:17). Because he became like us, he is able to help us when we face temptation: "For since he himself has suffered when he was tempted, he is able to help those who are tempted" (Heb 2:18; see Heb 4:15).

Because of the sympathy of Jesus as our high priest, we can "approach the throne of grace with boldness, so that we may receive mercy and find grace to help us in time of need" (Heb 4:15–16). In Christ, God draws us near to himself in kindness and love.

Jesus is the greater high priest who offered himself as a greater sacrifice.

The sacrifices that the law of Moses instructed Israel to perform could never truly atone for sin. Hebrews says, "For it is impossible for the blood of bulls and goats to take away sins" (Heb 10:4). God gave these instructions as a shadow of the heavenly things (Heb 8:5). These sacrifices pointed forward to the perfect sacrifice of Jesus for sins. Jesus is both the high priest who stands between humans and God and the sacrifice that is offered for human sin. Because Jesus' sacrifice has been completed, the old covenant sacrifices are no longer necessary.

Continue in faith, and don't turn back.

By reminding these Jewish Christians about the superiority of Jesus, Hebrews encourages them to persevere in faith in Christ. Hebrews says, "But we are not those who draw back and are destroyed, but those who have faith and are saved" (Heb 10:39). Hebrews repeatedly warns believers not to abandon Jesus (Heb 2:1–4; 3:7–4:13; 6:1–8; 10:26–39). These warnings are like signs protecting God's people from danger. True believers persevere in their faith for two reasons: First, true believers will listen to God's warnings in the book, and second God will lovingly discipline them as his children (Heb 12:3–11).

While God's warnings push us to persevere in faith, God's promises pull us toward the joys of faith. Hebrews repeatedly reminds us of the promises of God: God promises us rest (Heb 4:10). He promises a city he has built and a homeland (Heb 11:10, 14). He promises us "a kingdom that cannot be shaken" (Heb 12:28).[8]

The New Testament

James

Basic Facts
Author: James, the brother of Jesus and pastor of the Jerusalem Church
Original Audience: Christians who were scattered by persecution, possibly from Jerusalem
Place Written: probably Jerusalem
Date Written: about A.D. 40–45

The Main Idea
Joyfully endure every trial because trials test the quality of your faith.

Structure
- 1:1–18. Consider it a great joy when trials test your faith.
- 1:19–2:26. Faith without works is dead.
- 3:1–5:12. Everyday life tests your faith.
- 5:13–18. Faith is demonstrated through prayer.
- 5:19–20. Bring back those who wander from the truth.

Big Events & Ideas

Consider it a great joy when trials test your faith.

James announces his main idea clearly at the beginning of his letter. He wants Christians to endure their trials with joy because trials test the quality of their faith (Jas 1:2–4). James writes to people who have fled from persecution (possibly the persecution described in Acts 8:1–4). Life has been hard, and it is easy in those times to believe that suffering happens because God is punishing us. But James teaches that the Christian suffers as a test. True faith in Christ endures the test of suffering, while false faith will not pass the test. Even the demons believe in God (Jas 2:19), but true, saving faith is accompanied by works (Jas 2:8–26). While works do not save us, they are the evidence of genuine faith in Christ.

Live according to God's wisdom.

The letter of James is like a New Testament book of Proverbs. It contains wisdom about many topics in life, and it isn't always clear how the author has organized these different topics. James begins by ensuring his readers that God wants to give them wisdom. All they must do is ask in faith (Jas 1:5–8). Wisdom is not having the right solution to every problem. True wisdom is loving our neighbors. James writes, "But the wisdom from above is first pure, then peace-loving, gentle, compliant, full of mercy and good fruits, unwavering, without pretense" (Jas 3:17). Such wisdom is evident in the way we speak (Jas 3:1–12) and in the way we deal with conflict (Jas 4:1–11). It is also evident in the humble way we respond to God's word. "But be doers of the word and not hearers only, deceiving yourselves" (Jas 1:22).

Not many should become teachers.

James warns his readers against desiring to become a teacher or pastor. "Not many should become teachers, my brothers, because you know that we will receive a stricter judgment" (Jas 3:1). Many people desire positions of leadership in the church because they see church leadership as a pathway to fame, power, or money, but with greater responsibilities in the church comes a greater level of accountability to God. No one should pursue the position of pastor-teacher in the church apart from God's gifting and calling.

The New Testament

1 Peter

Basic Facts
Author: Peter, the former fisherman and disciple
Original Audience: churches in Asia Minor (Pontus, Galatia, Cappadocia, Asia, Bithynia)
Place Written: Rome
Date Written: about A.D. 62–63

The Main Idea
Live in the hope of your salvation in the midst of this hostile world.

Structure
- 1:1–2:10. God's chosen people possess an imperishable inheritance.
- 2:11–4:11. God's chosen people live differently from the world.
- 4:12–5:14. God's chosen people endure suffering from the world.

Big Events & Ideas

Live in the hope of your salvation.

Peter begins by reminding his readers that God has given them "new birth into a living hope through the resurrection of Jesus Christ from the dead" (1 Pet

1:3). This hope is an inheritance that they are waiting for, and it is kept securely in heaven (1 Pet 1:4). When Jesus returns, they will be saved from the suffering of this fallen world, but for now, God's people must suffer various trials (1 Pet 1:6). God is using our trials to prepare us for our inheritance in the same way that gold is refined by fire (1 Pet 1:7).

God has chosen his people out of the world.

Peter describes his readers as people who have been "chosen" by God yet they live "as exiles" in this world. The church is God's new temple, which is built on the cornerstone of Jesus himself (1 Pet 2:1–8). They "are a chosen race, a royal priesthood, a holy nation, a people for his possession," whom God has called out of darkness and into light (1 Pet 2:9). These people belong to God, but they continue to live on earth. Therefore, they are not at home in this sinful age. As a result, they must pursue holy living (1 Pet 1:15) and endure suffering from the world (1 Pet 3:17).

God has called pastors to shepherd his people.

God has not left his people without leadership. He has appointed pastors to care for his flock. They should do so with joy, seeking to please God, and serving with gentleness (1 Pet 5:2–3). If they serve Christ humbly, then they will receive a reward when Jesus, the Chief Shepherd, comes to claim his sheep (1 Pet 5:4). The sheep really belong to Jesus. He is the Chief Shepherd. Those called as pastor-teachers serve for Jesus' sake, and must one day give an account of their work to Jesus.

The devil prowls like a roaring lion.

At the end of his letter, Peter exhorts his readers to be humble and to trust God with all their cares because God "cares about you" (1 Pet 5:6–7). At the same time, we should always "be alert" because we have an enemy, the devil (the word "devil" simply means "adversary"). Satan is "like a roaring lion, looking for anyone he can devour" (1 Pet 5:7–8). He is hungry, ruthless, and dangerous.

While this should motivate us to stay alert, it should not discourage us. God has given us the ability to resist Satan: "Resist him, firm in the faith, knowing that the same kind of sufferings are being experienced by your fellow believers throughout the world" (1 Pet 5:9). While Satan can cause trials and persecutions to complicate our lives, we know that nothing can threaten our inheritance in heaven, and that these sufferings are actually preparing us for the inheritance (1 Pet 1:3–9).

The New Testament

2 Peter

Basic Facts
Author: Peter, the former fisherman and disciple
Original Audience: Unknown
Place Written: Rome
Date Written: about A.D. 64–67

The Main Idea
Resist false teachers by growing in the grace and knowledge of Christ.

Structure
- 1:1–15. Grace and knowledge produce a godly life.
- 1:16–21. We know that Christ will return in glory.
- 2:1–22. False teachers oppose the grace and knowledge of Christ.
- 3:1–13. We know that Christ will return to judge.
- 3:14–18. Live a godly life by growing in grace and knowledge.

Big Events & Ideas

Live a godly life by growing in grace and knowledge.

Peter calls on his readers to live godly lives. Such a life is characterized by self-control, endurance, brotherly affection, and love (2 Pet 1:5–6). This is the type of life that the grace and knowledge of Jesus should produce in believers. Peter writes, "For if you possess these qualities in increasing measure, they will keep you from being useless or unfruitful in the knowledge of our Lord Jesus Christ" (2 Pet 1:8). Believers should avoid lawlessness and "grow in the grace and knowledge of our Lord and Savior Jesus Christ" (2 Pet 3:18).

False teachers oppose the grace and knowledge of Christ.

In contrast with the true believer, false teachers do not live godly lives. These false teachers are motivated by greed, and they influence people to "follow their depraved ways" (2 Pet 2:2–3). They lack godliness because they have abandoned the truth about God's grace in Christ. They teach "destructive heresies, even denying the Master who bought them" (2 Pet 2:1). Such false teachers will face God's judgment.

We know that Christ will return.

The knowledge of Christ that motivates godly living is the knowledge of his return. Peter received a glimpse of Christ's glory on the Mount of Transfiguration (2 Pet 1:16–18; see Mark 9:2–8). Jesus will return in his glory to judge the earth. His return will come when it isn't expected (2 Pet 3:1–10). Peter concludes from this knowledge, "Since all these things are to be dissolved in this way, it is clear what sort of people you should be in holy conduct and godliness as you wait for the day of God and hasten its coming" (2 Pet 3:11–12). The return of Christ shouldn't fill us with fear. We eagerly desire to see Christ return, and because we do not know when he will come, we must always stay prepared by obeying his commands.

1 John

Basic Facts
Author: John, the former fisherman and disciple
Original Audience: churches in Asia Minor
Place Written: Ephesus
Date Written: about A.D. 85–95

The Main Idea
Practice faith, obedience, and love because God is light and love.

Structure
- 1:1–2:17. God is light, and his children confess their sins.
- 2:18–3:24. Antichrists do not practice faith, obedience, and love.
- 4:1–5:21. God is love, and his children practice faith, obedience, and love.

Big Events & Ideas
God is light and love.

John makes two statements about who God is. First, he writes, "God is light, and there is absolutely no darkness in him" (1 John 1:5), and second, he writes,

"God is love" (1 John 4:8). God's character is important because it is reproduced in the character of his children. God's children are those who "walk in the light as he himself is in the light" (1 John 1:7). God's children "love one another, because love is from God, and everyone who loves has been born of God and knows God" (1 John 4:7). God's children reflect the character of God himself, and will one day perfectly display the character of God. John explains, "Dear friends, we are God's children now, and what we will be has not yet been revealed. We know that when he appears, we will be like him because we will see him as he is" (1 John 3:2).

The antichrists are in the world already.

John warns God's children about the antichrists in the world. While the Antichrist will come at the end of history before the return of Christ, John warns that "even now many antichrists have come" (1 John 2:18). These antichrists are people who initially belonged to the church, but then left the church. By doing this, they showed that they were never truly believers (1 John 2:19). Even though the antichrists previously looked like Christians, it has become evident who they truly are. Those who have the Holy Spirit confess Jesus Christ is from God, but the antichrists oppose Jesus and the church (1 John 4:3). Christians should not fear this opposition. John writes, "You are from God, little children, and you have conquered them, because the one who is in you is greater than the one who is in the world" (1 John 4:4).

2 John

Basic Facts
Author: John, the former fisherman and disciple
Original Audience: a church in Asia Minor
Place Written: Ephesus
Date Written: about A.D. 85–95

The Main Idea
Churches must guard against deceptive teachers who deny the truth about Jesus.

Structure
- 1–3. People who know the truth love their church.
- 4–11. Deceptive teachers deny the truth about Jesus.
- 12–13. John wants to teach more to this church face to face.

Big Events & Ideas
Deceptive teachers deny the truth about Jesus.

John writes "to the elect lady and her children," which is code language for a church and its members (2 John 1). He warns this church, "Many deceivers have gone out into the world; they do not confess the coming of Jesus Christ in the flesh. This is the deceiver and the antichrist" (2 John 7). This church needs to remember that false teachers come to deceive them and to deny the truth about Jesus. Our relationship with God is demonstrated by our enduring faith in the truth. John writes, "Anyone who does not remain in Christ's teaching but goes beyond it does not have God" (2 John 9). The church must therefore guard itself by not allowing these deceptive teachers to teach.

3 John

Basic Facts
Author: John, the former fisherman and disciple
Original Audience: Gaius, a believer from a church, probably, in Asia Minor.
Place Written: Ephesus
Date Written: about A.D. 85–95

The Main Idea
Believers should support missionaries despite self-centered opposition.

Structure
- 1–4. John's greatest joy is children who walk in the truth.
- 5–12. Support missionaries despite self-centered opposition.
- 13–15. John wants to teach more face to face.

Big Events & Ideas
Support missionaries despite self-centered opposition.

John writes to a believer named Gaius who had shown hospitality to some missionaries John had sent out (3 John 5). John writes, "Therefore, we ought to support such people so that we can be coworkers with the truth" (3 John 8). By praying for, supporting, and showing hospitality to missionaries, we partner in their important work of taking the gospel to the unreached.

Not everyone has shown the same kind of support. Diotrephes has tried to stop the missionaries John has sent. His resistance comes from his self-centered attitude. John says that Diotrephes "loves to have first place" (3 John 9). Gaius shouldn't be intimidated by Diotrephes, but should continue to support missionaries who proclaim the gospel.

Jude

Basic Facts
Author: Jude, the brother of Jesus
Original Audience: Unknown
Place Written: Unknown
Date Written: about A.D. 50–65

The Main Idea
Those whom God has called, loved, and kept should keep themselves in the love of God by contending for the faith.

Structure
- 1–4. Contend for the faith!
- 5–16. Ungodly teachers are designated for judgment.
- 17–19. Remember that the apostles predicted the coming of these teachers.
- 20–23. Keep yourselves in the love of God.
- 24–25. God is able to protect you.

Big Events & Ideas

Keep yourselves in the love of God.

Jude commands his readers, "Keep yourselves in the love of God, waiting expectantly for the mercy of our Lord Jesus Christ for eternal life" (Jude 21). The challenge to their faith came from ungodly teachers who "have come in by stealth" and are "turning the grace of our God into sensuality and denying Jesus Christ, our only Master and Lord" (Jude 4). The way Jude's readers can keep themselves in God's love is by resisting these false teachers. Jude writes, "I found it necessary to write, appealing to you to contend for the faith that was delivered to the saints once for all" (Jude 3).

But even as Christians fight to remain faithful to the true gospel taught by the apostles, we do not persevere by our own strength. We are "kept for Jesus Christ" (Jude 1) and protected by God for the return of Jesus (Jude 24). Jude teaches both God's sovereignty and human responsibility. While we must do the hard work of remaining faithful to Christ and his gospel, it is ultimately God who keeps us for his glory.

Revelation

Basic Facts
Author: John, the former fisherman and disciple
Original Audience: seven churches in Asia Minor: Ephesus, Smyrna, Pergamum, Thyatira, Sardis, Philadelphia, Laodicea
Place Written: island of Patmos (off the coast of Asia Minor)
Date Written: about A.D. 95–96

The Main Idea
We overcome tribulation by faith in the Lion-like Lamb who has conquered all enemies by his suffering, who reigns in glory, and who will forever reign in the new creation.

Structure
- 1:1–8. John received a revelation of Jesus Christ.
- 1:9–22:9. John records the vision he received.
  - 1:9–3:22. Seven Churches: The glorified Christ speaks to his churches.
  - 4:1–5:14. The Lion-like Lamb is worthy to take the scroll.
  - 6:1–17. Seven Seals: The Lamb controls the suffering that comes.
  - 7:1–17. God seals his chosen people from every nation.
  - 8:1–9:21. Seven Trumpets: God judges the enemies of the saints.

- 10:1–11:19. God vindicates his prophetic word.
- 12:1–14:20. Seven Signs: Christ and Satan battle.
- 15:1–8. The conquerors worship their victorious God.
- 16:1–21. Seven Bowls: The seventh sign brings God's final plagues of wrath.
- 17:1–14. John sees the great prostitute, Babylon.
- 17:15–20:15. Seven Last Events: God triumphs over all enemies.
- 21:1–22:5. The Seventh Event: God makes all things new.
- **22:6–21. John gives a final warning: Jesus is coming soon.**

Big Events & Ideas

Jesus is the risen king.

The book of Revelation is "the revelation of Jesus Christ" (Rev 1:1). While it certainly does deal with future events, it is primarily about who Jesus is. John receives a stunning vision of Jesus in his heavenly glory in Revelation 1:9–20. This vision is meant to remind those who read Revelation that even though followers of Christ suffer in this world, Christ has already entered into his glory. Jesus is indeed the Lion of the tribe of Judah, the mighty king in the line of David, but he is also "a slaughtered lamb" (Rev 5:5–6). Jesus is the risen king who is in control of all the events of history. But he has received such authority because he first suffered as a sacrificial lamb for our sins.

God's people look like their Savior.

Revelation promises that God's people will be victorious over their enemies. Jesus describes his people as conquerors (Rev 2:7, 11, 17, 26; 3:5, 12, 21). But first, like Jesus, they must endure suffering. Jesus instructs the Smyrna church, "Be faithful to the point of death, and I will give you the crown of life" (Rev 2:10). When John sees a vision of God's people, he sees "a vast multitude from every nation, tribe, people, and language" (Rev 7:9). One of the elders from God's presence, however, makes clear that this beautiful multitude had first suffered for Christ (Rev 7:14). Through Christ, God's people will experience eternal victory, but first like Christ, they must suffer in a sinful world.

God triumphs over his enemies.

In Revelation 17:15–20:15, John sees the seven final events of human history: (1) Babylon will fall (17:15–19:5). Babylon represents the sinful world under Satanic domination. While the world is powerful now, the day is coming when the world will fall and God will rescue his people.

(2) The marriage supper of the lamb will come (19:6–10). After the destruction of the world, the church will be perfectly united with Christ forever.

(3) Christ will defeat his enemies (19:11–21). John sees Christ riding on a white horse as a victorious warrior who is pursuing his enemies. While Jesus already conquered through his death and resurrection, the day is coming when Jesus will complete his victory by destroying his enemies forever. Among these enemies will be the sinful kings of the earth, the Beast (also called the man of lawlessness and the antichrist; see 2 Thess 2:3; 1 John 2:18; 4:3), and the false prophet who will proclaim the superiority of the Beast.

(4) Christ will reign for 1,000 years (20:1–6). An angel will bind Satan. God will resurrect his people, and they will reign with Jesus on earth for a long period of time before the complete end of human history.

(5) God will defeat Satan and throw him in the lake of fire (20:7–10). After the end of the long period of Christ's earthly reign, Satan will be released and allowed to rebel against God once more. Then God will defeat him completely and throw him into the lake of fire.

(6) God will raise all other people and judge them (20:11–15). While God had raised his people for the millennium reign of Christ, all other people will be raised after Satan's defeat. They will be judged and thrown into the lake of fire with Satan. (7) Then God will make all things new.

God makes all things new.

After God has defeated every enemy, God will create a new heaven and a new earth with a new Jerusalem (Rev 21:1–2). This new creation is a new temple where God will dwell with his people (Rev 21:3). It will be perfectly free from sin, death, and suffering (Rev 21:4). God declares, "Look, I am making everything new" (Rev 21:4). This is the final place of victory and rest for God's people in the loving presence of God the Father and Jesus Christ. Finally, God's covenant goal will be perfectly fulfilled: "They will be his peoples, and God himself will be with them and will be their God" (Rev 21:3). The task of the believer is to remain faithful to Christ until God brings about this perfect ending. But this new world is coming soon, as Jesus closes the book, "Yes, I am coming soon." To this, God's people answer, "Amen! Come, Lord Jesus" (Rev 22:20)!

Extras

Extras

Bible Reading Plan

This Bible reading plan gives readings each day from four sections of the Bible: the Old Testament, Psalms, Proverbs, and the New Testament. By following this plan, you will read through the Old and New Testaments once and the Psalms and Proverbs twice each year.

For a printable copy of this Bible reading plan, visit: gospellife.org/biblereading

Extras

"Give me life through your word." Psalm 119:25

Week 1
- ☐ Ge 1-3, Mt 1, Ps 1, Pr 1:1-7
- ☐ Ge 4-6, Mt 2, Ps 2, Pr 1:8-9
- ☐ Ge 7-9, Mt 3, Ps 3, Pr 1:10-19
- ☐ Ge 10-12, Mt 4, Ps 4, Pr 1:20-23
- ☐ Ge 13-15, Mt 5, Ps 5, Pr 1:24-28

Week 2
- ☐ Ge 16-18, Mt 6, Ps 6, Pr 1:29-33
- ☐ Ge 19-21, Mt 7, Ps 7, Pr 2:1-5
- ☐ Ge 22-24, Mt 8, Ps 8, Pr 2:6-15
- ☐ Ge 25-27, Mt 9, Ps 9:1-10, Pr 2:16-22
- ☐ Ge 28-30, Mt 10, Ps 9:11-20, Pr 3:1-4

Week 3
- ☐ Ge 31-33, Mt 11, Ps 10, Pr 3:5-12
- ☐ Ge 34-36, Mt 12, Ps 11, Pr 3:13-18
- ☐ Ge 37-39, Mt 13, Ps 12, Pr 3:19-20
- ☐ Ge 40-42, Mt 14, Ps 13, Pr 3:21-26
- ☐ Ge 43-45, Mt 15, Ps 14, Pr 3:27-32

Week 4
- ☐ Ge 46-48, Mt 16, Ps 15, Pr 3:33-35
- ☐ Ge 49-50, Mt 17, Ps 16, Pr 4:1-6
- ☐ Ex 1-2, Mt 18, Ps 17, Pr 4:7-9
- ☐ Ex 3-5, Mt 19, Ps 18:1-6, Pr 4:10-13
- ☐ Ex 6-8, Mt 20, Ps 18:7-19, Pr 4:14-19

Week 5
- ☐ Ex 9-11, Mt 21, Ps 18:20-29, Pr 4:20-27
- ☐ Ex 12-14, Mt 22, Ps 18:30-42, Pr 5:1-6
- ☐ Ex 15-17, Mt 23, Ps 18:43-50, Pr 5:7-14
- ☐ Ex 18-20, Mt 24, Ps 19, Pr 5:15-19
- ☐ Ex 21-23, Mt 25, Ps 20, Pr 5:20-23

Week 6
- ☐ Ex 24-26, Mt 26, Ps 21, Pr 6:1-5
- ☐ Ex 27-29, Mt 27, Ps 22:1-10, Pr 6:6-11
- ☐ Ex 30-32, Mt 28, Ps 22:11-20, Pr 6:12-15
- ☐ Ex 33-35, Mk 1, Ps 22:21-31, Pr 6:16-19
- ☐ Ex 36-38, Mk 2, Ps 23, Pr 6:20-26

Week 7
- ☐ Ex 39-40, Mk 3, Ps 24, Pr 6:27-35
- ☐ Lev 1-2, Mk 4, Ps 25:1-11, Pr 7:1-5
- ☐ Lev 3-4, Mk 5, Ps 25:12-22, Pr 7:6-23
- ☐ Lev 5-7, Mk 6, Ps 26, Pr 7:24-27
- ☐ Lev 8-10, Mk 7, Ps 27, Pr 8:1-11

Week 8
- ☐ Lev 11-13, Mk 8, Ps 28, Pr 8:12-21
- ☐ Lev 14-16, Mk 9, Ps 29, Pr 8:22-31
- ☐ Lev 17-19, Mk 10, Ps 30, Pr 8:32-36
- ☐ Lev 20-22, Mk 11, Ps 31:1-13, Pr 9:1-6
- ☐ Lev 23-25, Mk 12, Ps 31:14-24, Pr 9:7-9

Week 9
- ☐ Lev 26-27, Mk 13, Ps 32, Pr 9:10-12
- ☐ Nu 1-3, Mk 14, Ps 33:1-9, Pr 9:13-18
- ☐ Nu 4-6, Mk 15, Ps 33:10-22, Pr 10:1-3
- ☐ Nu 7-9, Mk 16, Ps 34:1-10, Pr 10:4-6
- ☐ Nu 10-12, Lk 1, Ps 34:11-22, Pr 10:7-9

Week 10
- ☐ Nu 13-15, Lk 2, Ps 35:1-10, Pr 10:10-12
- ☐ Nu 16-18, Lk 3, Ps 35:11-21, Pr 10:13-15
- ☐ Nu 19-21, Lk 4, Ps 35:22-28, Pr 10:16-18
- ☐ Nu 22-24, Lk 5, Ps 36, Pr 10:19-21
- ☐ Nu 25-27, Lk 6, Ps 37:1-13, Pr 10:22-24

Week 11
- ☐ Nu 28-30, Lk 7, Ps 37:14-22, Pr 10:25-27
- ☐ Nu 31-33, Lk 8, Ps 37:23-31, Pr 10:28-30
- ☐ Nu 34-36, Lk 9, Ps 37:32-40, Pr 10:31-32
- ☐ Dt 1-2, Lk 10, Ps 38:1-12, Pr 11:1-3
- ☐ Dt 3-5, Lk 11, Ps 38:13-22, Pr 11:4-6

Week 12
- ☐ Dt 6-8, Lk 12, Ps 39, Pr 11:7-9
- ☐ Dt 9-10, Lk 13, Ps 40:1-5, Pr 11:10-12
- ☐ Dt 11-13, Lk 14, Ps 40:6-10, Pr 11:13-15
- ☐ Dt 14-16, Lk 15, Ps 40:11-17, Pr 11:16-18
- ☐ Dt 17-19, Lk 16, Ps 41, Pr 11:19-21

Week 13
- ☐ Dt 20-22, Lk 17, Ps 42, Pr 11:22-24
- ☐ Dt 23-25, Lk 18, Ps 43, Pr 11:25-27
- ☐ Dt 26-28, Lk 19, Ps 44:1-8, Pr 11:28-29
- ☐ Dt 29-31, Lk 20, Ps 44:9-16, Pr 11:30-31
- ☐ Dt 32-34, Lk 21, Ps 44:17-26, Pr 12:1-3

Week 14
- ☐ Josh 1-3, Lk 22, Ps 45:1-9, Pr 12:4-6
- ☐ Josh 4-6, Lk 23, Ps 45:10-17, Pr 12:7-9
- ☐ Josh 7-9, Lk 24, Ps 46, Pr 12:10-12
- ☐ Josh 10-12, Jn 1, Ps 47, Pr 12:13-15
- ☐ Josh 13-15, Jn 2, Ps 48, Pr 12:16-18

Week 15
- ☐ Josh 16-18, Jn 3, Ps 49:1-12, Pr 12:19-21
- ☐ Josh 19-21, Jn 4, Ps 49:13-20, Pr 12:22-24
- ☐ Josh 22-24, Jn 5, Ps 50:1-6, Pr 12:25-26
- ☐ Jdg 1-3, Jn 6, Ps 50:7-15, Pr 12:27-28
- ☐ Jdg 4-6, Jn 7, Ps 50:16-23, Pr 13:1-3

Week 16
- ☐ Jdg 7-9, Jn 8, Ps 51:1-9, Pr 13:4-6
- ☐ Jdg 10-12, Jn 9, Ps 51:10-19, Pr 13:7-9
- ☐ Jdg 13-15, Jn 10, Ps 52, Pr 13:10-12
- ☐ Jdg 16-18, Jn 11, Ps 53, Pr 13:13-15
- ☐ Jdg 19-21, Jn 12, Ps 54, Pr 13:16-18

Week 17
- ☐ Ru 1-2, Jn 13, Ps 55:1-7, Pr 13:19-21
- ☐ Ru 3-4, Jn 14, Ps 55:8-14, Pr 13:22-23
- ☐ 1Sa 1-3, Jn 15, Ps 55:15-23, Pr 13:24-25
- ☐ 1Sa 4-6, Jn 16, Ps 56, Pr 14:1-3
- ☐ 1Sa 7-9, Jn 17, Ps 57, Pr 14:4-6

Week 18
- ☐ 1Sa 10-12, Jn 18, Ps 58, Pr 14:7-9
- ☐ 1Sa 13-15, Jn 19, Ps 59:1-10, Pr 14:10-12
- ☐ 1Sa 16-18, Jn 20, Ps 59:11-17, Pr 14:13-15
- ☐ 1Sa 19-21, Jn 21, Ps 60, Pr 14:16-18
- ☐ 1Sa 22-24, Ac 1, Ps 61, Pr 14:19-21

Week 19
- ☐ 1Sa 25-27, Ac 2, Ps 62, Pr 14:22-24
- ☐ 1Sa 28-30, Ac 3, Ps 63, Pr 14:25-27
- ☐ 1Sa 31-2Sa 2, Ac 4, Ps 64, Pr 14:28-30
- ☐ 2Sa 3-5, Ac 5, Ps 65, Pr 14:31-33
- ☐ 2Sa 6-8, Ac 6, Ps 66:1-9, Pr 14:34-35

Week 20
- ☐ 2Sa 9-11, Ac 7, Ps 66:10-20, Pr 15:1-3
- ☐ 2Sa 12-14, Ac 8, Ps 67, Pr 15:4-6
- ☐ 2Sa 15-17, Ac 9, Ps 68:1-10, Pr 15:7-9
- ☐ 2Sa 18-20, Ac 10, Ps 68:11-27, Pr 15:10-12
- ☐ 2Sa 21-22, Ac 11, Ps 68:28-35, Pr 15:13-15

Week 21
- ☐ 2Sa 23-24, Ac 12, Ps 69:1-12, Pr 15:16-18
- ☐ 1Ki 1-2, Ac 13, Ps 69:13-18, Pr 15:19-21
- ☐ 1Ki 3-5, Ac 14, Ps 69:19-28, Pr 15:22-24
- ☐ 1Ki 6-8, Ac 15, Ps 69:29-36, Pr 15:25-27
- ☐ 1Ki 9-11, Ac 16, Ps 70, Pr 15:28-30

Week 22
- ☐ 1Ki 12-13, Ac 17, Ps 71:1-8, Pr 15:31-33
- ☐ 1Ki 14-16, Ac 18, Ps 71:9-24, Pr 16:1-3
- ☐ 1Ki 17-19, Ac 19, Ps 72:1-11, Pr 16:4-6
- ☐ 1Ki 20-22, Ac 20, Ps 72:12-20, Pr 16:7-9
- ☐ 1Ki 3, Ac 21, Ps 73:1-12, Pr 16:10-12

Week 23
- ☐ 2Ki 4-6, Ac 22, Ps 73:13-20, Pr 16:13-15
- ☐ 2Ki 7-9, Ac 23, Ps 73:21-28, Pr 16:16-18
- ☐ 2Ki 10-12, Ac 24, Ps 74:1-11, Pr 16:19-21
- ☐ 2Ki 13-14, Ac 25, Ps 74:12-23, Pr 16:22-24
- ☐ 2Ki 15-17, Ac 26, Ps 75, Pr 16:25-27

Week 24
- ☐ 2Ki 18-20, Ac 27, Ps 76, Pr 16:28-30
- ☐ 2Ki 21-23, Ac 28, Ps 77:1-12, Pr 16:31-33
- ☐ 2Ki 24-25, Rom 1, Ps 77:13-20, Pr 17:1-3
- ☐ 1Ch 1-3, Rom 2, Ps 78:1-8, Pr 17:4-6
- ☐ 1Ch 4-6, Rom 3, Ps 78:9-16, Pr 17:7-9

Week 25
- ☐ 1Ch 7-9, Rom 4, Ps 78:17-31, Pr 17:10-12
- ☐ 1Ch 10-12, Rom 5, Ps 78:32-39, Pr 17:13-15
- ☐ 1Ch 13-15, Rom 6, Ps 78:40-55, Pr 17:16-18
- ☐ 1Ch 16-18, Rom 7, Ps 78:56-64, Pr 17:19-21
- ☐ 1Ch 19-21, Rom 8, Ps 78:65-72, Pr 17:22-24

377

Bible Reading Plan

Week 26
- 1Ch 22-24, Rom 9, Ps 79, Pr 17:25-26
- 1Ch 25-27, Rom 10, Ps 80:1-11, Pr 17:27-28
- 1Ch 28-2Ch 1, Rom 11, Ps 80:12-19, Pr 18:1-3
- 2Ch 2-4, Rom 12, Ps 81, Pr 18:4-6
- 2Ch 5-6, Rom 13, Ps 82, Pr 18:7-9

Week 27
- 2Ch 7-9, Rom 14, Ps 83:1-8, Pr 18:10-12
- 2Ch 10-12, Rom 15, Ps 83:9-18, Pr 18:13-15
- 2Ch 13-15, Rom 16, Ps 84, Pr 18:16-18
- 2Ch 16-18, 1Cor 1, Ps 85, Pr 18:19-21
- 2Ch 19-21, 1Cor 2, Ps 86:1-10, Pr 18:22-24

Week 28
- 2Ch 22-24, 1Cor 3, Ps 86:11-17, Pr 19:1-3
- 2Ch 25-27, 1Cor 4, Ps 87, Pr 19:4-6
- 2Ch 28-30, 1Cor 5, Ps 88:1-9, Pr 19:7-9
- 2Ch 31-33, 1Cor 6, Ps 88:10-18, Pr 19:10-12
- 2Ch 34-36, 1Cor 7, Ps 89:1-4, Pr 19:13-15

Week 29
- Ez 1-3, 1Cor 8, Ps 89:5-12, Pr 19:16-18
- Ez 4-6, 1Cor 9, Ps 89:13-18, Pr 19:16-18
- Ez 7-9, 1Cor 10, Ps 89:19-29, Pr 19:19-21
- Ez 10-Neh 2, 1Cor 11, Ps 89:30-37, Pr 19:22-24
- Neh 3-5, 1Cor 12, Ps 89:38-45, Pr 19:25-27

Week 30
- Neh 6-8, 1Cor 13, Ps 89:46-52, Pr 19:28-29
- Neh 9-11, 1Cor 14, Ps 90:1-12, Pr 20:1-3
- Neh 12-13, 1Cor 15, Ps 90:13-17, Pr 20:4-6
- Est 1-2, 1Cor 16, Ps 91, Pr 20:7-9
- Est 3-5, 2Cor 1, Ps 92, Pr 20:10-12

Week 31
- Job 1-3, 2Cor 2, Ps 93, Pr 20:13-15
- Job 4-6, 2Cor 3, Ps 94:1-11, Pr 20:16-18
- Job 7-9, 2Cor 4, Ps 94:12-23, Pr 20:19-21
- Job 10-12, 2Cor 5, Ps 95, Pr 20:22-24
- Job 13-15, 2Cor 6, Ps 96, Pr 20:25-27

Week 32
- Job 16-18, 2Cor 7, Ps 97, Pr 20:28-30
- Job 19-21, 2Cor 8, Ps 98, Pr 21:1-3
- Job 22-24, 2Cor 9, Ps 99, Pr 21:4-6
- Job 25-27, 2Cor 10, Ps 100, Pr 21:7-9
- Job 28-30, 2Cor 11, Ps 101, Pr 21:10-12

Week 33
- Job 31-33, Gal 1, Ps 102:1-11, Pr 21:13-15
- Job 34-36, Gal 2, Ps 102:12-22, Pr 21:16-18
- Job 37-39, Gal 3, Ps 103:1-10, Pr 21:19-21
- Job 40-42, Gal 4, Ps 103:11-22, Pr 21:22-24
- Ecc 1-3, Gal 5, Ps 104:1-13, Pr 21:25-27

Week 34
- Ecc 4-6, Gal 6, Ps 104:14-23, Pr 21:28-29
- Ecc 7-9, Eph 1, Ps 104:24-35, Pr 21:30-31
- Ecc 10-12, Eph 2, Ps 105:1-6, Pr 22:1-3
- Song 1-3, Eph 3, Ps 105:7-15, Pr 22:4-6
- Song 4-6, Eph 4, Ps 105:16-22, Pr 22:7-9

Week 35
- Song 7-8, Eph 5, Ps 105:23-36, Pr 22:10-12
- Isa 1-3, Eph 6, Ps 105:37-45, Pr 22:13-14
- Isa 4-6, Phil 1, Ps 106:1-15, Pr 22:15-16
- Isa 7-9, Phil 2, Ps 106:16-23, Pr 22:17-21
- Isa 10-12, Phil 3, Ps 106:24-31, Pr 22:22-23

Week 36
- Isa 13-15, Phil 4, Ps 106:32-39, Pr 22:24-25
- Isa 16-18, Col 1, Ps 106:40-48, Pr 22:26-27
- Isa 19-21, Col 2, Ps 107:1-9, Pr 22:28-29
- Isa 22-24, Col 3, Ps 107:10-22, Pr 23:1-3
- Isa 25-27, Col 4, Ps 107:23-32, Pr 23:4-5

Week 37
- Isa 28-30, 1Th 1, Ps 107:33-43, Pr 23:6-8
- Isa 31-33, 1Th 2, Ps 108, Pr 23:9-11
- Isa 34-36, 1Th 3, Ps 109:1-20, Pr 23:12-14
- Isa 37-39, 1Th 4, Ps 109:21-31, Pr 23:15-16
- Isa 40-42, 1Th 5, Ps 109:26-31, Pr 23:17-18

Week 38
- Isa 43-45, 2Th 1, Ps 109:26-31, Pr 23:19-21
- Isa 46-48, 2Th 2, Ps 110, Pr 23:22-25
- Isa 49-51, 2Th 3, Ps 111, Pr 23:26-28
- Isa 52-54, 1Ti 1, Ps 112, Pr 23:29-35
- Isa 55-57, 1Ti 2, Ps 113, Pr 24:1-2

Week 39
- Isa 58-60, 1Ti 3, Ps 114, Pr 24:3-4
- Isa 61-63, 1Ti 4, Ps 115:1-8, Pr 24:5-6
- Isa 64-66, 1Ti 5, Ps 115:9-18, Pr 24:7-9
- Jer 1-3, 1Ti 6, Ps 116:1-11, Pr 24:10-12
- Jer 4-6, 2Ti 1, Ps 116:12-19, Pr 24:13-14

Week 40
- Jer 7-9, 2Ti 2, Ps 117, Pr 24:15-18
- Jer 10-12, 2Ti 3, Ps 118:1-9, Pr 24:19-22
- Jer 13-15, 2Ti 4, Ps 118:10-18, Pr 24:23-25
- Jer 16-18, Titus 1, Ps 118:19-29, Pr 24:26-29
- Jer 19-21, Titus 2, Ps 119:1-8, Pr 24:30-34

Week 41
- Jer 22-24, Titus 3, Ps 119:9-16, Pr 25:1-3
- Jer 25-27, Phm, Ps 119:17-24, Pr 25:4-7
- Jer 28-30, Heb 1, Ps 119:25-32, Pr 25:8-10
- Jer 31-33, Heb 2, Ps 119:33-40, Pr 25:11-13
- Jer 34-36, Heb 3, Ps 119:41-48, Pr 25:14-15

Week 42
- Jer 37-39, Heb 4, Ps 119:49-56, Pr 25:16-17
- Jer 40-42, Heb 5, Ps 119:57-64, Pr 25:18-19
- Jer 43-45, Heb 6, Ps 119:65-72, Pr 25:20-22
- Jer 46-48, Heb 7, Ps 119:73-80, Pr 25:23-25
- Jer 49-50, Heb 8, Ps 119:81-88, Pr 25:26-28

Week 43
- Jer 51-52, Heb 9, Ps 119:89-96, Pr 26:1-3
- Lam 1-2, Heb 10, Ps 119:97-104, Pr 26:4-5
- Lam 3-5, Heb 11, Ps 119:105-112, Pr 26:6-8
- Ezk 1-3, Heb 12, Ps 119:113-120, Pr 26:9-12
- Ezk 4-6, Heb 13, Ps 119:121-128, Pr 26:13-16

Week 44
- Ezk 7-9, Jas 1, Ps 119:129-136, Pr 26:17-19
- Ezk 10-12, Jas 2, Ps 119:137-144, Pr 26:20-22
- Ezk 12-14, Jas 3, Ps 119:145-152, Pr 26:23-26
- Ezk 15-17, Jas 4, Ps 119:153-160, Pr 26:27-28
- Ezk 18-20, Jas 5, Ps 119:161-168, Pr 27:1-3

Week 45
- Ezk 21-23, 1Pe 1, Ps 119:169-176, Pr 27:4-6
- Ezk 24-26, 1Pe 2, Ps 119:169-176, Pr 27:7-9
- Ezk 27-29, 1Pe 3, Ps 120, Pr 27:10-12
- Ezk 30-32, 1Pe 4, Ps 121, Pr 27:13-14
- Ezk 33-34, 1Pe 5, Ps 122, Pr 27:15-17

Week 46
- Ezk 35-37, 2Pe 1, Ps 123, Pr 27:18-20
- Ezk 38-40, 2Pe 2, Ps 124, Pr 27:21-22
- Ezk 41-43, 2Pe 3, Ps 125, Pr 27:23-27
- Ezk 44-46, 1Jn 1, Ps 126, Pr 28:1-3
- Ezk 47-48, 1Jn 2, Ps 127, Pr 28:4-6

Week 47
- Dan 1-3, 1Jn 3, Ps 128, Pr 28:7-9
- Dan 4-6, 1Jn 4, Ps 129, Pr 28:10-12
- Dan 7-9, 1Jn 5, Ps 130, Pr 28:13-15
- Hos 1-3, 3Jn, Ps 131, Pr 28:16-18
- Hos 4-6, 2Jn, Ps 132:1-10, Pr 28:19-21

Week 48
- Hos 7-9, Jude, Ps 132:11-18, Pr 28:22-24
- Hos 10-12, Rev 1, Ps 133, Pr 28:25-28
- Hos 13-14, Rev 2, Ps 134, Pr 29:1-3
- Joel 1-3, Rev 3, Ps 135:1-12, Pr 29:4-6
- Am 1-3, Rev 4, Ps 135:13-21, Pr 29:7-9

Week 49
- Am 4-6, Rev 5, Ps 136:1-12, Pr 29:10-12
- Am 7-9, Rev 6, Ps 136:13-26, Pr 29:13-15
- Ob-Jnh 2, Rev 7, Ps 137, Pr 29:16-18
- Jnh 3-Mic 1, Rev 8, Ps 138, Pr 29:19-21
- Mic 2-4, Rev 9, Ps 139:1-12, Pr 29:22-24

Week 50
- Mic 5-7, Rev 10, Ps 139:13-24, Pr 29:25-27
- Na 1-3, Rev 11, Ps 140, Pr 30:1-4
- Hab 1-3, Rev 12, Ps 141, Pr 30:5-6
- Zep 1-3, Rev 13, Ps 142, Pr 30:7-10
- Hag 1-2, Rev 14, Ps 143, Pr 30:11-14

Week 51
- Zec 1-3, Rev 15, Ps 144, Pr 30:15-17
- Zec 4-6, Rev 16, Ps 145:1-7, Pr 30:18-20
- Zec 7-9, Rev 17, Ps 145:8-21, Pr 30:21-23
- Zec 10-12, Rev 18, Ps 146, Pr 30:24-28
- Zec 13-14, Rev 19, Ps 147:1-11, Pr 30:29-31

Week 52
- Mal 1-2, Rev 20, Ps 147:12-20, Pr 30:32-33
- Mal 3-4, Rev 21, Ps 148, Pr 31:1-7
- Rev 22, Ps 149, Pr 31:8-9
- Ps 150, Pr 31:10-24
- Pr 31:25-31

Extras

Biblical Measurements

Biblical Unit	Metric System	English System
Weights		
Talent (60 minas)	34 kg	75 lbs
Mina (50 shekels)	560 g	1.25 lbs
Shekel (2 bekas)	11.5 g	0.4 oz
Pim ($2/3$ shekel)	7.8 g	0.25 oz
Beka (10 gerahs)	5.7 g	0.2 oz
Gerah	0.6 g	0.02 oz
Daric	8.4 g	0.33 oz
Length		
Cubit	45 cm	18 in
Span	23 cm	9 in
Handbreadth	7.5 cm	3 in
Stadion/Stadia	183 m	600 ft
Dry Measure		
Cor/Homer (10 ephahs)	220 L	6 bushels
Lethek (5 ephahs)	110 L	3 bushels
Ephah (10 omers)	22 L	0.6 bushel
Seah ($1/3$ ephah)	7.5 L	7 qts
Omer ($1/10$ ephah)	2 L	2 qts
Liquid Measure		
Bath (1 ephah)	22 L	6 gal
Hin ($1/6$ bath)	3.8 L	1 gal

Maps

Extras

Bible Lands Today

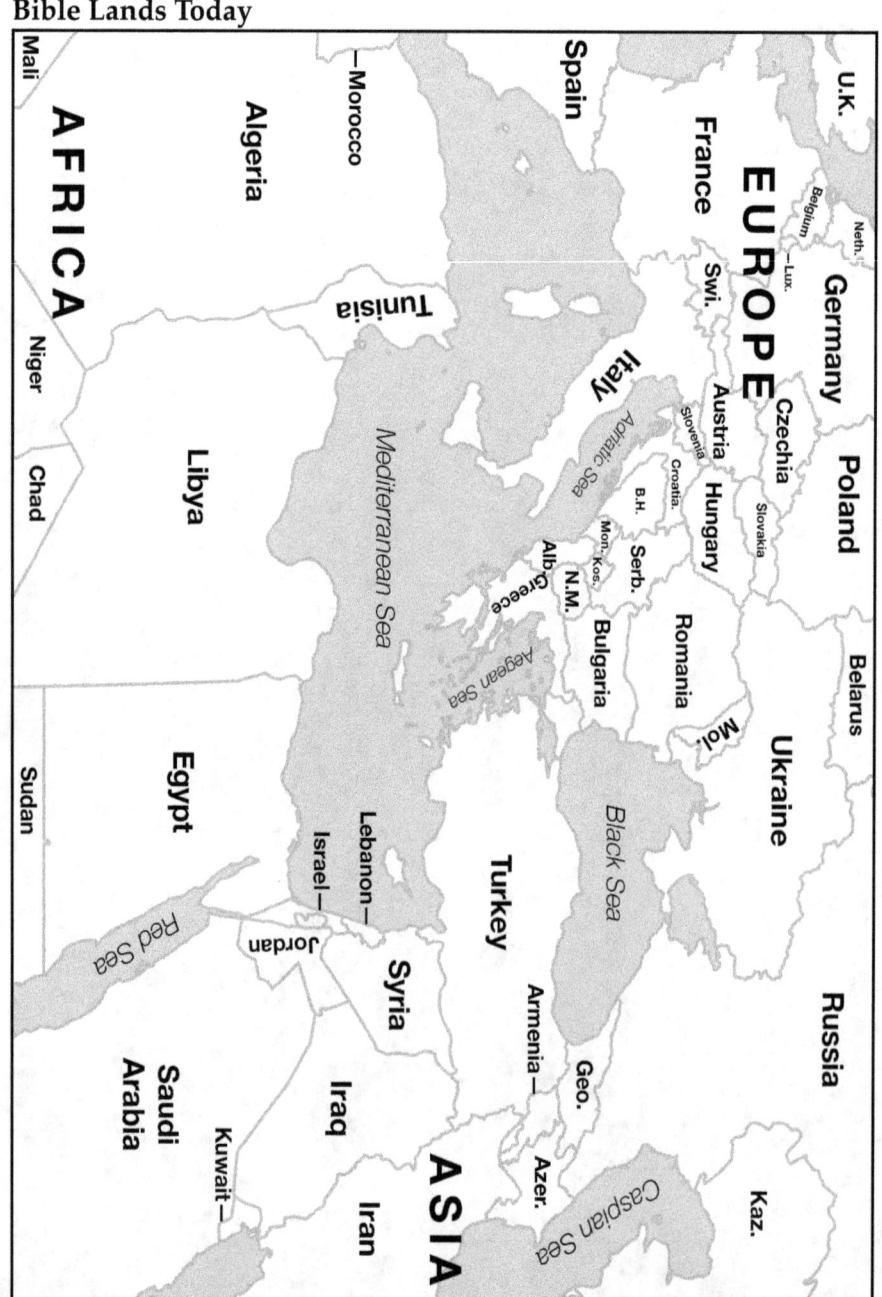

The Table of Nations (Genesis 10)

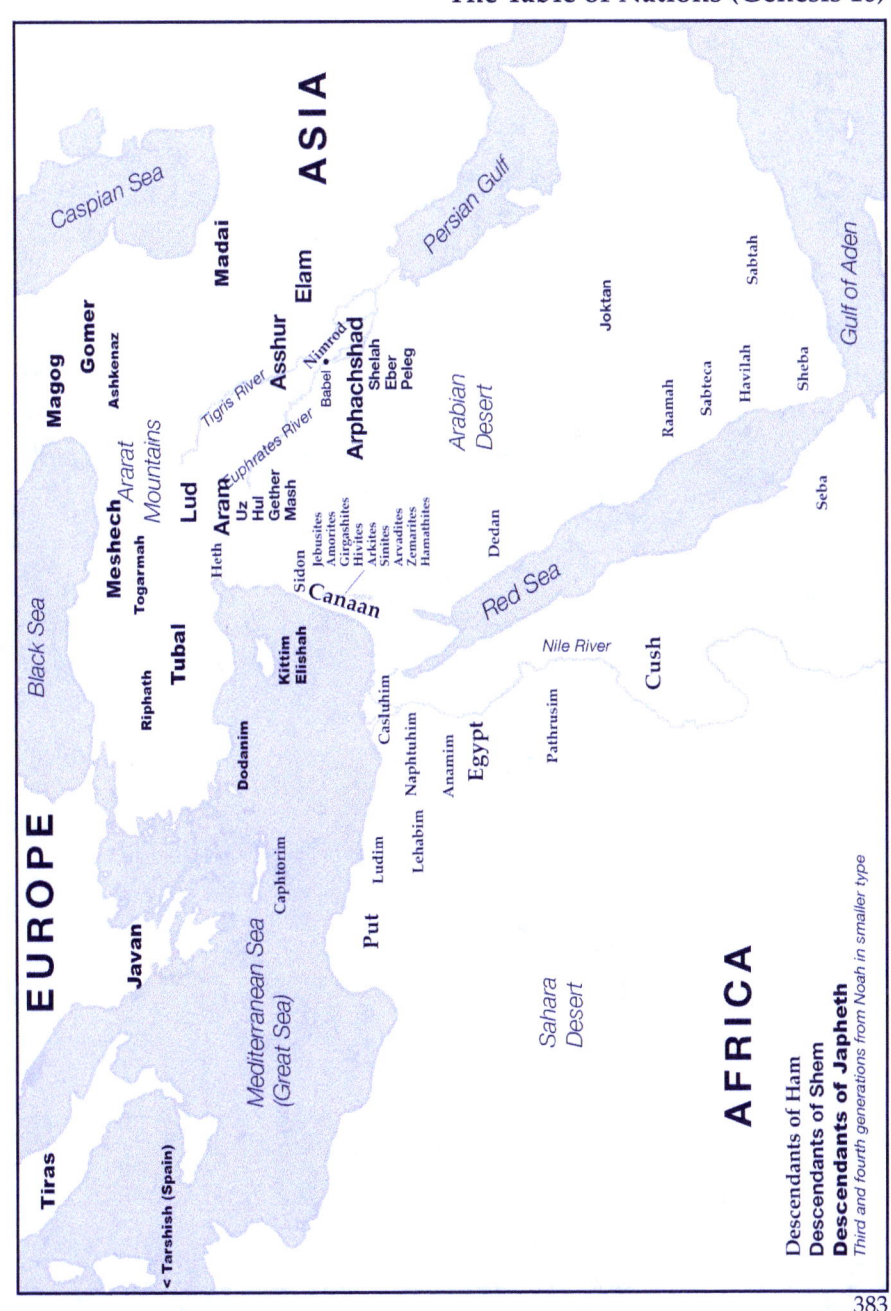

Extras

The World of Abraham, Isaac, and Jacob

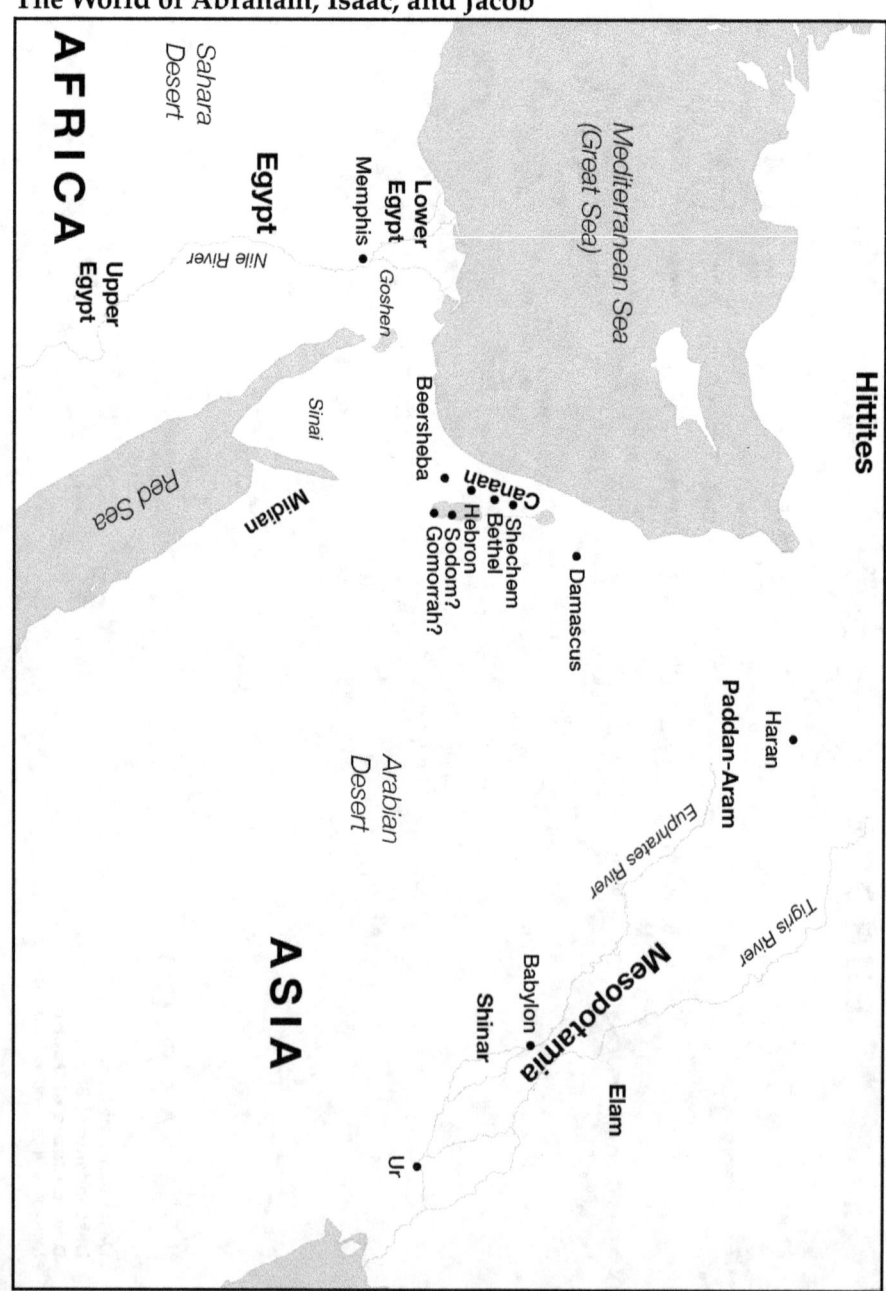

Maps

The Wilderness and Promised Land of Moses and Joshua

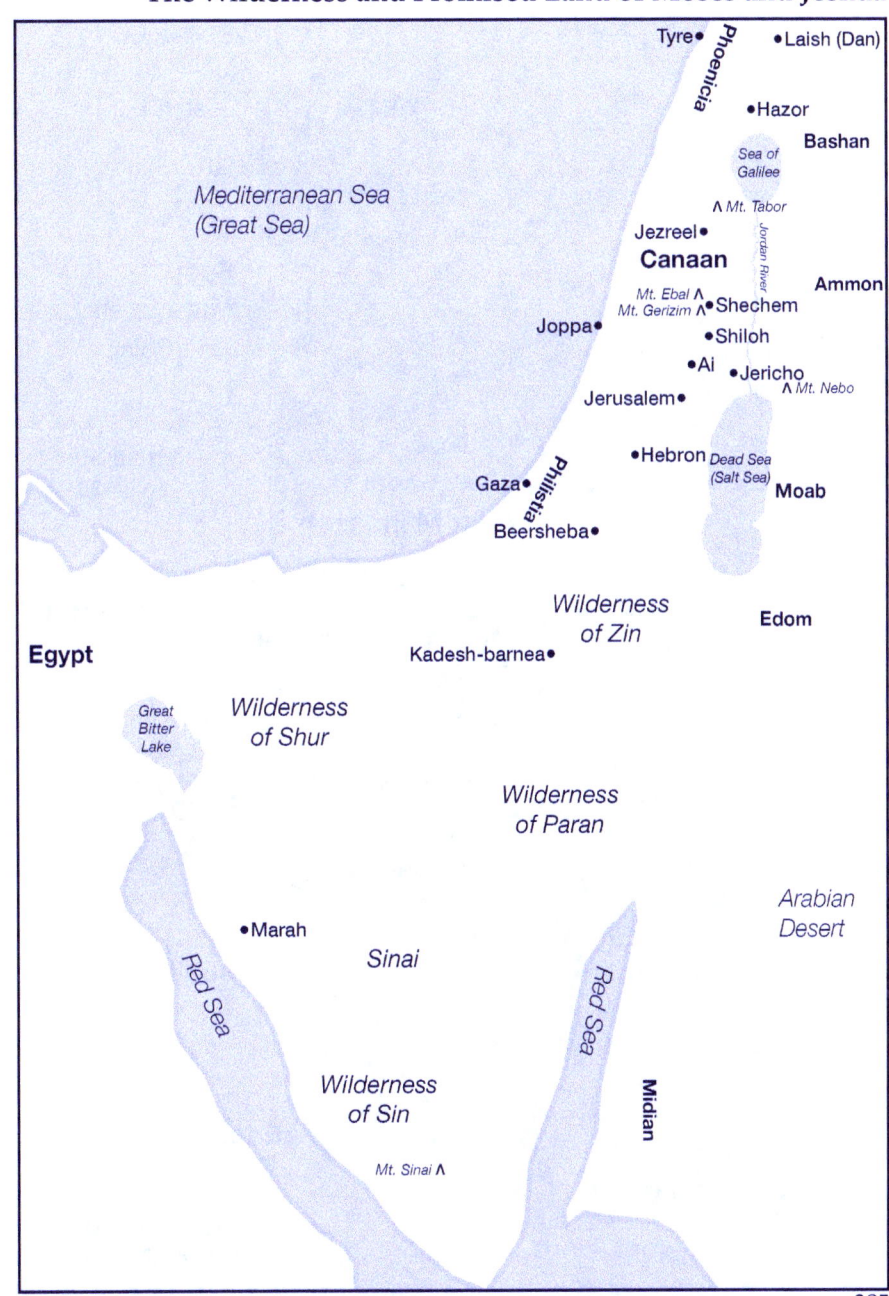

385

Extras

Tribal Lands and Cities of Refugee

Mt. Herman ∧
Tyre•
•Laish (Dan)
•<u>Kedesh</u>
•Hazor
Asher
Naphtali
East
Sea of **Manasseh**
Mediterranean Sea Galilee •<u>Golan</u>
(Great Sea) <u>Zebulun</u>
∧ Mt. Tabor
<u>Issachar</u>
Jezreel•
•<u>Ramoth</u>
Mt. Gilboah ∧ <u>Gilead</u>
West Manasseh
Mt. Ebal ∧
Mt. Gerizim ∧ •<u>Shechem</u>
Joppa• **Ammon**
•Shiloh **Gad**
<u>Ephraim</u>
Dan Ramah• •Jericho
Gibeah <u>Benjamin</u> •<u>Heshbon</u>
Jerusalem• ∧ Mt. Nebo
Ekron•
•Bethlehem •<u>Bezer</u>
Ashdod• •Gath **Judah** **Reuben**
•<u>Hebron</u>
Ashkelon• En Gedi• Dead Sea
Gaza• •Ziklag (Salt Sea)
Simeon
Beersheba• **Moab**

Wilderness
of Zin **Edom**
Kadesh-barnea•

Tribal Land
<u>City of Refugee</u>•

386

The Kingdom of David and Solomon

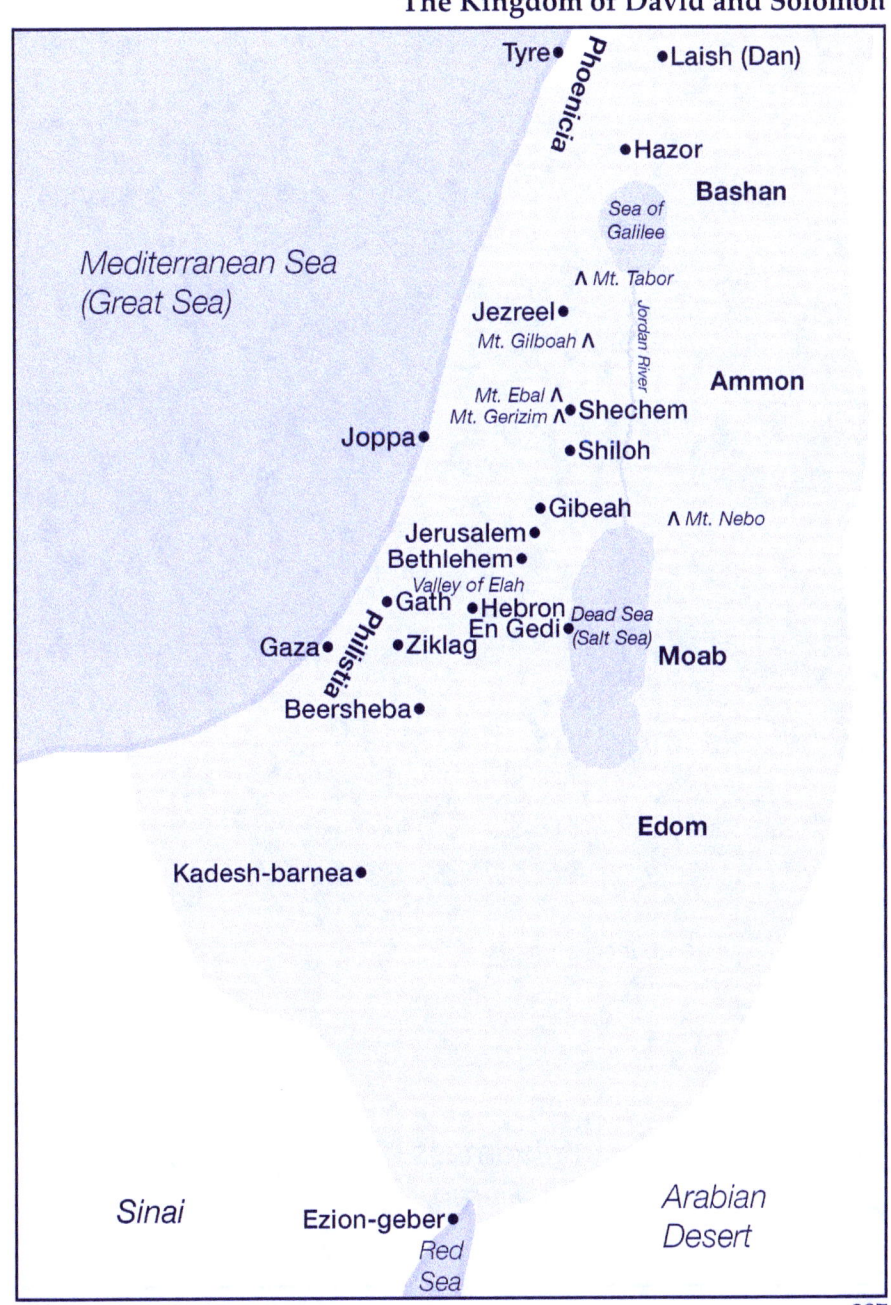

Extras

The Divided Kingdom of Judah and Israel

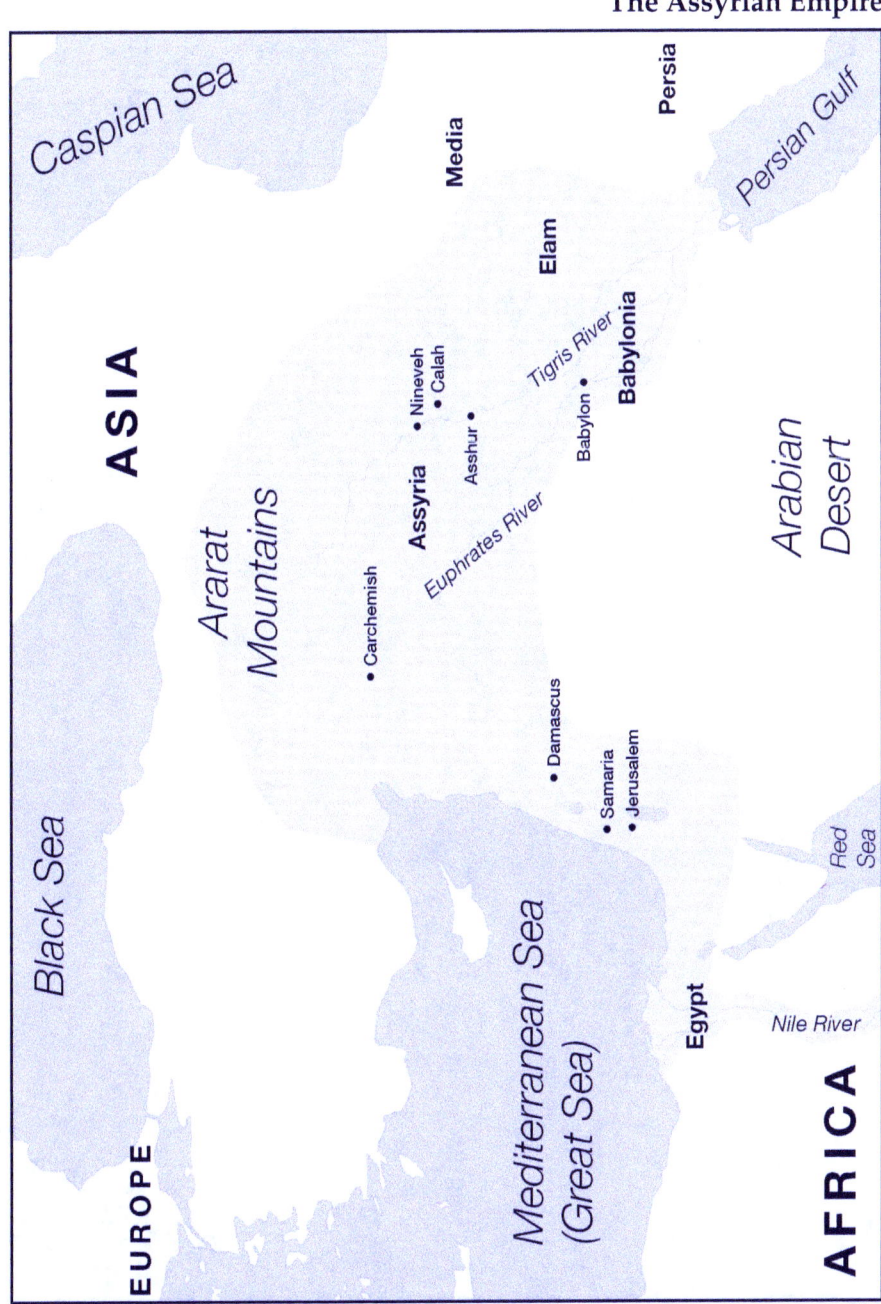

The Babylonian Empire

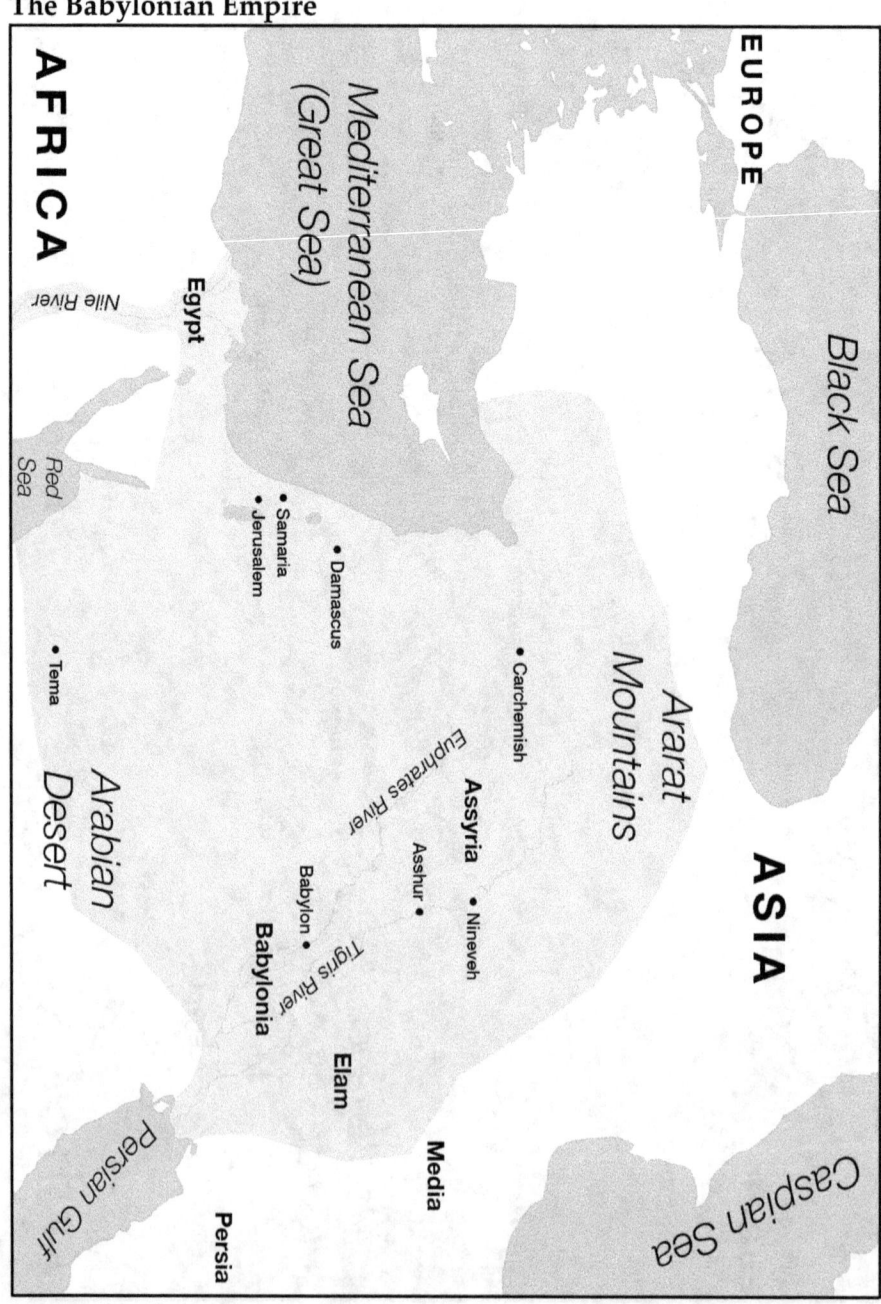

The Persian Empire

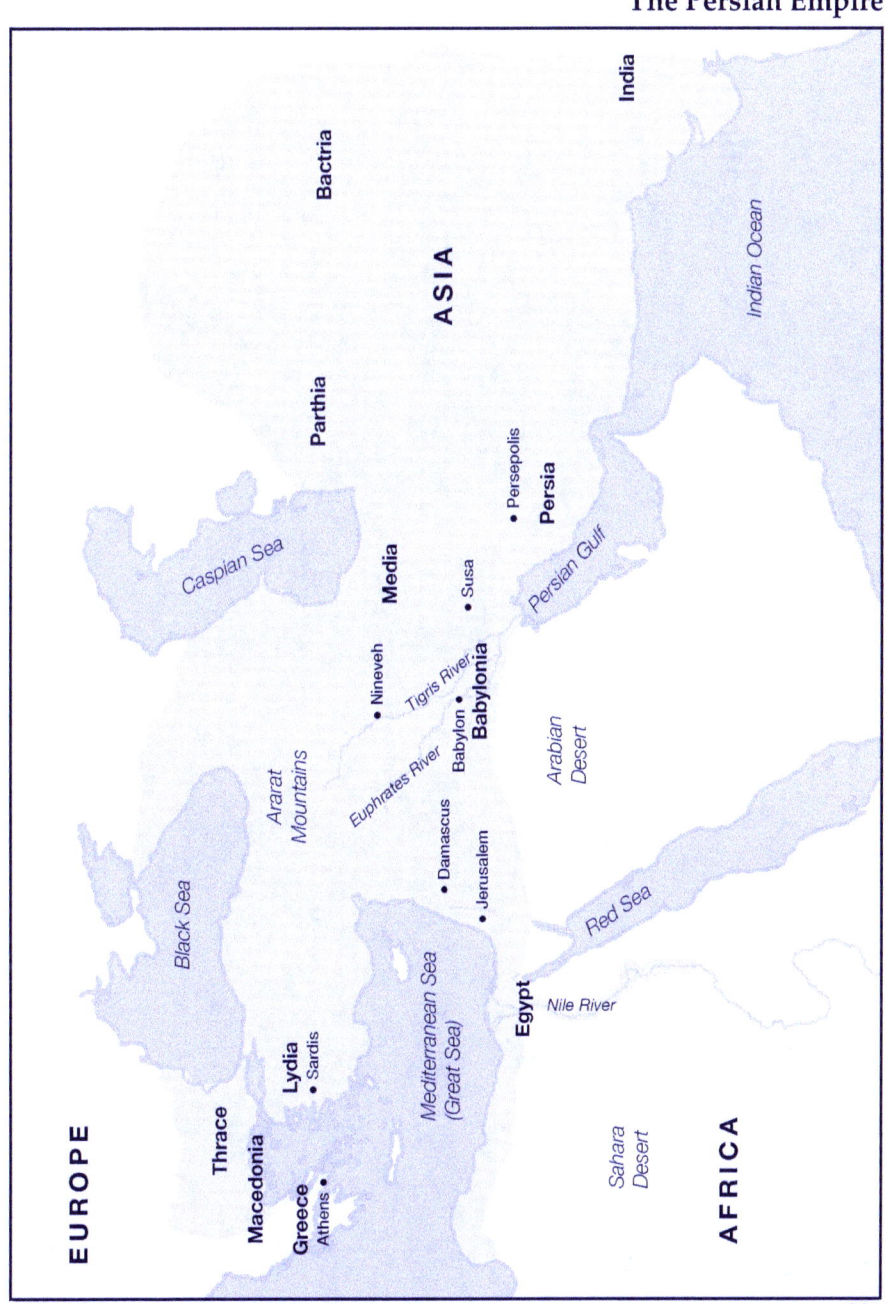

Extras

The Empire of Alexander the Great

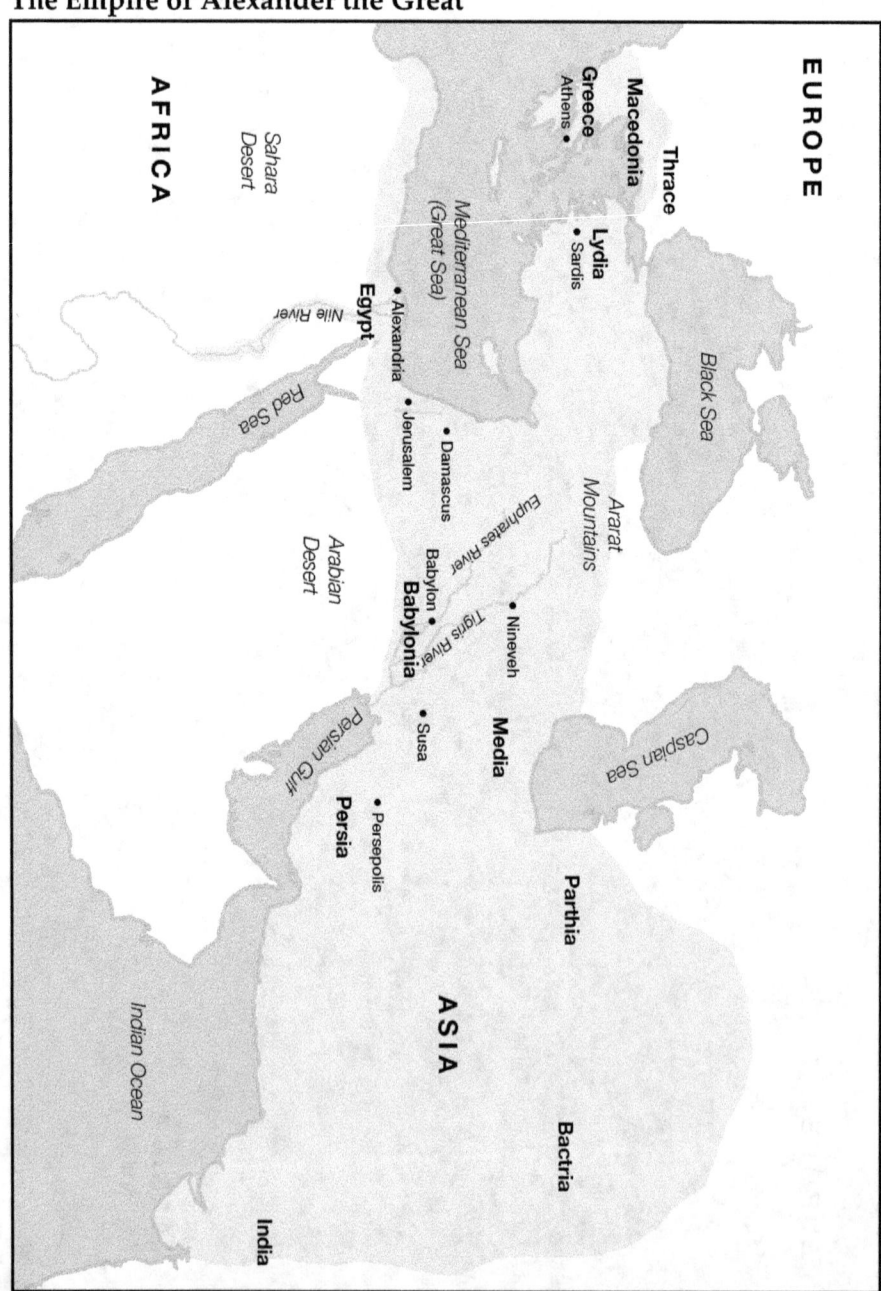

Maps

The Promised Land during the New Testament

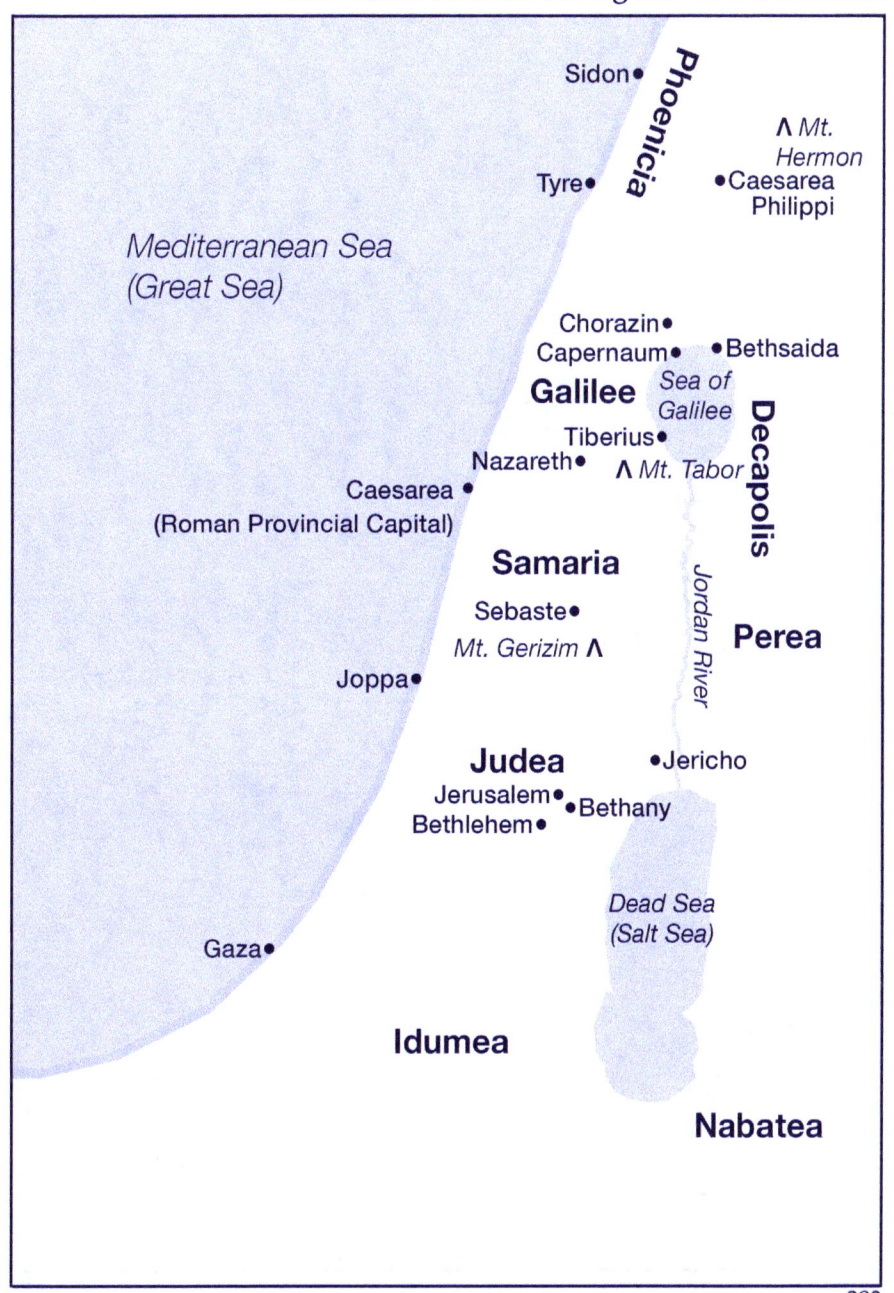

Extras

Paul's First and Second Missionary Journeys

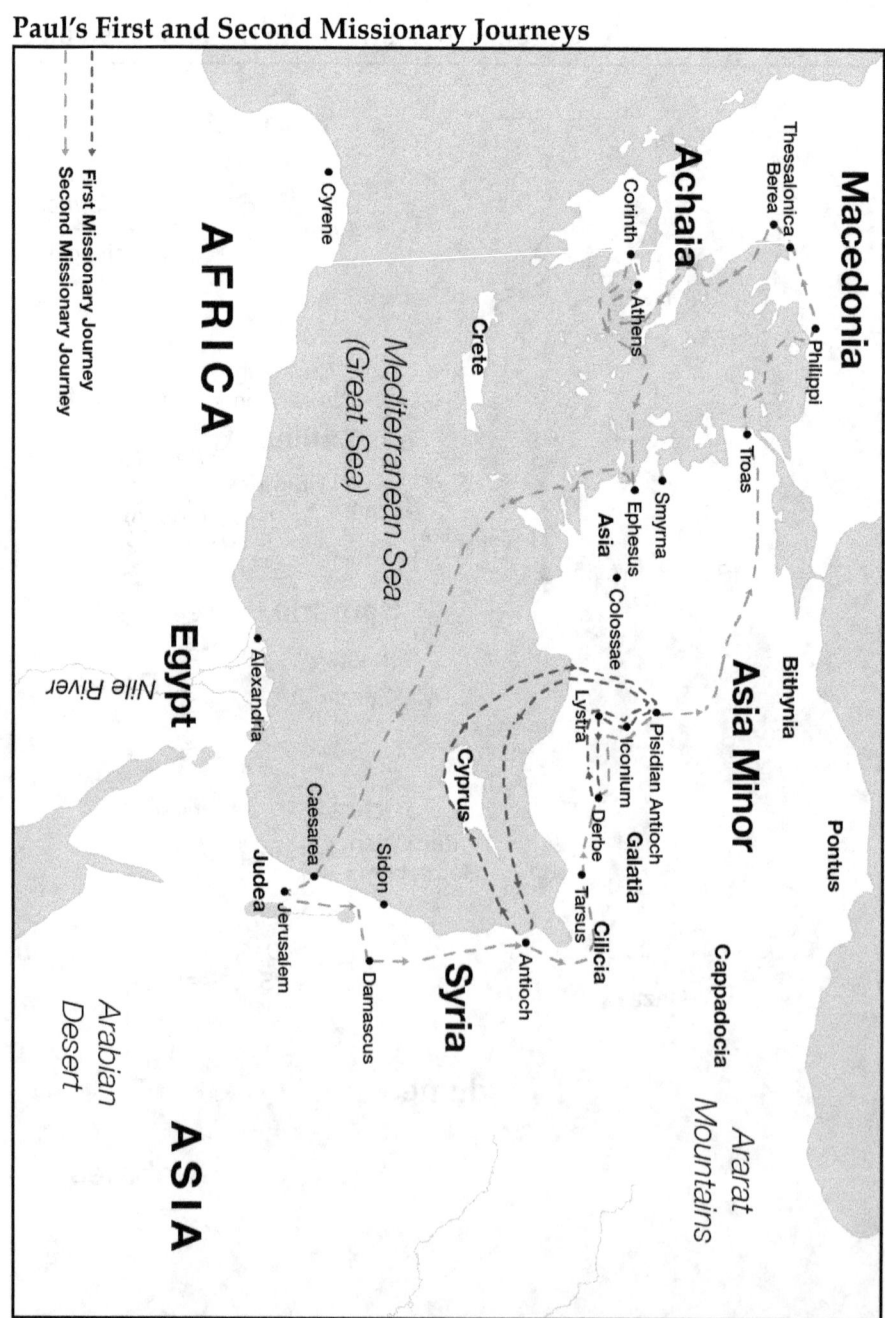

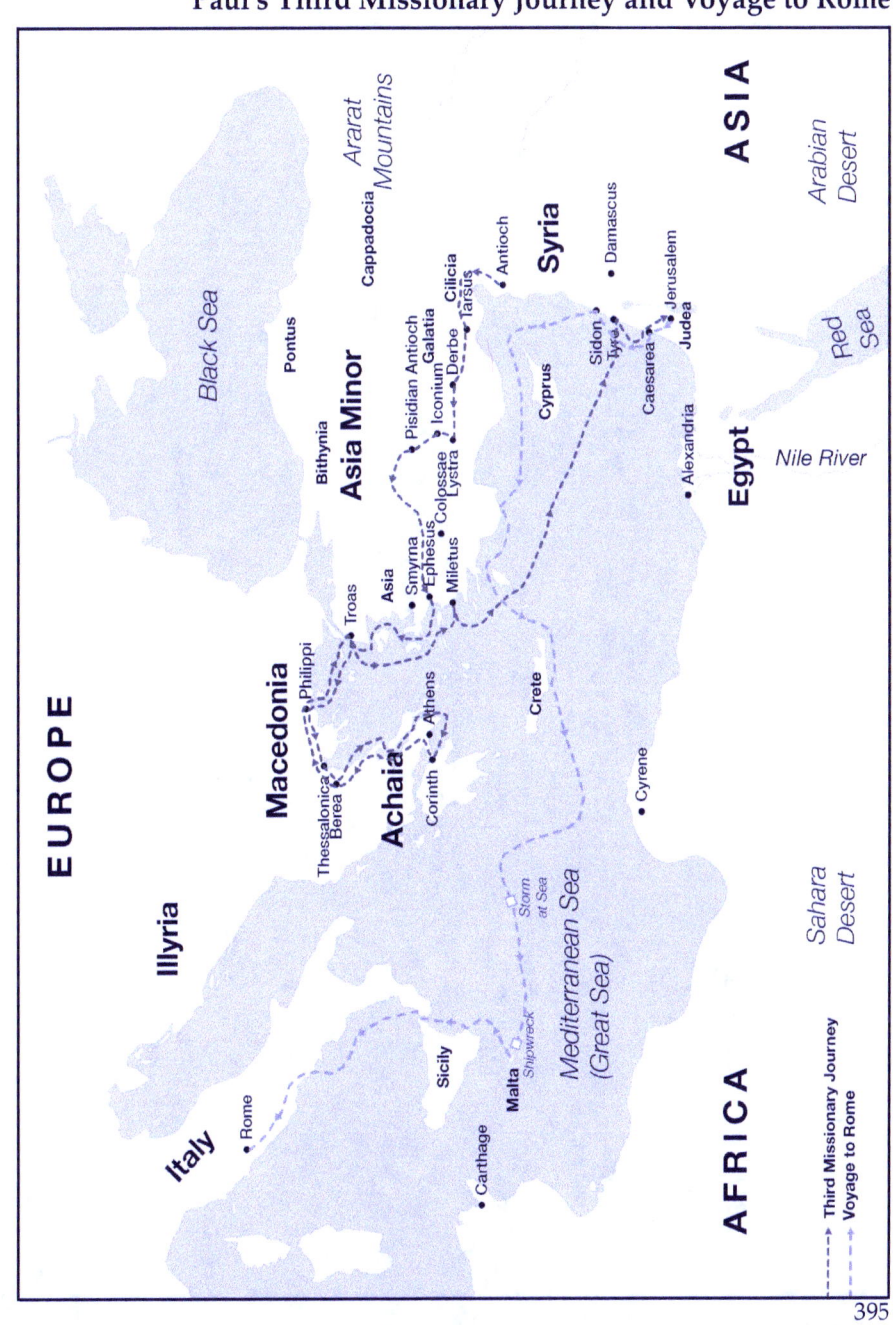

Extras

The Roman Empire during the New Testament

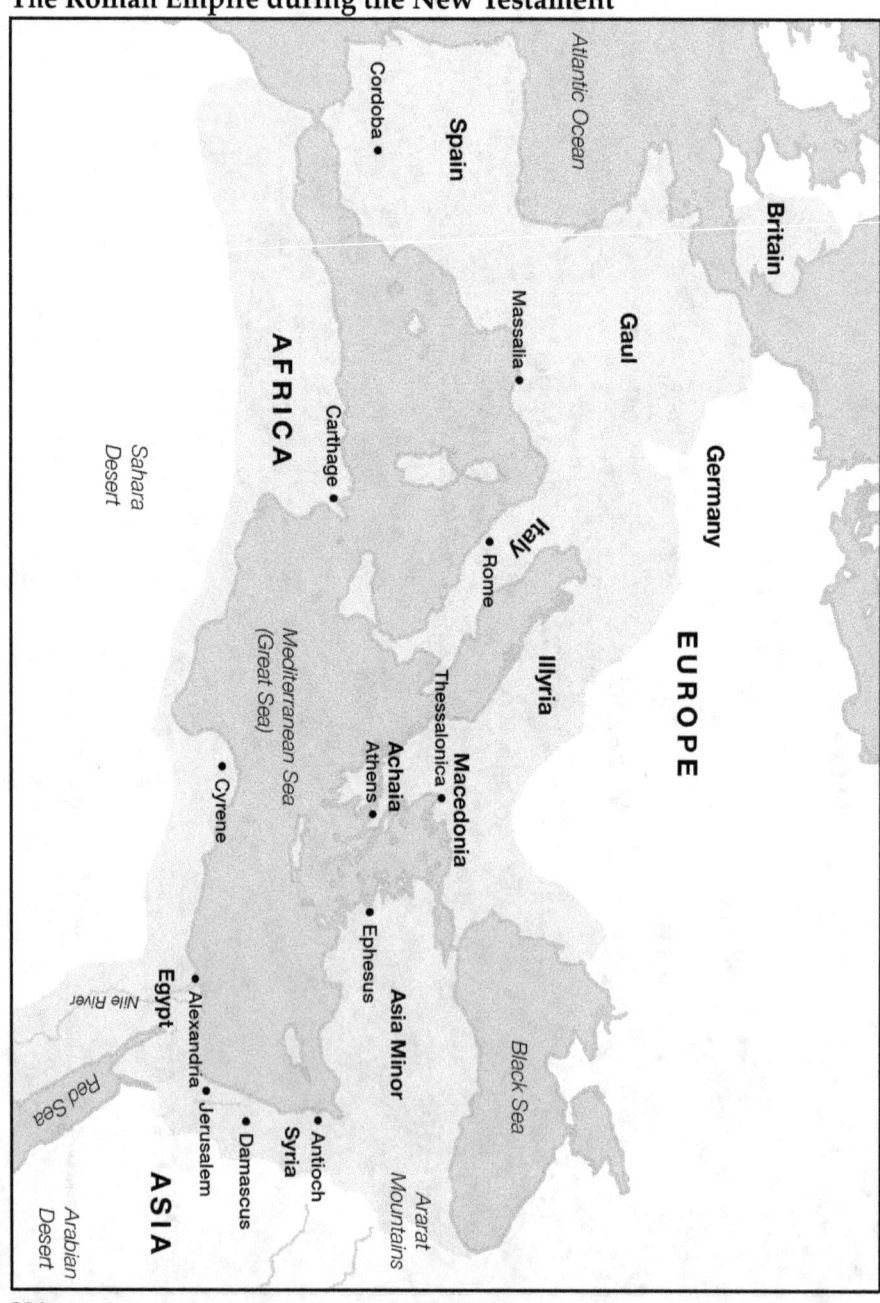

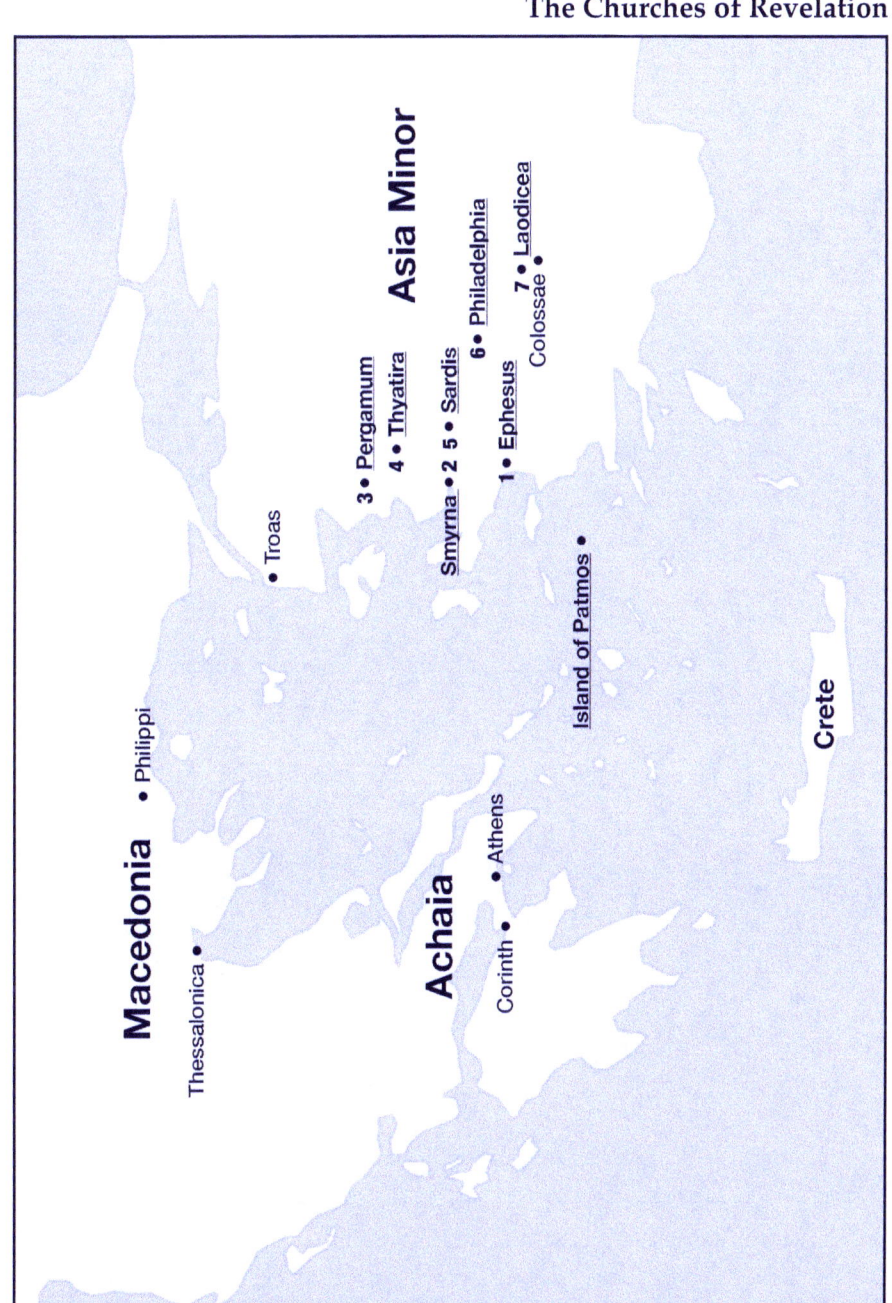

The Churches of Revelation

Extras

Picture Credits

p. 78, Hammurabi of Babylon, by ridaeology, in the Royal Ontario Museum, from Wikimedia Commons. p. 79, Cuneiform Tablet, public domain, in the Metropolitan Museum of Art, from Wikimedia Commons. p. 83, Amenhotep II, by Rama, in the Louvre Museum, from Wikimedia Commons. p. 84, Hieroglyphics, by Glenn Ashton, at the Karnak Temple, from Wikimedia Commons. p. 87, Baal, public domain, in the Louvre Museum, from Wikimedia Commons. p. 90, Ashurbanipal on a Lion Hunt, by Johnbod, in the British Museum, from Wikimedia Commons. p. 91, Assyrian Siege Tower, public domain from the Encyclopaedia Biblica (1903), from Wikimedia Commons. p. 93, Nebuchadnezzar II, public domain by Hedning, from Wikimedia Commons. p. 95, Ishtar Gate of Babylon, by Radomir Vrbovsky, in the Pergamon Museum, from Wikimedia Commons. p. 98, Darius I, public domain, from Wikimedia Commons. p. 99, Ahura Mazda, by A. Davey, in Taft, Iran, from Wikimedia Commons. p. 102, Alexander the Great, public domain, in the House of the Faun in Pompeii, from Wikimedia Commons. p. 103, The Parthenon, Temple of Athena, by Phanatic, in Athens, Greece, from Wikimedia Commons. p. 106, Augustus Caesar, public domain by Till Niermann, in the Chiaramonti Museum, from Wikimedia Commons. p. 108, Roman Road, by Bernard Gagnon, in Tall Aqibrin, Syria, from Wikimedia Commons. p. 112, An Ancient Scroll, by ArtMari, from Shutterstock. p. 132, The Tabernacle, by ArtMari, from Shutterstock. p. 133, The Divisions of the Tabernacle and Israel's Camp, by the author. p.

Extras

135, The Bronze Altar, by ArtMari, from Shutterstock. p. 135, The Table of the Bread of the Presence, by ArtMari, from Shutterstock. p. 135, The Lampstand, by ArtMari, from Shutterstock. p. 136, Altar of Incense, by ArtMari, from Shutterstock. p. 136, Ark of the Covenant, by ArtMari, from Shutterstock. p. 136, The Ark carried by Priests, by ArtMari, from Shutterstock. p. 137, The three divisions of Levi, by ArtMari, from Shutterstock. pp. 382–397, Maps designed by the author and based on maps from freevectormaps.com.

Notes

[1] This definition is inspired by Graeme Goldsworthy, *Gospel and Kingdom* in *The Goldsworthy Trilogy* (Carlisle: Paternoster, 2000), 54. But the definition and the overview of salvation history that follows has also been influenced by the following: Peter J. Gentry and Stephen J. Wellum, *Kingdom through Covenant: A Biblical-Theological Understanding of the Covenants* (Wheaton: Crossway, 2012); Vaughan Roberts, *God's Big Picture: Tracing the Storyline of the Bible* (Downers Grove, IL: IVP, 2008).

[2] These articles on interpreting the different genres of Scripture have been influenced by the following: Gordon D. Fee and Douglas K. Stuart, *How to Read the Bible for All Its Worth: A Guide to Understanding the Bible* (Grand Rapids: Zondervan, 2003); George H. Guthrie, *Read the Bible for Life: Your Guide to Understanding & Living God's Word* (Nashville: B&H, 2011); Robert L. Plummer, *40 Questions About Interpreting the Bible* (Grand Rapids: Kregel, 2010).

[3] Most of this article is a summary of Brian S. Rosner, *Paul and the Law: Keeping the Commandments of God*, New Studies in Biblical Theology (Downers Grove, IL: IVP Academic, 2013).

[4] Much of this article is inspired by D. A. Carson, *Exegetical Fallacies* (Grand Rapids: Baker, 1984).

[5] Paul R. House, *The Unity of the Twelve*, JSOT Supplement (Sheffield: Almond, 1990), 72.

[6] Westminster Confession of Faith (1646), 1.3; Second London Baptist Confession of Faith (1677), 1.3.

Notes

⁷ Patrick Schreiner, *Matthew, Disciple and Scribe: The First Gospel and Its Portrait of Jesus* (Grand Rapids: Baker Academic, 2019).

⁸ Thomas R. Schreiner and Ardel B. Caneday, *The Race Set before Us: A Biblical Theology of Perseverance & Assurance* (Downers Grove, IL: InterVarsity Press, 2001).